William Sharp

Lyra Celtica

An anthology of representative Celtic poetry

William Sharp

Lyra Celtica
An anthology of representative Celtic poetry

ISBN/EAN: 9783337295646

Printed in Europe, USA, Canada, Australia, Japan

Cover: Foto ©Thomas Meinert / pixelio.de

More available books at **www.hansebooks.com**

LYRA ☙ CELTICA

AN ANTHOLOGY OF REPRE-
SENTATIVE CELTIC POETRY

EDITED BY ELIZABETH A. SHARP · WITH IN-
TRODUCTION AND NOTES BY WILLIAM SHARP

ANCIENT IRISH ALBAN 𝕲
GAELIC BRETON CYMRIC
AND MODERN SCOTTISH
ᴬᴺᴰ IRISH CELTIC POETRY.

PATRICK GEDDES AND
COLLEAGUES ∞ THE
LAWNMARKET EDINBURGH
MDCCCXCVI

CONTENTS

" .   .   .   .   .   . a troubled Eden, rich
In throb of heart . . . . . ."

GEORGE MEREDITH

CONTENTS

vii

EARLY CYMRIC AND MEDIÆVAL WELSH

IRISH (MODERN AND CONTEMPORARY)

CONTENTS

ix

CONTENTS   xi

MODERN AND CONTEMPORARY SCOTO-CELTIC

CONTENTS xiii

CONTENTS

MODERN AND CONTEMPORARY BRETON

THE CELTIC FRINGE

xvi # CONTENTS

INTRODUCTION

INTRODUCTION

IN this foreword I must deal cursorily with a great
and fascinating subject, for "Lyra Celtica" has
extended beyond its original limits, and Text and
Notes have absorbed much of the space which had
been allotted for a preliminary dissertation on the
distinguishing qualities and characteristics of Celtic
literature.

For most readers, the interest of an anthology is
independent of any introductory remarks: the appeal is
in the wares, not in the running commentary of the
hawker. For those, however, who have looked for a
detailed synthesis, as well as for the Celticists who may
have expected an ample, or, at least, a more adequately
representative selection from the older Celtic literatures,
I have a brief word to say before passing on to the
matter in hand.

In the first place, this volume is no more than an
early, and, in a sense, merely arbitrary, gleaning from
an abundant harvest. For "Lyra Celtica" is not so
much the introduction to a much larger, more organic,
and more adequately representative work, to be called
"Anthologia Celtica," but is rather the outcome of the
latter, itself culled from a vast mass of material, ancient,
mediæval, and modern. It is, moreover, intentionally
given over mainly to modern poetry. "Anthologia
Celtica" may not appear for a year or two hence,
perhaps not for several years; for a systematic effort
to compile a scholarly anthology, on chronological and
comparative lines, of the ancient poetry of Irish and
Scottish Gaeldom, of the Cymric, Armorican, and other

Brythonic bards, is a task not to be lightly undertaken, or fulfilled in anything like satisfactory degree without that patience and care which only enthusiastic love of the subject can give, and for which the extrinsic reward is payable in rainbow-gold alone.

In the second place, all that was intended to be written here, will be given more fully and more systematically in a volume to be published later : "An Introduction to the Study of Celtic Literature." Therein an effort is made to illustrate the distinguishing imaginative qualities of the several Celtic races; to trace the origins, dispersion, interfusion, and concentration of the early Celtic, Picto-Celtic, and later Goidelic and Brythonic peoples, and to reflect Celtic mythopœic and authentic history through Celtic poetry and legendary lore. Concurrently there is an endeavour to relate, in natural order, the development of the literature of contemporary Wales, Brittany, Ireland, and Celtic Scotland, from their ancient Cymric, Armorican, Erse, and Alban-Gaelic congeners.

It is not yet thirty years ago since Matthew Arnold published his memorable and beautiful essay on Celtic Literature, so superficial in its knowledge, it is true, but informed by so keen and fine an interpretative spirit; yet already, since 1868, the writings of Celtic specialists constitute quite a library.

Of recent years we have had many works of the greatest value in Celtic ethnology, philology, history, archæology, art, legendary ballads and romances, folk-lore, and literature. Of all the Celtic literatures, that which was least known, when Arnold wrote, was the Scoto-Gaelic; but now with books such as Skene's "Celtic Scotland," Campbell's "Popular Tales of the West Highlands," with its invaluable supplementary matter, Dr Cameron's "Reliquiæ Celticæ," and many others, there is no difficulty for the would-be student. Again,

it is impossible to overrate the value of popular books
at once so able, so trustworthy, and so readily attainable,
as Professor Rhys's "Celtic Britain," or Dr Douglas
Hyde's "Story of Early Gaelic Literature"; while Breton
literature, ancient or modern, has found almost as many,
and certainly as able and enthusiastic, exponents as that
of Wales or that of Ireland. In Ireland there is, with
Mr Standish Hayes O'Grady, Dr Douglas Hyde, Dr
Sigerson, and many more, quite an army of workers in
every branch of Celtic science and literature ; in Scotland
one less numerous perhaps, but not less ardent and justly
enthusiastic ; and in Wales the old Cymric spirit survives
unabated, from the Butt of Anglesea to the marches of
Hereford. In Brittany there was, till the other day,
Hersart de la Villemarqué, and now there are M. de
Jubainville, M. Loth, M. Anatole Le Braz, M. Auguste
Brizeux, Charles Le Goffic, Louis Tiercelin, and many
more philologists and other students, poets, romancists,
and critics. Cornwall has not been neglected, nor has
Man, and even the outlying fringe of Celtdom has found
interpreters and expounders. In France the "Revue
Celtique"; in Ireland, Scotland, and Wales, Gaelic or
Welsh or Anglo-Celtic periodicals and "Transactions,"
stimulate a wider and deeper interest, and do inestim-
able service. The writings of men such as Renan, De
Jubainville, Valroger, and other French Celticists: of
Windisch, Kuno Meyer, and other Germans: of English
specialists such as Mr Whitley Stokes, Mr Alfred Nutt,
and others : these, together, and in all their different
ways of approach, are, along with the writings of native
specialists in Ireland, Wales, and Scotland, accomplish-
ing a work greater than is now to be measured or
even accurately apprehended.

To all who would know something authentic concerning the history of the Celtic race since its occupation
of these Isles, and of a large section, and latterly of a
corner, of Western Europe, I would recommend Professor

Rhys's admirable little book, "Celtic Britain," a volume within the reach of all. In the Irish National Library, the volumes of which are sold at a trifling sum, may be had Dr Douglas Hyde's lucid and excellent exposition of early Gaelic literature; and, among valuable popular contributions to Anglo-Celtic Literature, mention should be made of the Rev. Nigel MacNeill's "Literature of the Highlanders." These three books alone, each priced at a moderate sum, will give a reader, hitherto ignorant of the subject, much trustworthy information on the history, ethnology, and literature of the Irish and Scottish Gael. I know of no "popular" book on early Welsh literature, and certainly none that, in trustworthiness, has superseded Stephens's "Literature of the Cymri." Mr Norris has introduced us to much ancient Cornish writing which it would have been a pity to let lapse uncollected: and of MM. Villemarqué, De Jubainville, Valroger, Le Braz, and other Breton specialists I have already spoken.

It would seem reserved for this coming century, says Dr Hyde, unless a vigorous, sustained, and national effort at once be made, to catch the last tones of "that beautiful, unmixed Aryan language which, with the exception of that glorious Greek which has now renewed its youth like the eagle, has left the longest, most luminous, and most consecutive literary track behind it of any of the vernacular tongues of Europe." But, alas, a stronger law than that which man can make or unmake, or nations can resolve, is slowly disintegrating the subsoil wherefrom the roots of the Celtic speech draw the sole nurture which can give it the beauty and fragrance of life.

Some idea of the vastness of the mass of the as yet untranslated Celtic literature may be had from the notes in books by Dr Douglas Hyde, J. F. Campbell, Alfred Nutt, and other specialists. In the National Libraries in Great Britain alone it is estimated that, if all the inedited MSS. were printed, they would fill at least twelve hundred or fourteen hundred octavo volumes. Those who would realise more adequately the extent and importance of this early literature should, besides the authorities already mentioned, consult Eugene O'Curry's invaluable "Manners and Customs," and in particular the section of 130 pp. devoted to Education and Literature in Ancient Erinn, which deals with the most important Irish-Gaelic poets from the earliest times down to the eleventh century: the likewise invaluable "Myvyrian Archaiology," which sets forth an imposing list of Cymric poets, with much information concerning life in Ancient Wales: and books such as Campbell's "Leabhar na Féinne," and "Tales of the West Highlands," MacNeill's "Literature of the Highlanders," and (though for students rather than the general reader) the writings of Skene, Anderson, Whitley Stokes, Nutt, and many others.

Modern Irish-Celtic literature may be said to date from O'Donovan's superb redaction and amplification of "The Annals of the Four Masters," one of the monumental achievements in world-literature, on the side of scholarship; and from Keating's "History of Ireland," on the side of popular writing. Since O'Donovan and Keating, the literary activity of Ireland has again and again re-asserted itself, and is once more so much in evidence, in Celtic scholarship and in Anglo-Celtic romance and poetry, that the not over-ready attention of England is perforce drawn to it.

The contemporary Anglo-Celtic poetry of Ireland has a quality which no other English poetry possesses in like degree: the quality which Matthew Arnold defined as natural magic—"Celtic poetry drenched in the dew of natural magic." Obviously, the lover of poetry may at once object that Shakespere, Milton, Coleridge, Shelley, Keats, are English, and Byron, Burns, and Scott are Scottish, and not distinctively Anglo-Celtic. Well, of Shakespere's ancestry we know little; and if Celtic enthusiasts maintain that he must

have had a strong Celtic strain in his blood, they may
be innocent blasphemers, but do not deserve crucifixion
for their iniquity.   Milton was of Welsh blood through
his maternal descent; and Keats is a Celtic name.
Keats' mother's name is Welsh of the Welsh, while his
genius is as convincingly Celtic in its distinguishing
qualities as though he were able to trace his descent
from Oisìn or Fergus Honey-Mouth of "the Fingalians."
Keats, born a Cockney, is pre-eminently a Celtic poet,
by virtue of the nationality of the brain if for no other
authentic reason; while Moore, born in Ireland of Celtic
ancestry, is the least Celtic of all modern poets of eminence.   So far as we know, Coleridge and Shelley are of
unmixed English blood, though who can say there was
nothing atavistic in their genius, and that the wild lyricism
of the one and the glamour and magic of the other were
not in part the expression of some "ancestral voice"?

Of the three great modern Scots, it is still a debat-
able point if Burns was not more Celtic than "Lowland,"
that is, by paternal as well as by maternal descent;
and it surely is almost unquestionable that, in the geography of the soul, Burns' natal spot must be sought in
the Fortunate Isles of Celtdom.   Byron, of course, though
far more British than Scottish, and again more Scottish
than Celtic, had a strong Celtic strain in his blood;
and Scott, as it happens, was of the ancient stock, and
not "the typical Lowlander" he is so often designated.*

The truth is, that just as in Scotland we may come
upon a type which is unmistakably national without
being either Anglo-Saxon or Celtic or Anglo-Celtic,

---

*Apropos, let me quote a word or two from Dr
Douglas Hyde: "We all remember the inimitable
felicity with which that great English-speaking Gael,
Sir Walter Scott, has caught," &c. (with this note)
"Both the Buccleugh Scots, and the other four branches
of the name, were originally Gaelic-speaking Celts."

but which, rightly or wrongly, we take to be Pictish
(and possibly a survival of an older race still), so,
throughout our whole country, and in Sussex and
Hampshire, as well as in Connemara or Argyll, we
may at any moment encounter the Celtic brain in the
Anglo-Saxon flesh. In Scotland, in particular, it may
be doubted if there are many families native to the soil
who have not at least a Celtic strain. People are apt
to forget that Celtic Scotland does not mean only the
Western Isles and the Highlands, and that the whole
country was at one time Celtic (Goidelic), and before
that was again Celtic, when Brythonic or Cymric Scotland and the Dalriadic Scoto-Irish of Argyll, and the
northern Picts, who were probably Gaels, or of kindred
Celtic origin, held the land, and sowed the human seed
whence arose much of the finest harvest of a later
Scotland.

Here I may conveniently quote a significant passage
from "Celtic Britain":—

"This means, from the Celtic point of view, that the
Goidelic race of history is not wholly Celtic or Aryan,
but inherits in part a claim to the soil of these islands,
derived from possession at a time when, as yet, no
Aryan waggoner had driven into Europe; and it is,
perhaps, from their Kynesian ancestry that the Irish of
the present day have inherited the lively humour and
ready wit, which, among other characteristics, distinguish
them from the Celts of the Brythonic branch, most of
whom, especially the Kymry, are a people still more
mixed, as they consist of the Goidelic element of the
compound nature already suggested, with an ample
mixture of Brythonic blood, introduced mostly by the
Ordovices. And as to Welsh, it is, roughly speaking,
the Brythonic language, as spoken by the Ordovices, and
as learned by the Goidelic peoples they overshadowed
in the Principality of Wales. To this its four chief
dialects still correspond, being those, respectively, of

Powys, Gwent or Siluria, Dyved or Demetia, and Venedot or Gwynedd.

"Skulls are harder than consonants, and races lurk when languages slink away. The lineal descendants of the neolithic aborigines are ever among us, possibly even those of a still earlier race. On the other hand, we can imagine the Kynesian impatiently hearing out the last echoes of palæolithic speech ; we can guess dimly how the Goidel gradually silenced the Kynesian ; we can detect the former coming slowly round to the keynote of the Brython ; and, lastly, we know how the Englishman is engaged, linguistically speaking, in drowning the voice of both of them in our own day. Such, to take another metaphor, are some of the lines one would have to draw in the somewhat confused picture we have suggested of one wave of speech chasing another, and forcing it to dash itself into oblivion on the western confines of the Aryan world ; and that we should fondly dream English likely to be the last, comes only from our being unable to see into a distant future pregnant with untold changes of no less grave a nature than have taken place in the dreary wastes of the past."

To return : among the great English and Scottish writers of to-day two may be taken as examples of this brain-kinship with a race physically alien. Much of the poetry of Algernon Charles Swinburne is distinctively Celtic, particularly in its lyric fire and wonderful glow and colour, as well as its epithetical luxuriance ; but, indeed, this is hardly a good instance after all, for Mr Swinburne's north-country ancestry is not without definite Celtic admixture. "Tristram of Lyonesse" is, in its own way, as Celtic as "The Voyage of St Brendan," and with more of innate inevitableness than in those lovely Celtic reflections in the essentially English brain of Tennyson, "The Dream" and "The Voyage of Maelduin."

As for Robert Louis Stevenson, come of Lowland

stock, and, as he said himself once, "made up o' Lallan
dust, body and soul," there is not, so far as I know,
any proof that a near paternal or maternal ancestor
was of Celtic blood. But who, that has studied his
genius, can question the Celtic strain in him, or who
believe that, though "the Lallan dust" may have been
unadulterate for generations, the brain which conceived
and wrought "The Merry Men" and "Thrawn Janet"
was not attuned to Celtic music? There is a poem of
his which seems to me typically Celtic in its indescrib-
able haunting charm, its air of I know not what rare
music, its deep yearning emotion, and its cosmic note—

"In the highlands, in the country places,
Where the old plain men have rosy faces,
And the young fair maidens
Quiet eyes ;
Where essential silence cheers and blesses
And forever in the hill-recesses
Her more lovely music
Broods and dies,

O to mount again where erst I haunted ;
Where the old red hills are bird-enchanted,
And the low green meadows
Bright with sward ;
And when even dies, the million tinted,
And the night has come, and planets glinted,
Lo, the valley hollow
Lamp-bestarred !

O to dream, O to awake and wander
There, and with delight to take and render,
Through the trance of silence,
Quiet breath ;
Lo ! for there, among the flowers, and grasses,
Only the mightier movement sounds and passes ;
Only winds and rivers,
Life and death."

Of course there is a certain poignant note common to
all poetry, and he might be a zealous Celticist, but a
poor worshipper of Apollo, who would try to limit this
charm of exquisite regret and longing to Celtic poetry.
It is an unfrontiered land, this pleasant country in the
geography of the soul which we call Bohemia; and
here all parochial and national, and even racial distinctions fall away, and Firdausi and Oisin, Omar the
Tentmaker and Colum the Saint, and all and every
"Honey-Mouth" of every land and time, move in equal
fellowship.   Even in one of the most haunting quatrains
by any modern Anglo-Celtic poet—

> "O wind, O mighty melancholy wind,
>   Blow through me, blow!
> Thou blowest forgotten things into my mind,
>   From long ago "—

we must not forget the elder music of one who is
among the truest of the poets of Nature whom the
world has seen : though neither in brain nor, so far as
we know, in blood, had Wordsworth any kinship with
the Celt—the music "Of old, unhappy, far-off things."
By a natural association, "Ossian" comes to mind.
It is pleasant to think that a book like "Lyra Celtica"
appears just at the centenary of James Macpherson.
Macpherson died in 1796, but long before his death his
reputed "Ossian" had become one of the most vital
influences in literature.   This is not the occasion to go
into the "Ossian" dispute.   It must suffice to say that
the concensus of qualified opinion decides—(1) That
Macpherson's "Ossian" is not a genuine rendering of
ancient originals; (2) that he worked incoherently upon
a genuine but unsystematised, unsifted, and fragmentary
basis, without which, however, he could have achieved nothing; (3) that inherent evidence disproves Macpherson's
sole or even main authorship as well as "Ossian's," and
that he was at most no more than a skilful artificer;

(4) that, if he were the sole author, he would be one of the few poetic creators of the first rank, and worthy of all possible honour; (5) that no single work in our literature has had so wide-reaching, so potent, and so enduring an influence.

Much of the tragic gloom, of which "Ossian" is a true mirror, colours even contemporary Scoto-Celtic poetry; and though in Gaelic there is much humorous verse, and much poetry of a blithe, bright, and even joyous nature, the dominant characteristic is that of gloom, the gloom of unavailing regret, of mournful longing, a lament for what cannot be again. True, in a Gaelic poem by Mary Mackellar, a contemporary Highland poet, we hear of

> Spioraid aosmhoir tìr nan Gàidheal,
> Ciod an diugh a's fàth do 'n ghàirich
> 'Dhùisg thu comhdaichte le aighear,
> As an uaigh 's an robh thu'd 'chadal?

> (Spirit of the Gaelic earth
> Wherefore is this mirth unwonted
> That hath waked thee from the tomb,
> And to triumph turned thy gloom?)—

but, alas! that fine line, "Spioraid aosmhoir tìr nan Gàidheal" is not an invocation to the Gaelic muse to arouse herself to a new and blither music, but is simply part of some congratulatory lines of a "Welcome to the Marquis of Lorne on his union with the Princess Louise"!*

The "Spirit of the Gaelic earth" does not make for mirth, as a rule, at least in the Highlands, save in verse of a frankly Bacchanalian or satiric kind.

In this, there is a marked contrast with the Irish-

---

* "Failte do Mharcus Latharna 's do 'Mhnaoi oig Rioghail."

Gaelic, whose muse is laughter-loving though ever with "dewy dark eyes."

If, however, the blithe and delightful peasant poetry of Mr Alfred Percival Graves, and that so beautifully translated and paraphrased by Dr Douglas Hyde, be characteristically Irish, so also is such typically Celtic poetry as this lyric by the latest Irish singer, Miss Moira O'Neill—

"SEA WRACK."

The wrack was dark an' shiny where it floated in the sea,
There was no room in the brown boat but only him an' me ;
Him to cut the sea wrack—me to mind the boat,
An' not a word between us the hours we were afloat.
   The wet wrack,
   The sea wrack,
   The wrack was strong to cut.

We laid it on the grey rocks to wither in the sun ;
An' what should call my lad then to sail from Cushendun?
With a low moon, a full tide, a swell upon the deep,
Him to sail the old boat—me to fall asleep.
   The dry wrack,
   The sea wrack,
   The wrack was dead so soon.

There's a fire low upon the rocks to burn the wrack to kelp ;
There's a boat gone down upon the Moyle, an' sorra one to help.
Him beneath the salt sea—me upon the shore—
By sunlight or moonlight we'll lift the wrack no more.
   The dark wrack,
   The sea wrack,
   The wrack may drift ashore.

When we come to examine the literature of the four
great divisions of the Celtic race, a vast survey lies
before us, with innumerable vistas. A lifetime might
well be given to the study of any one of the ancient
Erse, Alban-Gaelic, Cymric, and Armorican literatures:
a lifetime that would yet have to leave much undis-
covered, much unrelated. There is room for every
student. In old Irish literature alone, though so many
enthusiasts are now working towards its greater eluci-
dation and the transference of the better part of it into
Anglo-Celtic literature, there remain whole tracts, and
even regions, of unexploited land. In a score of ways,
pioneers have been clearing the ground for us: philologists like Windisch, Loth, Kuno Meyer, Whitley Stokes;
literary scholars like S. Hayes O'Grady, Campbell of
Islay, Cameron of Brodick, Dr Douglas Hyde; folk-
lorists innumerable, in Scotland, Wales, and Ireland;
romancists like Standish O'Grady, who write across
the angle of the historic imagination, and romancists
like W. B. Yeats, who write across the angle of the
poetic imagination; and poets, an ever - growing band
of sweet singers, who catch for us the fugitive airs,
the exquisite fleeting cadences, the haunting, indefinable
music of an earlier day.

From Ireland the Neo-Celtic Renascence has extended
through Gaeldom. The concurrent Welsh development
may be independent of this Irish influence, and probably
is: largely because the poetic imagination of the Cymri
of to-day was stirred from within, by the stimulus to the
national genius through the world-wide attention drawn
by the publication of the "Mabinogion," as in turn the
Gaelic imagination was stirred by the incalculable influence
of "Ossian"—an influence so great, so deep, so wide-reaching, that, as already said, were Macpherson to be proved
the sole author, were it convincingly demonstrable that
he was, not a more or less confused and unscholarly
interpreter, but himself a creator, himself "Ossian," he

would deserve to rank with the three or four great
ancients and moderns who have dug, deep and wide,
new channels for the surging flow of human thought.
Possibly, at any rate, this may prove to be one good
reason for the independence of the Welsh development
from any Irish stimulus—an impulse from within always
being more potent and enduring than one from without;
but, fundamentally, this independence is due to an organic
difference. In a word, the Celtic genius is broadly divi-
sible, even at this day, into two great sections: the Goidelic
and the Brythonic or Cymric—let us say, is represented
by the Welsh Celt and the Gaelic Celt. Those readers
or students who approach the literature of either, ancient
or modern, but particularly the latter, and expect to find
identity both of sentiment and in method of expression,
will ultimately be as disappointed as one who should,
with the same idea, approach Spanish and Portuguese,
or Dutch and German, or Provençal and French. In
every respect, save that of ancient kinship, the Welsh
and the Gaels differ materially. There is, perhaps, more
likeness between the Highlander and the Welshman
than between the latter and the Irishman; but even
here the distinctions are considerable, and the Gaelic
islesman of Barra or Uist is as different a creature
from the native of Glamorgan or Caermarthen as though
no racial cousinship united them. But, in the instance
of Welsh and Irish, the unlikeness is so marked that
the best analogue is that of the Frenchman and the
German. The Irish are the French of the Celtic races,
the Welsh the Germans. The two people are distinct
in their outer and inner life as well as in their literature;
and for a Connaught man or a Hebridean to go through
Wales would be as foreign an experience as for a
Welshman to find himself among the Catholic islesmen
of South Uist, or among the moorside villages of
Connemara.

To-day the Gael and Cymri are foreigners. Strangely

enough, the section of the Celtic race most akin to the
Welsh is the Manx—a Goidelic people, and with a
Gaelic dialect. The Gael himself, however, does not
stand out distinctly. Although there is a far greater
likeness between the Scoto-Celt and the Irish-Celt than
between either and the Welshman, there are traits which
unmistakably distinguish them. In Ireland itself, the
Celt of the south-east and south differs in more respects
than mere dialect from his kinsman by the Connaught
shore or of the hills of Connemara; as, in Scotland,
there is a marked distinction between the "Tuathach"
(North Highlander) and the "Deasach" (the South and
West Highlander). A Farquharson or a Gordon from
Aberdeenshire has to shake hands across the arms of
many a Mackenzie and Macgregor, many a Cameron
and Macpherson, before he can link in brotherly grip
with a MacNeill of Barra, a Macdonald of Skye, a
Macleod of the Lewis. These distinctions, of course, are
in their nature parochial rather than racial; but they are
highly indicative of a fundamental weakness in the Celtic
nature, and suggest a cogent reason for the failure of
the race to cohere into one compact and indispersable
nation, as the central Teutonic races merged into
"Germany," as Gauls, Normans, and Provençals merged
into "France," and as the Brythons, the Teutonic outlanders (Frisians, Angles, Jutes, &c.), Saxons, Danes,
Normans, and Anglo-Celts merged into "England,"
and, later, into "Great Britain," into the "British
Empire."

The most marked Celtic national homogeneity is to
be found in Wales. Wales has ever persisted, and
still persists in her moat and her drawbridge. In the
preservation of her language is her safeguard. Without
Welsh, Wales would be as English as Cumberland or
Cornwall. In this way only, knit indissolubly to the
flank of England as she is, and without any natural
eastern frontier of mountain range or sea, can she

isolate herself; and I am convinced that herein we have one main reason for the passionate attachment of the Cymri of to-day to their ancient language — an attachment as strong among the unlettered as among ardent scholars, and even among those who have no heed for the beauty of traditional literature or, indeed, heed of any kind other than for the narrow personal interests of domesticity.

But this very isolation of Wales, through her language, has, no doubt, interfered materially with the development of her Anglo-Celtic literature.   Contrasted with that of Ireland or that of Scotland, how astonishingly meagre it is.   All Ireland is aflame with song ; Scotland is again becoming the land of old romance.   Here and there are a few writers, a poet-romancist like Mr Ernest Rhys, a poet like the late Emily Davis, a few novelists who are Welsh by the accident of birth rather than by the nationality of the brain.   For, of course, Mr George Meredith stands so far above all localisation of this kind that it would be out of place to rank him merely as the head of contemporary Wales.   He is the foremost Anglo-Celtic voice of to-day ; so emphatically foremost, by the distinguishing qualities of his genius, that if to-morrow he were proved to be come of a stock of long unmixed Saxon ancestry never dissociated from that southern country of which he is by birth a native, we should be justified in abiding by the far more significant and important lineage of the brain.

But this great exception apart, the difference alluded to is extraordinary.   Wales is so animated by national enthusiasms, pride, and incalculable hereditary uplift, that her silence—in English, that is—can hardly be accounted for away from the supposition that, in closing her ears against English, she has also set her lips against utterance in that tongue.

The Scoto-Celtic writers of to-day, both in prose and poetry, have produced more Anglo-Celtic literature than

Wales has done since the beginning of the century, and with a range, a vitality, a beauty, far beyond anything that has come forth from modern Cymru ; and Ireland, again, in poetry at any rate, has given us even more than Scotland.

The Celtic Renascence, of which so much has been written of late—that is, the re-birth of the Celtic genius in the brain of Anglo-Celtic poets and the brotherhood of dreamers—is, fundamentally, the outcome of "Ossian," and, immediately, of the rising of the sap in the Irish nation.

Of the immense and never yet approximately defined Irish-Celtic influence in literature a fine and true word has been said by one of the ablest of the Irish fellow-ship ; and I would strongly urge every reader to obtain Mr Stopford Brooke's admirable and stimulating little essay "On the Need and Use of getting Irish Literature into the English Tongue." *   With its conclusion, every lover of English poetry and romance will agree.

"When we have got the old [Celtic] legendary tales rendered into fine prose and verse, I believe we shall open out English poetry to a new and exciting world, an immense range of subjects, entirely fresh and full of inspiration.   Therefore, as I said, get them out into English, and then we may bring England and [Celtdom] into a union which never can suffer separation, and send another imaginative force on earth which may (like Arthur's tale) create Poetry for another thousand years."

These are inspiring words, and should find an eager response.

----

* Published by Mr Fisher Unwin at a shilling.   The reader will have to discount Mr Brooke's over-emphasis on the word Irish, which he frequently uses instead of Celtic, even when alluding to Scoto - Celtic literature and influence.

More and more we may hope that the beautiful poetry of Ireland, ancient and modern, with its incommunicable charm and exquisite spontaneity; that the strange, elemental, sombre imagination of the West Highlander and of the Gael of the Isles; and that the vivid spell of the old Welsh bards, will, before long, become a still greater, a still more regenerating, and a lasting force and influence in our English literature.

In the Notes I have something to say concerning each of the many ancient and modern writers drawn upon for this representative anthology, so need not here enter into further detail of the kind.

Obviously, it would be impossible to make a work of this nature as welcome to the Celtic scholar as to the general reader.   No one in the least degree acquainted with ancient Gaelic and Cymric literature could fail to note how merely superficial this section of " Lyra Celtica " is.   Therefore, let me again aver that this anthology has been compiled, not for the specialist, but for the lover of poetry; and to serve, for the many who have no knowledge of "Anglo-Celtic" as distinct from "Anglo-Saxon" poetry, as a small Pisgah whence to gain a glimpse into a strange and beautiful land, a land wherein, as in a certain design by William Blake, the sun, the moon, and the morning star all shine together, and where the horizons are spanned by fugitive rainbows ever marvellously dissolving and more marvellously re-forming.

The effort of the Editor has been to give, not always the finest or most unquestionably authentic examples of early Celtic poetry, but the most characteristic.   Thus only could some idea be conveyed of the physiognomy of this ancient literature.

In the first section, that representative of Early Gaelic, a long period of time is covered.   A whole

heroic age lies between that strange pantheistic utterance
of Amergin, who is now accepted as the earliest Erse
poet of whom we have authentic record, and the hymns
of Columba : and the quaint " Shaving Hymn " of
Murdoch the Monk, though it precedes the Ossianic
fragments, relates to a much nearer period of history
than they do.   Of these Ossianic fragments, it is not
needful to say more here than that, in their actual form,
they are no more genuinely old than, for example, are
many of the lovely fantasias on old themes by modern
Irish poets.   They are, at most, fundamentally ancient,
and are given here on this plea, and not as the translations of Macpherson.   The day is gone when the
stupid outcry against Macpherson's "Ossian," as no
more than a gigantic fraud, finds a response among
lovers of literature.   We all know, now, that Macpherson's "Ossian" is not a genuine translation of
authentic Dana Oisin mhic Fhionn, but, for all its
great and enduring beauty, a clumsily - constructed,
self-contradictory, and sometimes grotesquely impossible
rendering of disconnected, fugitive, and, for the most
part, oral lore.   Of the genuineness of this legendary
lore there is no longer any doubt in the minds of those
native and alien students, who alone are qualified to
pronounce a definite verdict on this long disputed point.
It would have been easy to select other Ossianic
fragments ; but as, in this anthology, the spirit and not
the letter was everything, it was considered advisable
to make as apt a compromise with Macpherson's
"Ossian" as practicable.   Ancient poetry of the nature
of pieces such as " The Song of Fionn " (page 4)
convey little to the ordinary reader, not only on
account of their puzzling allusions to events and per-
sons of whom the Englishman is not likely to have
heard, or from the strangeness of their style, as
because of the remoteness of the underlying sentiment
and mental standpoint.   And of this there can be no

question : that the ancient poetry, the antique spirit, breathes throughout this eighteenth-century restoration, and gives it enduring life, charm, and all the spell of cosmic imagination. It may well be, indeed, that the literary historian has another signal discovery to make, and, in definitively dissociating Oisìn of the Féinn and Ossian of Badenoch, prove convincingly that James Macpherson was not even the author (of the greater part at any rate) of the matter that has been interpolated into the original, inchoate, traditional bardic lore.

However much or little appeal "Ossian" may have for English readers of to-day, there can surely be no doubt that all who have the spirit of poetry must recognise the charm of the ancient Celtic imagination in compositions such as "Credhe's Lament" (page 5). This lovely haunting lament, from the "Book of Lismore," comes in its English form from that invaluable work of Mr S. Hayes O'Grady, "Silva Gadelica." Of how much Celtic poetry, modern as well as ancient, is not this, though variously expressed, the refrain : "Melodious is the crane, and O melodious is the crane, in the marshlands of Druim-dá-thrén ! 'tis she that may not save her brood alive !"

For the remarkable continuity of both expression and sentiment which characterises Celtic poetry, ancient and modern, let the student turn, for example, to the most famous Gaelic poem in Scotland to-day, Duncan Bàn Macintyre's "Ben Dorain," and compare it with this "Lay of Arran" by Caeilte, the Ossianic bard—Arran, no longer Arran of the many stags, but still one of the loveliest of the Scottish isles, and touched on every headland and hill with the sunset glamour of the past.

CAEILTE—LAY OF ARRAN.*

"Arran of the many stags—the sea impinges on her
very shoulders! an island in which whole companies
were fed—and with ridges among which blue spears
were reddened! Skittish deer are on her pinnacles,
soft blackberries upon her waving heather; cool water
there is upon her rivers, and mast upon her russet oaks!
Greyhounds there were in her, and beagles; blaeberries
and sloes of the blackthorn; dwellings with their backs
set close against her woods, and the deer fed scattered
by her oaken thickets! A crimson crop grew on her
rocks, in all her glades a faultless grass; over her crags
affording friendly refuge, leaping went on and fawns
were skipping! Smooth were her level spots—her wild
swine they were fat; cheerful her fields (this is a tale
that may be credited), her nuts hung on her forest
hazel's boughs, and there was sailing of long galleys
past her! Right pleasant their condition all when the
fair weather sets in: under her rivers' brinks trouts lie;
the sea-gulls wheeling round her grand cliff answer one
the other—at every fitting time delectable is Arran!"

Again, most readers will be able to apprehend the
delight of the barbaric outlook in compositions such as
"Cuchullin in His Chariot," which has been excerpted

---

* "On the first day of the Trogan-month, we, to the
number of Fianna's three battalions, practised to repair
to Arran, and there to have our fill of hunting until such
time as from the tree-tops the cuckoo would call in
Ireland. More melodious than all birds whatsoever, it
was to give ear to the voices of the birds as they
rose from the billows, and from the island's coast line;
thrice fifty separate flocks there are that encircled her,
and they clad in all brilliance of all colours; as blue, and
green, and azure, and yellow."

from Hector MacLean's "Ultonian Hero Ballads"; or
the fantastic beauty of "The March of the Faerie
Host," as rendered by Prof. Kuno Meyer after the
original in "The Book of Lismore"; or the lovely portrait
of a beautiful woman, by a Highland poet of old, the
"Aisling air Dhreach Mna; or, Vision of a Fair
Woman." Possibly, too, even Celtic scholars may
not be displeased to read here English metrical paraphrases, such as Sir Samuel Ferguson's "Lament of
Deirdrê for the Sons of Usnach,"* or Mr T. W.
Rolleston's haunting "The Lament of Queen Maev";
or, again, in dubiously authentic fragments such as
"Fingal and Ros-crana," to have an opportunity to trace
the "inner self" of many a familiar ballad or legend.

The Breton section, also, is represented equally slightly,
though perhaps not inadequately, all things considered.
"The Dance of the Sword" is, probably, fundamentally
one of the most ancient of Celtic bardic utterances. In the
modern selection, it will be a surprise to many readers
to encounter names so familiar to lovers of French
poetry as Leconte de Lisle and Villiers de l'Isle-Adam.
There are many contemporary Breton poets of distinction, but it was feasible to select no more than one or
two. Auguste Brizeux and Charles Le Goffic may be
taken as typical exemplars of the historically re-creative
and the individually impressionistic methods. Unfortun-
ately neither is represented here. It was desirable to
select at least one poet who still uses the old Armorican
tongue; but in my translation from Leo-Kermorvan's
"Taliesen" (as again in that of Tiercelin's "By
Menec'hi Shore"), I have not attempted a rhymed
version, as in the original, or in the French version

---

* Readers should obtain Dr Hyde's "Three Sorrows
of Story-Telling" (1/-), wherein the beautiful old tale
of Deirdrê is re-told by one who is at once a poet and
a scholar.

published in the "Anthologie." There are very few
translators who can be faithful both to the sound and
sense, in the attempt concurrently to reproduce identity
of form, music, and substance; and, as a rule, therefore,
rhythmic prose, or an unrhymed metrical version, is
likely to prove more interesting as well as more truly
interpretative.

Out of the rich garth of ancient and mediæval Welsh
poetry, the Editor has culled only a few blossoms.
They contain, at least, something of that lyric love of
Nature which is so distinctively Celtic, and is the chief
charm of the poetic literature of Wales.   It is earnestly
to be hoped that some poet-scholar will give us before
long, in English, an anthology of the best contemporary
Welsh poetry.

Of living poets who write in Gaelic, there are more
in Scotland than in Ireland.   The Hebrides have been
a nest of singers, since Mary Macleod down to the
youngest of the Uist poets of to-day; and though there
is not at present any Alexander Macdonald or Duncan
Bàn Macintyre, there are many singers who have a
sweet and fine note, and many writers whose poems
have beauty, grace, and distinction.   Perhaps the last
fine product of the pseudo-antique school is the "Sean
Dàna"* of Dr John Smith, late in the last century; but
occasionally there occurs in our own day a noteworthy
instance of the re-telling of the old tales in the old way.
In "The Celtic Monthly," and other periodicals, much
good Gaelic verse is to be found, and it is no exaggeration to say that at this moment there are more than a
hundred Gaelic singers in Western Scotland whose poetry
is as fresh and winsome, and, in point of form as well
as substance, as beautiful, as any that is being produced
throughout the rest of the realm.   The Gaelic Muse has

* Whence comes the "Prologue to Gaul," given at
p. 187 of this book.

also found a home in Canada, and it is interesting to note that one of the longest of recent Gaelic poems was written by a Highlander in far-away Burmah.

"The Highlander" (and in this and the following passage I quote the words of Professor Mackinnon, from his Inaugural Address on his succession to the Celtic Chair at Edinburgh University) "The Highlander may be truly described as the child of music and song. For many a long year his language is the language, for the most part, of the uneducated classes. And yet, amid surroundings which too often are but mean and wretched, without the advantages of education beyond what his native glen supplied, he has contrived to enliven his lot by the cultivation of such literature as the local bards, the traditions of the clan, and the popular tales of the district supplied. He has attempted, not unsuccessfully, to live not for the day and hour alone, but, in a true sense, to live the life of the spirit! He has produced a mass of lyric poetry which, in rhythmical flow, purity of sentiment, and beauty of expression, can compare favourably with the literature of more powerful and more highly-civilised communities.

"In the highest efforts of Gaelic literature, in the prose of Norman Macleod, in the masterpieces of the lyric poets, in the "Sean Dàna" of Dr Smith, and above all, in the poems of Ossian, whether composed by James Macpherson or the son of Fingal, the intellect of the Scottish Celt, in its various moods and qualities, finds its deepest and fullest expression. Here we have humour, pathos, passion, vehemence, a rush of feeling and emotion not always under restraint, and apt to run into exaggeration and hyperbole—characteristics which enter largely into the mental and spiritual organisation of the people. But above and beneath all these, there is a touch of melancholy, a 'cry of the weary,' pervading the spirit of the Celt. Ossian gives expression to this sentiment in the touching line which Matthew Arnold, the most sympathetic and penetrating critic of the Celtic imagination, with the true instinct of genius, prefixes to his charming volume, ' On the Study of Celtic Literature ' :

"'They went forth to the war, but they always fell.'"

Professor Mackinnon goes on to adduce a familiar legend, which may again be quoted, for we are all now waiting for that longed-for blast which shall arouse the spell-bound trance wherein sleeps "Anima Celtica." The Féinn, he says, were laid spell-bound in a cave which no man knew of. At the mouth of the cave hung a horn, which if ever any man should come and blow three times, the spell would be broken, and the Féinn would arise, alive and well. A hunter, one day wandering in the mist, came on this cave, saw the horn, and knew what it meant. He looked in and saw the Féinn lying asleep all round the cave. He lifted the horn and blew one blast. He looked in again, and saw that the Féinn had wakened, but lay still with their eyes staring, like those of dead men. He took the horn again, blew another blast, and instantly the Féinn all moved, each resting on his elbow. Terrified at their aspect, the hunter turned and fled homewards. He told what he had seen, and, accompanied by friends, went to search for the cave. They could not find it ; it has never again been found ; and so there still sit, each resting on his elbow, waiting for the final blast to rouse them into life, the spell-bound heroes of the old Celtic world.

Of the modern and larger section of "Lyra Celtica" I need say little here. To avoid confusion, the Editor has refrained from representing poets whose "Celtic strain" is more or less obviously disputable ; hence the wise ignoring of the claims even of Scott and Burns. Byron was more Celtic in blood than in brain, and is represented really by virtue of this accidental kinship.

Ireland, Scotland, Wales, Man, Cornwall, and Brittany are all more or less adequately represented; and among the poets are some whose voices will be new to most readers. One or two writers, also, have been drawn upon as representatives of the distinctively Anglo-Celtic section of England. Finally, "greater Gaeldom" —the realm of the Irish and Scottish Gaels in the United States, Canada, and Australasia—is also represented; and one, at any rate, of these outlanders is a poet who has won distinction on both sides of the Atlantic.

If it be advisable to select one poet, still "with a future," as pre-eminently representative of the Celtic genius of to-day, I think there can be little doubt that W. B. Yeats' name is that which would occur first to most lovers of contemporary poetry. He has grace of touch and distinction of form beyond any of the younger poets of Great Britain, and there is throughout his work a haunting beauty, and a haunting sense of beauty everywhere perceived with joy and longing, that make its appeal irresistible for those who feel it at all. He is equally happy whether he deals with antique or with contemporary themes, and in almost every poem he has written there is that exquisite remoteness, that dream-like music, and that transporting charm which Matthew Arnold held to be one of the primary tests of poetry, and, in particular, of Celtic poetry.

As an example of Mr Yeats' narrative method, with legendary themes, I may quote this from his beautiful "Wanderings of Oisin" (rather affectedly and quite needlessly altered to Usheen in the latest version)—

"Fled foam underneath us, and round us a wandering and milky smoke,
High as the saddle-girth, covering away from our glances the tide;
And those that fled, and that followed, from the foam-pale distance broke;
The immortal desire of immortals we saw in their faces, and sighed.

I mused on the chase with the Fenians, and Bran,
Sgeolan, Lomair,
And never a song sang Neave, and over my finger-
tips
Came now the sliding of tears and sweeping of mist-
cold hair,
And now the warmth of sighs, and after the quiver of
lips.

Were we days long or hours long in riding, when
rolled in a grisly peace,
An isle lay level before us, with dripping hazel and
oak ?
And we stood on a sea's edge we saw not; for
whiter than new washed fleece
Fled foam underneath us, and round us a wandering
and milky smoke.

And we rode on the plains of the sea's edge—the sea's
edge barren and gray,
Gray sands on the green of the grasses and over the
dripping trees,
Dripping and doubling landward, as though they
would hasten away
Like an army of old men longing for rest from the
moan of the seas.

But the trees grew taller and closer, immense in their
wrinkling bark ;
Dropping—a murmurous dropping—old silence and that
one sound ;
For no live creatures lived there, no weasels moved
in the dark—
Long sighs arose in our spirits, beneath us bubbled
the ground.

And the ears of the horse went sinking away in the
hollow night,
For, as drift from a sailor slow drowning the gleams
of the world and the sun,

Ceased on our hands and our faces, on hazel and oak
   leaf, the light,
And the stars were blotted above us, and the whole
   of the world was one."

Often, too, there occur in his verse new and striking
imagery, as in the superb epithetical value of the fourth
line in the concluding stanza of "The Madness of King
Goll," one of the most beautiful of his poems—

"And now I wander in the woods
   When summer gluts the golden bees,
Or in autumnal solitudes
   Arise the leopard-coloured trees ;
Or when along the wintry strands
   The cormorants shiver on their rocks ;
I wander on, and wave my hands,
   And sing, and shake my heavy locks.
The gray wolf knows me ; by one ear
I lead along the woodland deer ;
The hares ran by me growing bold.
They will not hush, the leaves a-flutter
   round me, the beech leaves old."

Indeed, through all his work, "They will not hush ; the
leaves a-flutter, the beech leaves old"—the mystic leaves
of life, touched by the wind of old romance. We can
imagine him hearing often that fairy lure which his
"Stolen Child" listed and yielded to—

" Come away, O human child !
   To the waters and the wild
With a fairy, hand in hand,
For the world 's more full of weeping than
   you can understand."

For him always there is the Beauty of Beauty, the
Passion of Passion : the "Rose of the World."

"Who dreamed that beauty passes like a dream?
For these red lips, with all their mournful pride,
Mournful that no new wonder may betide,
Troy passed away in one high funeral gleam,
And Usna's children died.

We and the labouring world are passing by:
Amid men's souls, that waver and give place,
Like the pale waters in their wintry race,
Under the passing stars, foam of the sky,
Lives on this lonely face."

It is the lonely face that haunts the dreams of poets of
all races and ages: that "Lady Beauty" enthroned

" Under the arch of life, where love and death,
Terror and mystery, guard her shrine. . . ."

The vision of which we follow—

" How passionately, and irretrievably,
In what fond flight, how many ways and days!"

And of all races, none has so worshipped the "Rose of
the World" as has the Celt.

"No other human tribe," says Renan, "has carried
so much mystery into love. No other has conceived
with more delicacy the ideal of woman, nor been more
dominated by her. It is a kind of intoxication, a madness, a giddiness. Read the strange mabinogi of
'Pérédur,' or its French imitation, 'Parceval le Gallois';
these pages are dewy, so to say, with feminine
sentiment. Woman appears there as a sort of
vague vision intermediate between man and the super-
natural world. There is no other literature which offers
anything analagous to this. Compare Guinevere and
Iseult to those Scandinavian furies Gudruna and
Chrimhilde, and you will acknowledge that woman,
as chivalry conceived her—that ideal of sweetness and

beauty set up as the supreme object of life—is a creation neither classic, Christian, nor Germanic, but in reality Celtic."

And having quoted from Ernest Renan, himself one of the greatest of modern Celts, and a Celt in brain and genius as well as by blood, race, and birth, let me interpolate here a paraphrase of some words of his in that essay on "La Poesie de la Race Celtique," which was to intellectual France what Matthew Arnold's essay was to intellectual England.

If, he says, the eminence of races should be estimated according to the purity of their blood and inviolability of national character, there could be none able to dispute supremacy with the Celtic race. Never has human family lived more isolated from the world, nor less affected by foreign admixture.

Restricted by conquest to forgotten isles and peninsulas, the Celtic race has habitually striven to oppose an impassable barrier to all alien influences. It has ever trusted in itself, and in itself alone, and has drawn its mental and spiritual nurture from its own resources.

Hence that powerful individuality, that hatred of the stranger, which up to our day has formed the essential characteristic of the Celtic peoples. The civilisation of Rome hardly reached them, and left among them but few traces. The Germanic invasion flowed back on them, but it did not affect them at all. At the present hour they still resist an invasion, dangerous in quite another way, that of modern civilisation, so destructive of local varieties and national types. Ireland in particular (and there, perhaps, is the secret of her irremediable weakness) is the sole country of Europe where the native can produce authentic documents of his remote unbroken lineage, and designate with certainty, up to pre-historic ages, the race from which he sprang.

One does not enough reflect on how strange it is that an ancient race should continue down to our day, and almost under our eyes, in some islands and peninsulas of the West, its own life, more and more diverted from it, it is true, by the noise from without, but still faithful to its language, its memories, its ideals, and its genius. We are especially apt to forget that this small race, contracted now to the extreme confines of Europe, in the midst of those rocks and mountains where its enemies have driven it, is in possession of a literature, which in the Middle Ages exerted an immense influence, changed the current of European imagination, and imposed upon almost the whole of Christianity its poetical motifs. It is, however, only necessary to open authentic monuments of Celtic genius to convince oneself that the race which created these has had its own original method of thought and feeling ; and that nowhere does the eternal illusion dress itself in more seductive colours. In the grand concert of the human species, no family equals this, for penetrating voices which go to the heart. Alas ! if it, also, is condemned to disappear, this fading glory of the West ! Arthur will not return to his enchanted isle, and Saint Patrick was right in saying to Ossian : " The heroes whom you mourn are dead ; can they live again ? "

A strange melancholy characterises the genius of the Celtic race. For all the blithe songs and happy abandon of so many Irish singers, the Irish themselves have given us the most poignant, the most hauntingly-sad lyric cries in all modern literature. Renan fully recognises this, and how, even in the heroic age, the melancholy of inappeasible regret, of insatiable longing, is as obvious as in our own day, when spiritual weariness is as an added crown of thorns. Whence comes this sadness, he asks ? Take the songs of the sixth century bards ; they mourn more defeats than they sing victories. The history of the Celtic race itself is but a long com-

plaint, the lament of exiles, the grief of despairing flights
beyond the seas. If occasionally it seems to make merry,
a tear ever lurks behind the smile ; it rarely knows
that singular forgetfulness of the human state and of its
destinies which is called gaiety. But, if its songs of
joy end in elegies, nothing equals the delicious sadness
of these national melodies.

Nevertheless, concludes the most famous of modern
Breton writers, we are still far from believing that the
Celtic race has said its last word. After having exer-
cised all the godly and worldly chivalries, sought with
Pérédur the Holy Graal and the Beautiful, dreamed
with Saint Brandan of mystical Atlantides, who knows
what the Celtic genius would produce in the domain of
the intelligence if it should embolden itself to make its
entrance into the world, and if it subjected its rich and
profound nature to the conditions of modern thought ?
Few races have had a poetical infancy as complete as
the Celtic—mythology, lyricism, epic, romanesque imagination, religious enthusiasm, nothing have they lacked.
Why should philosophic thought be lacking? Germany,
which had begun by science and criticism, has finished
with poetry ; why should not the Celtic races, which
began with poetry, not end with a new and vivid
criticism of actual life as it now is?   It is not so far
from the one to the other as we are apt to suppose ; the
poetical races are the philosophical races, and philosophy is
at bottom but a manner of poetry like any other. When
one thinks that Germany fronted, less than a century ago,
the revelation of its genius ; that everywhere national
idiosyncrasies, which seemed effaced, have suddenly
risen again in our day more alive than ever, one is
persuaded that it is rash to set a law for the discon-
tinuances and awakenings of races. Modern civilisation,
which seemed made to absorb them, may, perhaps, be
but the forcing-house for a new and more superb efflor-
escence.

No, it is no "disastrous end": whether the Celtic peoples be slowly perishing or are spreading innumerable fibres of life towards a richer and fuller, if a less national and distinctive existence. From Renan, the high priest of the Breton faith, to the latest of his kindred of the Gael, there is a strange new uprising of hope. It is realised that the Dream is nigh dreamed: and then . . .

> " Till the soil—bid cities rise—
> Be strong, O Celt—be rich, be wise—
> But still, with those divine grave eyes,
> Respect the realm of Mysteries."

Let me conclude, then, in the words of the most recent of those many eager young Celtic writers whose songs and romances are charming the now intent mind of the Anglo-Saxon. "A doomed and passing race. Yes, but not wholly so. The Celt has at last reached his horizon. There is no shore beyond. He knows it. This has been the burden of his song since Malvina led the blind Oisìn to his grave by the sea. 'Even the Children of Light must go down into darkness.' But this apparition of a passing race is no more than the fulfilment of a glorious resurrection before our very eyes. For the genius of the Celtic race stands out now with averted torch, and the light of it is a glory before the eyes, and the flame of it is blown into the hearts of the mightier conquering people. The Celt falls, but his spirit rises in the heart and the brain of the Anglo-Celtic peoples, with whom are the destinies of the generations to come."

WILLIAM SHARP.

Read these faint runes of Mystery,
O Celt, at home and o'er the sea;
The bond is loosed—the poor are free—
The world's great future rests with thee!

Till the soil—bid cities rise—
Be strong, O Celt—be rich, be wise—
But still, with those divine grave eyes,
Respect the realm of Mysteries.

The Book of Orm.

I

ANCIENT IRISH
AND SCOTTISH

A

The Mystery of Amergin.

I am the wind which breathes upon the sea,
I am the wave of the ocean,
I am the murmur of the billows,
I am the ox of the seven combats,
I am the vulture upon the rocks,
I am a beam of the sun,
I am the fairest of plants,
I am a wild boar in valour,
I am a salmon in the water,
I am a lake in the plain,
I am a word of science,
I am the point of the lance of battle,
I am the God who creates in the head [i. e. of
    man] the fire [i. e. the thought].
Who is it who throws light into the meeting on the
    mountain?
Who announces the ages of the moon [If not I]?
Who teaches the place where couches the sun [If not I]?

The Song of Fionn.

May-day, delightful time! How beautiful the colour!
The blackbirds sing their full lay. Would that Læg
were here!
The cuckoos sing in constant strains. How welcome is
the noble
Brilliance of the seasons ever! On the margin of the
branching woods
The summer swallows skim the stream: the swift
horses seek the pool:
The heather spreads out her long hair: the weak fair
bog-down grows.
Sudden consternation attacks the signs; the planets, in
their courses running, exert an influence:
The sea is lulled to rest, flowers cover the earth.

Credhe's Lament.

The haven roars, and O the haven roars, over the rushing race of Rinn-dá-bharc! the drowning of the warrior of loch dá chonn, that is what the wave impinging on the strand laments. Melodious is the crane, and O melodious is the crane, in the marshlands of Druim-dá'-thrén! 'tis she that may not save her brood alive: the wild dog of two colours is intent upon her nestlings. A woeful note, and O a woeful note is that which the thrush in Drumqueen emits! but not more cheerful is the wail that the blackbird makes in Letterlee. A woeful sound, and O a woeful sound, is that the deer utters in Drumdaleish! dead lies the doe of Druim Silenn: the mighty stag bells after her. Sore suffering to me, and O suffering sore, is the hero's death—his death, that used to lie with me!... Sore suffering to me is Cael, and O Cael is a suffering sore, that by my side he is in dead man's form! That the wave should have swept over his white body—that is what hath distracted me, so great was his delightfulness. A dismal roar, and O a dismal roar, is that the shore-surf makes upon the strand! seeing that the same hath drowned the comely noble man, to me it is an affliction that Cael ever sought to encounter it. A woeful booming, and O a boom of woe, is that which the wave makes upon the northward beach! beating as it does against the polished rock, lamenting for Cael, now that he is gone. A woeful fight, and O a fight of woe, is that the wave wages against the southern shore! As for me my span is determined!... A woeful melody, and O a melody of woe, is that which the heavy surge of Tullachleish emits! As for me: the calamity that is fallen upon me having shattered me, for me prosperity exists no more. Since now Crimthann's son is drowned, one that I may love after him there is not in being. Many a chief is fallen by his hand, and in the battle his shield never uttered outcry!

Cuchullin in his Chariot.

"What is the cause of thy journey or thy story?"

The cause of my journey and my story
The men of Erin, yonder, as we see them,
Coming towards you on the plain.
The chariot on which is the fold, figured and cerulean,
Which is made strongly, handy, solid;
Where were active, and where were vigorous;
And where were full-wise, the noble hearted folk;
In the prolific, faithful city;—
Fine, hard, stone-bedecked, well-shafted;
Four large-chested horses in that splendid chariot;
Comely, frolicsome.

"What do we see in that chariot?"

The white-bellied, white-haired, small-eared,
Thin-sided, thin-hoofed, horse-large, steed-large horses;
With fine, shining, polished bridles;
Like a gem; or like red sparkling fire;—
Like the motion of a fawn, wounded;
Like the rustling of a loud wind in winter;—
Coming to you in that chariot.—

"What do we see in that chariot?"

We see in that chariot,
The strong, broad-chested, nimble, gray horses,—
So mighty, so broad-chested, so fleet, so choice;—
Which would wrench the sea skerries from the rocks.—
The lively, shielded, powerful horses;—
So mettlesome, so active, so clear-shining;—
Like the talon of an eagle 'gainst a fierce beast;
Which are called the beautiful Large-Gray—
The fond, large Meactroigh.

"What do we see in that chariot?"

We see in that chariot,
The horses; which are white-headed, white-hoofed, slender-legged,
Fine-haired, sturdy, imperious;
Satin-bannered, wide-chested;
Small-aged, small-haired, small-eared;
Large-hearted, large-shaped, large-nostriled;
Slender-waisted, long-bodied,—and they are foal-like;
Handsome, playful, brilliant, wild-leaping;
Which are called the Dubh-Seimhlinn.

"Who sits in that chariot?"

He who sits in that chariot,
Is the warrior, able, powerful, well-worded,
Polished, brilliant, very graceful.—
There are seven sights on his eye;
And we think that that is good vision to him;
There are six bony, fat fingers,
On each hand that comes from his shoulder;
There are seven kinds of fair hair on his head;—
Brown hair next his head's skin,
And smooth red hair over that;
And fair-yellow hair, of the colour of gold;
And clasps on the top, holding it fast;—
Whose name is Cuchullin, Seimh-suailte,
Son of Aodh, son of Agh, son of other Aodh.—
His face is like red sparkles;—
Fast-moving on the plain like mountain fleet-mist;
Or like the speed of a hill hind;
Or like a hare on rented level ground.—
It was a frequent step—a fast step—a joyful step;—
The horses coming towards us :—
Like snow hewing the slopes;—
The panting and the snorting,
Of the horses coming towards thee.

Deirdrê's Lament for the Sons of Usnach.

The lions of the hill are gone,
And I am left alone—alone—
Dig the grave both wide and deep,
For I am sick, and fain would sleep !

The falcons of the wood are flown,
And I am left alone—alone—
Dig the grave both deep and wide,
And let us slumber side by side.

The dragons of the rock are sleeping,
Sleep that wakes not for our weeping—
Dig the grave, and make it ready,
Lay me on my true-love's body.

Lay their spears and bucklers bright
By the warriors' sides aright;
Many a day the three before me
On their linkèd bucklers bore me.

Lay upon the low grave floor,
'Neath each head, the blue claymore ;
Many a time the noble three
Reddened their blue blades for me.

Lay the collars, as is meet,
Of the greyhounds at their feet ;
Many a time for me have they
Brought the tall red deer to bay.

In the falcon's jesses throw,
Hook and arrow, line and bow ;
Never again, by stream or plain,
Shall the gentle woodsmen go.

Sweet companions, were ye ever—
Harsh to me, your sister, never ;

ANCIENT ERSE

Woods and wilds, and misty valleys,
Were with you as good's a palace.

O, to hear my true-love singing,
Sweet as sounds of trumpets ringing ;
Like the sway of ocean swelling
Rolled his deep voice round our dwelling.

O! to hear the echoes pealing
Round our green and fairy shealing,
When the three, with soaring chorus,
Passed the silent skylark o'er us.

Echo now, sleep, morn and even—
Lark alone enchant the heaven !
Ardan's lips are scant of breath,
Neesa's tongue is cold in death.

Stag, exult on glen and mountain—
Salmon, leap from loch to fountain—
Heron, in the free air warm ye—
Usnach's sons no more will harm ye !

Erin's stay no more you are,
Rulers of the ridge of war ;
Never more 'twill be your fate
To keep the beam of battle straight !

Woe is me ! by fraud and wrong,
Traitors false and tyrants strong,
Fell Clan Usnach, bought and sold,
For Barach's feast and Conor's gold !

Woe to Eman, roof and wall !
Woe to Red Branch, hearth and hall !—
Tenfold woe and black dishonour
To the foul and false Clan Conor !

Dig the grave both wide and deep,
Sick I am, and fain would sleep !
Dig the grave and make it ready,
Lay me on my true-love's body.

The Lament of Queen Maev.

Raise the Cromlech high!
Mac Moghcorb is slain,
And other men's renown
Has leave to live again.

Cold at last he lies
'Neath the burial stone.
All the blood he shed
Could not save his own.

Stately, strong he went,
Through his nobles all,
When we paced together
Up the banquet-hall.

Dazzling white as lime,
Was his body fair,
Cherry-red his cheeks,
Raven-black his hair.

Razor-sharp his spear,
And the shield he bore,
High as champion's head—
His arm was like an oar.

Never aught but truth
Spake my noble king;
Valour all his trust
In all his warfaring.

As the forkèd pole
Holds the roof-tree's weight,
So my hero's arm
Held the battle straight.

Terror went before him,
Death behind his back,
Well the wolves of Erinn
Knew his chariot's track.

Seven bloody battles
  He broke upon his foes,
In each a hundred heroes
  Fell beneath his blows.

Once he fought at Fossud,
  Thrice at Ath-finn-fail.
'Twas my king that conquered
  At bloody Ath-an-Scail.

At the Boundary Stream
  Fought the Royal Hound,
And for Bernas battle
  Stands his name renowned.

Here he fought with Leinster—
  Last of all his frays—
On the Hill of Cucorb's Fate
  High his Cromlech raise.

The March of the Faerie Host.

In well-devised battle array,
Ahead of their fair chieftain
They march amidst blue spears,
White curly-headed bands.

They scatter the battalions of the foe,
They ravage every land I have attacked,
Splendidly they march to combat
An impetuous, distinguished, avenging host!

No wonder though their strength be great:
Sons of kings and queens are one and all.
On all their heads are
Beautiful golden-yellow manes:

With smooth, comely bodies,
With bright blue-starred eyes,
With pure crystal teeth,
With thin red lips:

Good they are at man-slaying.

Vision of a Fair Woman.

(Aisling air Dhreach Mna.)

Tell us some of the charms of the stars:
Close and well set were her ivory teeth;
White as the canna upon the moor
Was her bosom the tartan bright beneath.

Her well-rounded forehead shone
Soft and fair as the mountain-snow;
Her two breasts were heaving full;
To them did the hearts of heroes flow.

Her lips were ruddier than the rose;
Tender and tunefully sweet her tongue;
White as the foam adown her side
Her delicate fingers extended hung.

Smooth as the dusky down of the elk
Appeared her shady eyebrows to me;
Lovely her cheeks were, like berries red;
From every guile she was wholly free.

Her countenance looked like the gentle buds
Unfolding their beauty in early spring;
Her yellow locks like the gold-browed hills;
And her eyes like the radiance the sunbeams
    bring.

The Fian Banners.

The Norland King stood on the height
  And scanned the rolling sea;
He proudly eyed his gallant ships
  That rode triumphantly.

And then he looked where lay his camp,
  Along the rocky coast,
And where were seen the heroes brave
  Of Lochlin's famous host.

Then to the land he turn'd, and there
  A fierce-like hero came;
Above him was a flag of gold,
  That waved and shone like flame.

"Sweet bard," thus spoke the Norland King,
  "What banner comes in sight?
The valiant chief that leads the host,
  Who is that man of might?"

"That," said the bard, "is young MacDoon
  His is that banner bright;
When forth the Féinn to battle go,
  He's foremost in the fight."

"Sweet bard, another comes; I see
  A blood-red banner toss'd
Above a mighty hero's head
  Who waves it o'er a host?"

"That banner," quoth the bard, "belongs
  To good and valiant Rayne;
Beneath it feet are bathed in blood
  And heads are cleft in twain."

"Sweet bard, what banner now I see
  A leader fierce and strong

Behind it moves with heroes brave
Who furious round him throng?"

" That is the banner of Great Gaul :
That silken shred of gold,
Is first to march and last to turn,
And flight ne'er stained its fold."

" Sweet bard, another now I see,
High o'er a host it glows,
Tell whether it has ever shone
O'er fields of slaughtered foes?"

" That gory flag is Cailt's," quoth he,
" It proudly peers in sight ;
It won its fame on many a field
In fierce and bloody fight."

" Sweet bard, another still I see ;
A host it flutters o'er ;
Like bird above the roaring surge
That laves the storm-swept shore.'

"The Broom of Peril," quoth the bard,
"Young Oscur's banner, see :
Amidst the conflict of dread chiefs
The proudest name has he."

The banner of great Fionn we raised ;
The Sunbeam gleaming far,
With golden spangles of renown
From many a field of war.

The flag was fastened to its staff
With nine strong chains of gold,
With nine times nine chiefs for each chain ;
Before it foes oft rolled.

" Redeem your pledge to me," said Fionn;
"And show your deeds of might
To Lochlin as you did before
In many a gory fight."

Like torrents from the mountain heights
That roll resistless on ;
So down upon the foe we rushed,
And victory won.

The Rune of St Patrick.

"The Faedh Fiada"; or, "The Cry of the Deer."

At Tara to-day in this fateful hour
I place all Heaven with its power,
And the sun with its brightness,
And the snow with its whiteness,
And fire with all the strength it hath,
And lightning with its rapid wrath,
And the winds with their swiftness along their path,
And the sea with its deepness,
And the rocks with their steepness,
And the earth with its starkness :
  All these I place,
  By God's almighty help and grace,
Between myself and the powers of darkness.

Columcille cecenit.

O, Son of my God, what a pride, what a pleasure
  To plough the blue sea !
The waves of the fountain of deluge to measure
  Dear Eiré to thee.

We are rounding Moy-n-Olurg, we sweep by its head, and
  We plunge through Loch Foyle,
Whose swans could enchant with their music the dead, and
  Make pleasure of toil.

The host of the gulls come with joyous commotion
  And screaming and sport,
I welcome my own "Dewy-Red" from the ocean
  Arriving in port.*

O Eiré, were wealth my desire, what a wealth were
  To gain far from thee,
In the land of the stranger, but there even health were
  A sickness to me !

Alas for the voyage O high King of Heaven
  Enjoined upon me,
For that I on the red plain of bloody Cooldrevin
  Was present to see.

How happy the son is of Dima ; no sorrow
  For him is designed,
He is having, this hour, round his own hill in Durrow
  The wish of his mind.

The sounds of the winds in the elms, like the strings of
  A harp being played,
The note of the blackbird that claps with the wings of
  Delight in the glade.

---

* Dearg-drúchtach—i.e. "Dewy-Red"—was the
name of St Columba's boat.

With him in Ros-Grencha the cattle are lowing
    At earliest dawn,
On the brink of the summer the pigeons are cooing
    And doves in the lawn.

Three things am I leaving behind me, the very
    Most dear that I know,
Tir-Leedach I'm leaving, and Durrow and Derry,
    Alas, I must go!

Yet my visit and feasting with Comgall have eased me
    At Cainneach's right hand,
And all but thy government, Eiré, has pleased me,
    Thou waterfall land.

Columcille fecit.

Delightful would it be to me to be in Uchd Ailiun
    On the pinnacle of a rock,
That I might often see
    The face of the ocean;
That I might see its heaving waves
    Over the wide ocean,
When they chant music to their Father
    Upon the world's course;
That I might see its level sparkling strand,
    It would be no cause of sorrow;
That I might hear the song of the wonderful birds,
    Source of happiness;
That I might hear the thunder of the crowding waves
    Upon the rocks;
That I might hear the roar by the side of the church
    Of the surrounding sea;
That I might see its noble flocks
    Over the watery ocean;
That I might see the sea-monsters,
    The greatest of all wonders;
That I might see its ebb and flood
    In their career;
That my mystical name might be, I say,
    Cul ri Erin;*
That contrition might come upon my heart
    Upon looking at her;
That I might bewail my evils all,
    Though it were difficult to compute them;
That I might bless the Lord
    Who conserves all,
Heaven with its countless bright orders,
    Land, strand and flood;

---

* That is, " Back turned to Ireland."

That I might search the books all,
That would be good for my soul;
At times kneeling to beloved Heaven;
At times psalm singing;
At times contemplating the King of Heaven,
Holy the chief;
At times at work without compulsion,
This would be delightful.
At times plucking duilisc from the rocks;
At times at fishing;
At times giving food to the poor;
At times in a carcair :*
The best advice in the presence of God
To me has been vouchsafed.
The King whose servant I am will not let
Anything deceive me.

---

* Solitary cell.

The Song of Murdoch the Monk.

Murdoch, whet thy knife, that we may shave our
crowns to the Great King.

Let us sweetly give our vow, and the hair of both our
heads to the Trinity.

I will shave mine to Mary; this is the doing of a true
heart:

To Mary shave thou these locks, well-formed, soft-eyed
man.

Seldom hast thou had, handsome man, a knife on thy
hair to shave it;

Oftener has a sweet, soft queen comb'd her hair beside
thee.

Whenever it was that we did bathe, with Brian of the
well-curled locks,

And once on a time that I did bathe at the well of the
fair-haired Boroimhe,

I strove in swimming with Ua Chais, on the cold
waters of the Fergus.

When he came ashore from the stream, Ua Chais and
I strove in a race :

These two knives, one to each, were given us by
Duncan Cairbreach;

No knives were better: shave gently then, Murdoch.

Whet your sword, Cathal, which wins the fertile Banva;

Ne'er was thy wrath heard without fighting, brave, red-
handed Cathal.

Preserve our shaved heads from cold and from heat,
gentle daughter of Iodehim,

Preserve us in the land of heat, softest branch of Mary.

The Aged Bard's Wish.

(Miann a' Bhàird Aosda.)

O, lay me by the gentle stream
Which glides with stealing course;
Lay my head beneath the shady boughs,
And thou, O sun, be mild upon my rest.

There, in the flowery grass,
Where the breeze sighs softly on the bank,
My feet shall be bathed with the dew
When it falls on the silent vale.

There, on my lone green heap,
The primrose and the daisy shall bloom over my head,
And the wild bright star of St John
Shall bend beside my cheek.

Above, on the steeps of the glen,
Green flowering boughs shall spread,
And sweet, from the still grey craigs,
The birds shall pour their songs.

There, from the ivied craig,
The gushing spring shall flow,
And the son of the rock shall repeat
The murmur of its fall.

The hinds shall call around my bed;
The hill shall answer to their voice,
When a thousand shall descend on the field,
And feed around my rest.

The calves shall sport beside me
By the stream of the level plain,
And the little kids, weary of their strife,
Shall sleep beneath my arm.

Far in the gentle breeze
The stag cries on the field;
The herds answer on the hill,
And descend to meet the sound.

I hear the steps of the hunter!
His whistling darts—his dog upon the hill.
The joy of youth returns to my cheek
At the sound of the coming chase!

My strength returns at the sounds of the wood;
The cry of hounds—the thrill of strings.
Hark! the death-shout—"The deer has fallen!"
I spring to life on the hill!

I see the bounding dog,
My companion on the heath;
The beloved hill of our chase,
The echoing craig of woods.

I see the sheltering cave
Which often received us from the night,
When the glowing tree and the joyful cup
Revived us with their cheer.

Glad was the smoking feast of deer,
Our drink was from Loch Treig, our music its hum of
    waves;
Though ghosts shrieked on the echoing hills,
Sweet was our rest in the cave.

I see the mighty mountain,
Chief of a thousand hills;
The dream of deer is in its locks,
Its head is the bed of clouds.

I see the ridge of hinds, the steep of the sloping glen,
The wood of cuckoos at its foot,
The blue height of a thousand pines,
Of wolves, and roes, and elks.

Like the breeze on the lake of firs
The little ducks skim on the pool,
At its head is the strath of pines,
The red rowan bends on its bank.

There, on the gliding wave,
The fair swan spreads her wing,
The broad white wing which never fails
When she soars amidst the clouds.

Far wandering over ocean
She seeks the cold dwelling of seals,
Where no sail bends the mast,
Nor prow divides the wave.

Come to the woody hills
With the lament of thy love;
Return, O swan, from the isle of waves,
And sing from thy course on high.

Raise thy mournful song—
Pour the sad tale of thy grief;
The son of the rock shall hear the sound,
And repeat thy strain of woe.

Spread thy wing over ocean,
Mount up on the strength of the winds;
Pleasant to my ear is thy sound,
The song of thy wounded heart.

O youth! thou who hast departed,
And left my grey and helpless hairs,
What land has heard on its winds
Thy cry come o'er its rocks?

Are the tears in thy eye, O maiden?
Thou of the lovely brow and lily hand;
Brightness be around thee for ever!
Thou shalt return no more from the narrow bed!

Tell me, O winds! since now I see them not,
Where grow the murmuring reeds?
The reeds which sigh where rest the trout
On their still transparent fins.

O raise and bear me on your hands,
Lay my head beneath the young boughs,
That their shade may veil my eyes
When the sun shall rise on high.

And thou, O gentle sleep!
Whose course is with the stars of night;
Be near with thy dreams of song
To bring back my days of joy.

My soul beholds the maid!
In the shade of the mighty oak,
Her white hand beneath her golden hair,
Her soft eye on her beloved.

He is near—but she is silent,
His beating heart is lost in song,
Their souls beam from their eyes—
Deer stand on the hill!

The song has ceased!—
Their bosoms meet ;—
Like the young and stainless rose
Her lips are pressed to his!—

Blessed be that commune sweet!
Recalling the joy which returns no more—
Blessed be thy soul, my love!
Thou maid with the bright flowing locks.

Hast thou forsaken me, O dream!
Once more return again!
Alas! thou art gone, and I am sad—
Bless thee, my love—farewell!

Friends of my youth, farewell!
Farewell, ye maids of love!
I see you now no more—with you is summer still,
With me—the winter night!

O lay me by the roaring fall,
By the sound of the murmuring craig,
Let the cruit and the shell be near,
And the shield of my father's wars.

O breeze of Ocean come,
With the sound of thy gentle course,
Raise me on thy wings, O wind,
And bear me to the isle of rest ;

Where the heroes of old are gone,
To the sleep which shall wake no more
Open the hall of Ossian and Daol—
The night is come—the bard departs!

Behold my dim grey mist !—
I go to the dwelling of bards on the hill!
Give me the airy cruit and shell for the way—
And now—my own loved cruit and shell—farewell!

Ossian Sang.

Sweet is the voice in the land of gold,
  And sweeter the music of birds that soar,
When the cry of the heron is heard on the wold,
  And the waves break softly on Bundatrore.

Down floats on the murmuring of the breeze
  The call of the cuckoo from Cossahun,
The blackbird is warbling among the trees,
  And soft is the kiss of the warming sun.

The cry of the eagle of Assaroe
  O'er the court of Mac Morne to me is sweet,
And sweet is the cry of the bird below
  Where the wave and the wind and the tall cliff meet.

Finn mac Cool is the father of me,
  Whom seven battalions of Fenians fear:
When he launches his hounds on the open lea
  Grand is their cry as they rouse the deer.

Fingal and Ros-crana.

ROS-CRANA.

By night, came a dream to Ros-crana! I feel my beating soul. No vision of the forms of the dead came to the blue eyes of Erin. But, rising from the wave of the north, I beheld him bright in his locks. I beheld the son of the king. My beating soul is high. I laid my head down in night: again ascended the form. Why delayest thou thy coming, young rider of stormy waves!

But, there, far-distant, he comes; where seas roll their green ridges in mist! Young dweller of my soul; why dost thou delay ——

FINGAL.

It was the soft voice of Moi-lena! the pleasant breeze of the valley of roes! But why dost thou hide thee in shades? Young love of heroes, rise. Are not thy steps covered with light? In thy groves thou appearest, Ros-crana, like the sun in the gathering of clouds. Why dost thou hide thee in shades? Young love of heroes, rise.

ROS-CRANA.

My fluttering soul is high! Let me turn from steps of the king. He has heard my secret voice, and shall my blue eyes roll in his presence? Roe of the hill of moss, toward thy dwelling I move. Meet me, ye breezes of Mora! as I move through the valley of the winds. But why should he ascend his ocean? Son of heroes, my soul is thine! my steps shall not move to the desert; the light of Ros-crana is here.

FINGAL.

It was the light tread of a ghost, the fair dweller of eddying winds. Why deceivest thou me with thy voice?

Here let me rest in shades. Shouldst thou stretch thy white arm from thy grove, thou sunbeam of Cormac of Erin——

ROS-CRANA.

He is gone; and my blue eyes are dim; faint-rolling, in all my tears. But, there, I behold him, alone; king of Selma, my soul is thine. Ah me! what clanging of armour! Colc-ulla of Atha is near!

The Night-Song of the Bards.

[Five bards passing the night in the house of a chief, who was a poet himself, went severally to make their observations on, and returned with an extempore description of, night.]

FIRST BARD.

Night is dull and dark. The clouds rest on the hills. No star with green trembling beam; no moon looks from the sky. I hear the blast in the wood, but I hear it distant far. The stream of the valley murmurs; but its murmur is sullen and sad. From the tree at the grave of the dead the long-howling owl is heard. I see a dim form on the plain! It is a ghost! it fades, it flies. Some funeral shall pass this way: the meteor marks the path.

The distant dog is howling from the hut of the hill. The stag lies on the mountain moss: the hind is at his side. She hears the wind in his branchy horns. She starts, but lies again.

The roe is in the cleft of the rock; the heath-cock's head is beneath his wing. No beast, no bird is abroad, but the owl and the howling fox: she on a leafless tree; he in a cloud on the hill.

Dark, panting, trembling, sad, the traveller has lost his way. Through shrubs, through thorns, he goes, along the gurgling rill. He fears the rock and the fen. He fears the ghost of night. The old tree groans to the blast; the falling branch resounds. The wind drives the withered burrs, clung together, along the grass. It is the light tread of a ghost! He trembles amidst the night.

Dark, dusky, howling, is night, cloudy, windy, and full of ghosts! The dead are abroad! my friends, receive me from the night.

SECOND BARD.

The wind is up, the shower descends. The spirit of the mountain shrieks. Woods fall from high. Windows

flap.* The growing river roars. The traveller attempts
the ford.   Hark! that shriek! he dies!   The storm
drives the horse from the hill, the goat, the lowing cow.
They tremble as drives the shower, beside the shoulder-
ing bank.

The hunter starts from sleep, in his lonely hut; he
wakes the fire decayed.   His wet dogs smoke around him.
He fills the chinks with heath.   Loud roar two mountain streams which meet beside his booth. †

Sad on the side of a hill the wandering shepherd sits.
The tree resounds above him.   The stream roars down
the rock.   He waits for the rising moon to guide him to
his home.

Ghosts ride on the storm to-night.   Sweet is their
voice between the squalls of wind.   Their songs are of
other worlds.

The rain is past.   The dry wind blows.   Streams
roar, and windows flap.   Cold drops fall from the roof.
I see the starry sky.   But the shower gathers again.
The west is gloomy and dark.   Night is stormy and
dismal; receive me, my friends, from night.

THIRD BARD.

The wind still sounds between the hills, and whistles
through the grass of the rock.   The firs fall from their
place.   The turfy hut is torn.   The clouds, divided, fly
over the sky, and show the burning stars.   The meteor,
token of death! flies sparkling through the gloom.   It
rests on the hill.   I see the withered fern, the dark-
browed rock, the fallen oak.   Who is that in his shroud
beneath the tree, by the stream?

The waves dark-tumble on the lake, and lash its
rocky sides.   The boat is brimful in the cove; the oars
on the rocking tide.   A maid sits sad beside the rock,

---

* i.e. the sheepskin or deerskin coverings for aper-
tures, still used in some remote shealings and bothain.
† Shed.

and eyes the rolling stream. Her lover promised to come. She saw his boat, when yet it was light, on the lake. Is this his broken boat on the shore? Are these his groans on the wind?

Hark! the hail rattles around. The flaky snow descends. The tops of the hills are white. The stormy winds abate. Various is the night and cold; receive me, my friends, from night.

FOURTH BARD.

Night is calm and fair; blue, starry, settled is night. The winds, with the clouds, are gone. They sink behind the hill. The moon is up on the mountain. Trees glister, streams shine on the rock. Bright rolls the settled lake; bright the stream of the vale.

I see the trees overturned; the shocks of corn on the plain. The wakeful hind rebuilds the shocks, and whistles on the distant field.

Calm, settled, fair is night! Who comes from the place of the dead? That form with the robe of snow, white arms, and dark-brown hair! It is the daughter of the chief of the people: she that lately fell! Come, let us view thee, O maid! Thou that hast been the delight of heroes! The blast drives the phantom away; white, without form, it ascends the hill.

The breezes drive the blue mist, slowly, over the narrow vale. It rises on the hill, and joins its head to heaven. Night is settled, calm, blue, starry, bright with the moon. Receive me not, my friends, for lovely is the night.

FIFTH BARD.

Night is calm, but dreary. The moon is in a cloud in the west. Slow moves that pale beam along the shaded hill. The distant wave is heard. The torrent murmurs on the rock. The cock is heard from the booth.* More than half the night is past. The house-wife, groping in

---

* Here probably the byre.

the gloom, re-kindles the settled fire. The hunter thinks
that day approaches, and calls his bounding dogs. He
ascends the hill, and whistles on his way. A blast re-
moves the cloud. He sees the starry plough of the north.
Much of the night is to pass. He nods by the mossy rock.

Hark! the whirlwind is in the wood! A low murmur in the vale! It is the mighty army of the dead
returning from the air.

The moon rests behind the hill. The beam is still on
that lofty rock. Long are the shadows of the trees.
Now it is dark over all. Night is dreary, silent, and
dark; receive me, my friends, from night.

THE CHIEF.

Let clouds rest on the hills: spirits fly, and travellers
fear. Let the winds of the woods arise, the sounding
storms descend. Roar streams and windows flap, and
green-winged meteors fly! Rise the pale moon from
behind her hills, or inclose her head in clouds! Night is
alike to me, blue, stormy, or gloomy the sky. Night
flies before the beam, when it is poured on the hill. The
young day returns from his clouds, but we return no more.

Where are our chiefs of old? Where are our kings
of mighty name? The fields of their battles are silent.
Scarce their mossy tombs remain. We shall also be
forgot. This lofty house shall fall. Our sons shall not
behold the ruins in grass. They shall ask of the aged,
"Where stood the walls of our fathers?"

Raise the song, and strike the harp; send round the
shells of joy. Suspend a hundred tapers on high.
Youths and maids begin the dance. Let some grey bard
be near me, to tell the deeds of other times; of kings
renowned in our land, of chiefs we behold no more.
Thus let the night pass until morning shall appear in
our halls. Then let the bow be at hand, the dogs, the
youths of the chase. We shall ascend the hill with day,
and awake the deer.

Comala.

FINGAL	MELILCOMA	} Daughters of
HYDALLAN	DERSAGRENA	Morni
COMALA	BARDS	

DERSAGRENA.

The chase is over. No noise on Ardven but the torrent's roar! Daughter of Morni, come from Crona's banks. Lay down the bow and take the harp. Let the night come on with songs, let our joy be great on Ardven.

MELILCOMA.

Night comes apace, thou blue-eyed maid! Grey night grows dim along the plain. I saw a deer at Crona's stream; a mossy bank he seemed through the gloom, but soon he bounded away. A meteor played round his branching horns! The awful faces of other times looked from the clouds of Crona!

DERSAGRENA.

These are the signs of Fingal's death. The king of shields is fallen! and Caracul prevails. Rise, Comala, from thy rock: daughter of Sarno, rise in tears! The youth of thy love is low; his ghost is on our hills.

MELILCOMA.

There Comala sits forlorn! two grey dogs near shake their rough ears, and catch the flying breeze. Her red cheek rests upon her arm, the mountain-wind is in her hair. She turns her blue eyes toward the fields of his promise. Where art thou, O Fingal? The night is gathering around!

COMALA.

O Carun of the streams! Why do I behold thy waters rolling in blood? Has the noise of the battle

been heard; and sleeps the King of Morven? Rise,
moon, thou daughter of the sky! Look from between
thy clouds, rise that I may behold the gleam of his
steel, on the field of his promise. Or rather let the
meteor, that lights our fathers through the night, come,
with its red beam, to show me the way to my fallen
hero. Who will defend me from sorrow? Who from
the love of Hydallan? Long shall Comala look before
she can behold Fingal in the midst of his host; bright
as the coming forth of the morning, in the cloud of an
early shower.

HYDALLAN.
Dwell, thou mist of gloomy Crona, dwell on the path
of the king! Hide his steps from mine eyes, let me
remember my friend no more. The bands of battle are
scattered, no crowding tread is round the noise of his
steel. O Carun! roll thy streams of blood, the chief of
the people is low.

COMALA.
Who fell on Carun's sounding banks, son of the
the cloudy night? Was he white as the snow of
Ardven? Blooming as the bow of the shower? Was
his hair like the mist of the hill, soft and curling in the
day of the sun? Was he like the thunder of heaven in
battle? Fleet as the roe of the desert?

HYDALLAN.
O that I might behold his love, fair leaning from her
rock! Her red eye dim in tears, her blushing cheek half
hid in her locks! Blow, O gentle breeze! Lift thou
the heavy locks of the maid, that I may behold her
white arm, her lovely cheek in her grief.

COMALA.
And is the son of Comhal fallen, chief of the mournful tale? The thunder rolls on the hill! The lightning

flies on wings of fire! They frighten not Comala; for Fingal is low. Say, chief of the mournful tale, fell the breaker of the shields?

HYDALLAN.

The nations are scattered on their hills; they shall hear the voice of the king no more.

COMALA.

Confusion pursue thee over thy plains! Ruin overtake thee, thou king of the world! Few be thy steps to thy grave; and let one virgin mourn thee! Let her be like Comala, tearful in the days of her youth! Why hast thou told me, Hydallan, that my hero fell? I might have hoped a little while his return, I might have thought I saw him on the distant rock; a tree might have deceived me with his appearance; the wind of the hill might have been the sound of his horn in mine ear. O that I were on the banks of Carun! that my tears might be warm on his cheek!

HYDALLAN.

He lies not on the banks of Carun; on Ardven heroes raise his tomb. Look on them, O moon! from thy clouds; be thy beam bright on his breast, that Comala may behold him in the light of his armour!

COMALA.

Stop, ye sons of the grave, till I behold my love! He left me at the chase alone. I knew not that he went to war. He said he would return with the night; the King of Morven is returned! Why didst thou not tell me that he would fall, O trembling dweller of the rock? Thou sawest him in the blood of his youth; but thou didst not tell Comala!

MELILCOMA.
What sound is that on Ardven? Who is that, bright
in the vale? Who comes like the strength of rivers,
when their crowded waters glitter to the moon?

COMALA.
Who is it but the foe of Comala, the son of the
king of the world? Ghost of Fingal! Do thou from
thy cloud direct Comala's bow. Let him fall like the
hart of the desert. It is Fingal in the crowd of his
ghosts. Why dost thou come, my love, to frighten and
please my soul?

FINGAL.
Raise, ye bards, the song; raise the wars of the
streamy Carun! Caracul has fled from our arms along
the fields of his pride. He sets far distant like a meteor,
that incloses a spirit of night, when the winds drive it
over the heath, and the dark woods are gleaming around.
I heard a voice, or was it the breeze of my hills? Is
it the huntress of Ardven, the white-handed daughter of
Sarno? Look from thy rocks, my love; let me hear
the voice of Comala!

COMALA.
Take me to the cave of my rest, O lovely son of
death!

FINGAL.
Come to the cave of my rest. The storm is past,
the sun is on our fields. Come to the cave of my rest,
huntress of echoing Ardven!

COMALA.
He is returned with his fame. I feel the right hand
of his wars. But I must rest beside the rock till my
soul returns from my fear. O let the harp be near!
Raise the song, ye daughters of Morni!

DERSAGRENA.

Comala has slain three deer on Ardven, the fire ascends on the rock ; go to the feast of Comala, king of the woody Morven!

FINGAL.

Raise, ye sons of song, the wars of the streamy Carun ; that my white-handed maid may rejoice : while I behold the feast of my love.

BARDS.

Roll, streamy Carun, roll in joy, the sons of battle are fled ! The steed is not seen on our fields ; the wings of their pride spread in other lands. The sun will now rise in peace, and the shadows descend in joy. The voice of the chase will be heard ; the shields hang in the hall. Our delight will be in the war of the ocean, our hands shall grow red in the blood of Lochlin. Roll, streamy Carun, roll in joy, the sons of battle fled !

MELILCOMA.

Descend, ye light mists from high ! Ye moonbeams, lift her soul ! Pale lies the maid at the rock. Comala is no more !

FINGAL.

Is the daughter of Sarno dead, the white-bosomed maid of my love ? Meet me, Comala, on my heaths, when I sit alone at the streams of my hills !

HYDALLAN.

Ceased the voice of the huntress of Ardven ? Why did I trouble the soul of the maid ? When shall I see thee, with joy, in the chase of the dark-brown hinds ?

FINGAL.

Youth of the gloomy brow ! No more shalt thou feast in my halls. Thou shalt not pursue my chase, my

foes shall not fall by thy sword. Lead me to the place
of her rest that I may behold her beauty. Pale she lies
at the rock, cold winds lift her hair. Her bow-string
sounds in the blast, her arrow was broken in her fall.
Raise the praise of the daughter of Sarno! Give her
name to the winds of Heaven!

BARDS.

See! Meteors gleam around the maid! See! Moon-
beams lift her soul! Around her, from their clouds, bend
the awful faces of her fathers; Sarno of the gloomy
brow! The red-rolling eyes of Fidallan! When shall
thy white hand arise? When shall thy voice be heard
on our rocks? The maids shall seek thee on the heath
but they shall not find thee. Thou shalt come, at times,
to their dreams, to settle peace in their soul. Thy voice
shall remain in their ears, they shall think with joy on
the dreams of their rest. Meteors gleam around the
maid, and moon-beams lift her soul.

The Death-Song of Ossian.

Such were the words of the bards in the days of song; when the king heard the music of harps, the tales of other times! The chiefs gathered from all their hills, and heard the lovely sound. They praised the Voice of Cona! The first among a thousand bards! But age is now on my tongue; my soul has failed! I hear, at times, the ghosts of the bards, and learn their pleasant song. But memory fails on my mind. I hear the call of years! They say, as they pass along, why does Ossian sing? Soon shall he lie in the narrow house, and no bard shall raise his fame! Roll on, ye dark-brown years; ye bring no joy on your course! Let the tomb open to Ossian, for his strength has failed. The sons of song are gone to rest. My voice remains, like a blast, that roars, lonely, on a sea-surrounded rock, after the winds are laid. The dark moss whistles there; the distant mariner sees the waving trees!

II

ANCIENT
CORNISH

The Pool of Pilate.

[Wayfarer loq.

Guel yv thy'mmo vy may fe
mos the wolhy ow dule
    a Thesempes
me a vyn omma yn dour
may fons y guyn ha glan lour
    a vostethes

.   .   .   .   .   .

Ellas pan fema gynys
ancow sur yw dynythys
    Scon thy'mmo vy
ny'm bus bywe na fella
an dour re wruk thy'm henna
    yn pur deffry.

The Pool of Pilate.

[Wayfarer loq.

It is best to me that it be so
Go to wash my hands
    Immediately
I will, here in the water,
That they may be white, and clean enough
    From dirt.

[He washes his hands in the water and dies
    immediately.]

Alas that I was born!
Death surely is come
    Soon to me.
Life is no longer for me,
The water has done that to me
    Very clearly.

Merlin the Diviner.

Merlin! Merlin! where art thou going
So early in the day, with thy black dog?
Oi! oi! oi! oi! oi! oi! oi! oi! oi! oi!
Oi! oi! oi! ioi! oi!

I have come here to search the way,
To find the red egg;
The red egg of the marine serpent,
By the sea-side in the hollow of the stone.
I am going to seek in the valley
The green water-cress, and the golden grass,
And the top branch of the oak,
In the wood by the side of the fountain.

Merlin! Merlin! retrace your steps;
Leave the branch on the oak,
And the green water-cress in the valley,
As well as the golden grass;
And leave the red egg of the marine serpent,
In the foam by the hollow of the stone.
Merlin! Merlin! retrace thy steps,
There is no diviner but God.

The Vision of Seth.

[Adam bids Seth journey to the Gate of Paradise—
the way to be known to him because of the burnt im-
prints of the feet of himself and Eve on the day they
were driven forth, sere marks never grass-grown since—
and, after telling him to ask for the oil of mercy, blesses
him, and sees him go.]

CHERUBIN.
　　Seth, what is thy errand,
　　That thou wouldst come so long a way?
　　Tell me soon.

SETH.
　　O angel, I will tell thee:
　　My father is old and weary,
　　　He would not wish to live longer;

　　And through me he prayed thee
　　　To tell the truth
　　Of the oil promised to him
　　　Of mercy in the last day.

CHERUBIN.
　　Within the gate put thy head,
　　And behold it all, nor fear,
　　　Whatever thou seest,
　　And look on all sides;
　　Examine well every particular;
　　　Search out everything diligently.

SETH.
　　Very joyfully I will do it;
　　　I am glad to have permission
　　To know what is there,
　　　To tell it to my father.

[And he looks, and turns round, saying :—]
    Fair field is this ;
      Unhappy he who lost the country :
    And the tree, it is to me
      A great wonder that it is dry ;
    But I believe that it is dry,
    And all made bare, for the sin
      Which my father and mother sinned.
    Like the prints of their feet,
    They are all dry, like herbs.
      Alas, that the morsel was eaten.

CHERUBIN.
    O Seth, thou art come
    Within the Gate of Paradise ;
      Tell me what thou sawest.

SETH.
    All the beauty that I saw
    The tongue of no man in the world can
      Tell it ever.
    Of good fruit, and fair flowers,
    Minstrels and sweet song,   `
      A fountain bright as silver ;
    And four springs, large indeed,
    Flowing from it,
      That there is a desire to look at them.

    In it there is a tree,
    High with many boughs ;
      But they are all bare, without leaves.
    And around it, bark
    There was none, from the stem to the head
      All its boughs are bare.

    And at the bottom, when I looked,
      I saw its roots
    Even into hell descending,
      In the midst of great darkness.

And its branches growing up,
Even to heaven high in light;
And it was without bark altogether,
Both the head and the boughs.

CHERUBIN.
Look yet again within,
And all else thou shalt see
Before thou come from it.

SETH.
I am happy that I have permission;
I will go to the gate immediately,
That I may see further good.
[He goes, and looks, and returns.

CHERUBIN.
Dost thou see more now,
Than what there was just now?

SETH.
There is a serpent in the tree;
An ugly beast, without fail.

CHERUBIN.
Go yet a third time to it,
And look better at the tree.
Look, what you can see in it,
Besides roots and branches.
[Again he goes up.

SETH.
Cherub, angel of the God of grace,
In the tree I saw,
High up on the branches,
A little child newly born;
And he was swathed in cloths,
And bound fast with napkins.

D

CHERUBIN.
>The Son of God it was whom thou sawest,
>Like a little child swathed.
>>He will redeem Adam, thy father,
>With his flesh and blood too,
>When the time is come,
>>And thy mother, and all the good people.

>He is the oil of mercy,
>>Which was promised to thy father ;
>Through his death, clearly,
>>All the world will be saved.

SETH.
>Blessed be he :
>>O God, now I am happy ;
>Knowing the truth all plainly,
>I will go from thee.

CHERUBIN.
>Take three kernels of the apple,
>>Which Adam, thy father, ate.
>When he dies, put them, without fail,
>>Between his teeth and tongue.
>From them thou wilt see
>>Three trees grow presently ;
>For he will not live more than three days
>After thou reachest home.

SETH.
>Blessed be thou every day ;
>>I honour thee ever very truly :
>My father will be very joyful,
>>If he soon passes from life.

III

ANCIENT
ARMORICAN

(Breton)

The Dance of the Sword.

(Ha Korol ar C'Hleze.)

Blood, wine, and glee,
Sun, to thee,—
Blood, wine, and glee !
    Fire ! fire ! steel, Oh ! steel !
    Fire, fire ! steel and fire !
    Oak ! oak, earth, and waves !
    Waves, oak, earth and oak !

Glee of dance and song,
And battle-throng,—
Battle, dance, and song !
    Fire ! fire ! steel, etc.

Let the sword blades swing
In a ring,—
Let the sword blades swing !
    Fire ! fire ! steel, etc.

Song of the blue steel,
Death to feel,—
Song of the blue steel !
    Fire ! fire ! steel, etc.

Fight, whereof the sword
Is the Lord,—
Fight of the fell sword !
    Fire ! fire ! steel, etc.

Sword, thou mighty king
Of battle's ring,—
Sword thou mighty king !
    Fire ! fire ! steel, etc.

With the rainbow's light
 Be thou bright,—
With the rainbow's light!
        Fire! fire! steel, Oh! steel!
        Fire, fire! steel and fire!
        Oak! oak, earth and waves!
        Waves, oak, earth, and oak!

The Lord Nann and the Fairy.
(Aotron Nann Hag ar Gorrigan.)

The good Lord Nann and his fair bride
Were young when wedlock's knot was tied—
Were young when death did them divide.

But yesterday that lady fair
Two babes as white as snow did bear ;
A man-child and a girl they were.

" Now, say what is thy heart's desire,
For making me a man-child's sire ?
'Tis thine, whate'er thou may'st require,—

" What food soe'er thee lists to take,
Meat of the woodcock from the lake,
Meat of the wild deer from the brake."

" Oh, the meat of the deer is dainty food !
To eat thereof would do me good,
But I grudge to send thee to the wood."

The Lord of Nann, when this he heard,
Hath gripp'd his oak spear with never a word ;
His bonny black horse he hath leap'd upon,
And forth to the greenwood hath he gone.

By the skirts of the wood as he did go,
He was ware of a hind as white as snow.

Oh, fast she ran, and fast he rode,
That the earth it shook where his horse-hoofs trode.

Oh, fast he rode, and fast she ran,
That the sweat to drop from his brow began—

That the sweat on his horse's flank stood white ;
So he rode and rode till the fall o' the night.

When he came to a stream that fed a lawn,
Hard by the grot of a Corrigaun.

The grass grew thick by the streamlet's brink,
And he lighted down off his horse to drink.

The Corrigaun sat by the fountain fair,
A-combing her long and yellow hair.

A-combing her hair with a comb of gold,—
(Not poor, I trow, are those maidens cold).—

" Now who's the bold wight that dares come here
To trouble my fairy fountain clear?

" Either thou straight shall wed with me,
Or pine for four long years and three ;
Or dead in three days' space shall be."

" I will not wed with thee, I ween,
For wedded man a year I've been ;

" Nor yet for seven years will I pine,
Nor die in three days for spell of thine ;

" For spell of thine I will not die,
But when it pleaseth God on high.

" But here, and now, I'd leave my life,
Ere take a Corrigaun to wife.

.   .   .   .

" O mother, mother ! for love of me,
Now make my bed, and speedily,
For I am sick as a man can be.

" Oh, never the tale to my lady tell ;
Three days and ye'll hear my passing bell ;
The Corrigaun hath cast her spell."

Three days they pass'd, three days were sped,
To her mother-in-law the ladye said :

" Now tell me, madam, now tell me, pray,
Wherefore the death-bells toll to-day ?

" Why chaunt the priests in the street below,
All clad in ' their vestments white as snow ? "

" A strange poor man, who harbour'd here,
He died last night, my daughter dear."

" But tell me, madam, my lord, your son—
My husband—whither is he gone ? "

" But to the town, my child, he 's gone ;
And at your side he 'll be back anon."

" What gown for my churching were 't best to wear,—
My gown of grain, or of watchet fair ? "

" The fashion of late, my child, hath grown,
That women for churching black should don."

As through the churchyard porch she stept,
She saw the grave where her husband slept.

" Who of our blood is lately dead,
That our ground is new raked and spread ? "

" The truth I may no more forbear,
My son—your own poor lord—lies there ! "

She threw herself on her knees amain,
And from her knees ne'er rose again.

That night they laid her, dead and cold,
Beside her lord, beneath the mould ;
When, lo !—a marvel to behold !—

Next morn from the grave two oak-trees fair,
Shot lusty boughs high up in air ;

And in their boughs—oh wondrous sight !—
Two happy doves, all snowy white—

That sang, as ever the morn did rise,
And then flew up—into the skies !

Alain the Fox.

The bearded fox is yelping, yelp, yelping through the
    glades ;
Woe to the foreign rabbits ! His eyes are two keen
    blades.

His teeth are keen ; his feet are swift ; his nails are red
    with blood.
Alain the fox is yelping war : yelp, yelping in the wood.

The Bretons making sharp their arms of terror I did see,
It was on cuirasses of Gaul, not stones of Brittany.

The Bretons reaping did I see, upon the fields of war ;
It was not notched reaping-hooks, but swords of steel
    they bore.

They reapt no wheat of our own land, they reaped not
    our rye ;
But the beardless ears, the beardless ears of Gaul and
    Saxony.

I saw upon the threshing-floor the Bretons threshing
    corn :
I saw the beaten chaff fly out from beardless ears off-
    torn.

It was not with their wooden flails the Bretons thresht
    the wheat ;
But with their iron boar-spears and with their horses'
    feet.

I heard the cry when threshing 's done, the joy-cry
    onward borne
Far, far from Mont-Saint-Michel to the valleys of Elorn :

From the abbey of Saint Gildas far on to the Land's-
    End rocks.
In Brittany's four corners give a glory to the Fox !

From age to age give glory to the Fox a thousand
times!
But weep ye for the rhymer, though he recollect his
rhymes!

For he that sang this song the first since then hath
never sung:
Ah me, alas! Unhappy man! The Gauls cut out his
tongue.

But though no more he hath a tongue, a heart is
always his:
He has both hand and heart to shoot his arrowy
melodies.

Bran.

(The Crow.)

Wounded full sore is Bran the knight;
For he was at Kerloan fight;
At Kerloan fight, by wild seashore
Was Bran-Vor's grandson wounded sore;
And, though we gained the victory,
Was captive borne beyond the sea.
He when he came beyond the sea,
In the close keep wept bitterly.
"They leap at home with joyous cry
While, woe is me, in bed I lie.
Could I but find a messenger,
Who to my mother news would bear!"
They quickly found a messenger;
His hest thus gave the warrior:
"Heed thou to dress in other guise,
My messenger, dress beggar-wise!
Take thou my ring, my ring of gold,
That she thy news as truth may hold!
Unto my country straightway go,
It to my lady mother show!
Should she come free her son from hold,
A flag of white do thou unfold!
But if with thee she come not back,
Unfurl, ah me, a pennon black!"

So, when to Leon-land he came,
At supper table sat the dame,
At table with her family,
The harpers playing as should be.
"Dame of the castle, hail! I bring
From Bran your son this golden ring,
His golden ring and letter too;
Read it, oh read it, straightway through!"

"Ye harpers, cease ye, play no more,
For with great grief my heart is sore!
My son (cease harpers, play no more!)
In prison, and I did not know!
Prepare to-night a ship for me!
To-morrow I go across the sea."

The morning of the next, next day
The Lord Bran question'd, as he lay :
"Sentinel, sentinel, soothly say!
Seest thou no vessel on its way?"
"My lord the knight, I nought espy
Except the great sea and the sky."
The Lord Bran askt him yet once more,
Whenas the day's course half was o'er ;
"Sentinel, sentinel, soothly say!
Seest thou no vessel on its way?"
"I can see nothing, my lord the knight,
Except the sea-birds i' their flight."
The Lord Bran askt him yet again,
Whenas the day was on the wane ;
"Sentinel, sentinel, soothly say!
Seest thou no vessel on its way?"
Then that false sentinel, the while
Smiling a mischief-working smile ;
"I see afar a misty form—
A ship sore beaten by the storm."
"The flag? Quick give the answer back!
The banner? Is it white or black?"
"Far as I see, 'tis black, Sir knight,
I swear it by the coal's red light."
When this the sorrowing knight had heard
Again he never spoke a word ;
But turn'd aside his visage wan ;
And then the fever fit began.

Now of the townsmen askt the dame,
When at the last to shore she came,

"What is the news here, townsmen, tell!
That thus I hear them toll the bell?"
An aged man the lady heard,
And thus he answer'd to her word:
"We in the prison held a knight;
And he hath died here in the night."
Scarcely to end his words were brought,
When the high tower that lady sought;
Shedding salt tears and running fast,
Her white hair scatter'd in the blast,
So that the townsmen wonderingly
Full sorely marvell'd her to see;
Whenas they saw a lady strange,
Through their streets so sadly range,
Each one in thought did musing stand;
"Who is the lady, from what land?"
Soon as the donjon's foot she reacht,
The porter that poor dame beseecht;
"Ope, quickly ope, the gate for me!
My son! My son! Him would I see!"
Slowly the great gate open drew;
Herself upon her son she threw,
Close in her arms his corpse to strain,
The lady never rose again.

There is a tree, that doth look o'er
From Kerloan's battle-field to th' shore;
An oak. Before great Evan's face
The Saxons fled in that same place.
Upon that oak in clear moonlight,
Together come the birds at night;
Black birds and white, but sea birds all;
On each one's brow a blood-stain small,
With them a raven gray and old;
With her a crow comes young and bold.
Both with soil'd wings, both wearied are;
They come beyond the seas from far:

And the birds sing so lovelily
That silence comes on the great sea.
All sing in concert sweet and low
Except the raven and the crow.
Once was the crow heard murmuring:
"Sing, little birds, ye well may sing!
Sing, for this is your own countrie!
Ye died not far from Brittany!"

IV

EARLY CYMRIC AND
MEDIÆVAL WELSH

The Soul.

(From "The Black Book of Caermarthen.")

Soul, since I was made in necessity blameless
True it is, woe is me that thou shouldst have come to
   my design,
Neither for my own sake, nor for death, nor for end,
   nor for beginning.
It was with seven faculties that I was thus blessed,
With seven created beings I was placed for purification;
I was gleaming fire when I was caused to exist;
I was dust of the earth, and grief could not reach me;
I was a high wind, being less evil than good;
I was a mist on a mountain seeking supplies of stags;
I was blossoms of trees on the face of the earth.
If the Lord had blessed me, He would have placed me
   on matter.

                    Soul, since I was made——

The Gorwynion.

The tops of the ash glisten, that are white and stately,
When growing on the top of the dingle:
The breast rackt with pain, longing is its complaint.

Brightly glitters the top of the cliff at the long midnight
  hour;
Every ingenious person will be honoured:
'Tis the duty of the fair, to afford sleep to him that is
  in pain.

Brightly glistens the willow tops; the fish are merry in
  the lakes,
Blustering is the wind over the tops of the small
  branches:
Nature over learning doth prevail.

Brightly glisten the tops of the furze; have confidence
  with the wise,
But from the unwise tear thyself afar;
Besides God there is none that sees futurity.

Brightly glisten the clover tops: the timid has no heart;
Wearied out are the jealous ones:
Cares attend the weak.

Brightly glisten the tops of reed-grass; furious is the
  jealous,
If any should perchance offend him:
'Tis the maxim of the prudent to love with sincerity.

Brightly glare the tops of the mountains from the blus-
  tering of winter,
Full are the stalks of reeds; heavy is oppression:
Against famine bashfulness will vanish.

Brightly glare the tops of mountains assail'd by winter
  cold;
Brittle are the reeds; the mead is incrusted over;
Playful is the heedless in banishment.

Bright are the tops of the oaks, bitter are the ash
   branches ;
Before the duck, the dividing waves are seen :
Confident is deceit ; care is deeply rooted in my heart.

Brightly glisten the tops of the oaks, bitter are the ash
   branches ;
Sweet is the sheltering hedge ; the wave is a noisy
   grinner ;
The cheek cannot conceal the trouble of the heart.

Bright is the top of the eglantine ; hardship dispenses
   with forms,
Let everyone keep his fire-side :
The greatest blemish is ill-manners.

Brightly glitters the top of the broom ; may the lover
   have a home ;
Very yellow seem the clustered branches ;
Shallow is the ford ; sleep visits the contented mind.

Brightly glitters the top of the apple-tree ; the prosperous
   is circumspect.
In the long day the stagnant pool is warm ;
Thick is the veil on the light of the blind prisoner.

Very glittering are the hazel-tops by the hill of Dig ;
Every prudent one will be free from harm ;
'Tis the act of the mighty to keep a treaty.

Glittering are the tops of the reeds ; the fat are drowsy
And the young imbibe instruction ;
None but the foolish will break faith.

Glittering is the top of the lily ; let every bold one be
   a drinker ;
The word of a tribe is superior ;
'Tis usual for the unjust to break his word.

Bright are the tops of heath; miscarriage attends the
  timid;
Boldly laves the water on its banks.
'Tis the maxim of the just to keep his word.

The tops of the rushes glitter; the kine are gentle;
Running are my tears this day,
Social comfort from man there is not.

Glittering are the tops of fern, yellow is the wild mary-
  gold;
The sea is a fence for blind ones:
Swift and active are the young men.

Glittering are the tops of the service-tree; care attends
  the old;
The bees frequent the wilds;
Vengeance only to God belongs.

Brightly glitters the tops of the oak; incessant is the
  tempest;
The bees are high in their flight, brittle is the charr'd
  brushwood,
The wanton is apt to laugh too frequently.

The hazel grove brightly glitters, even and uniform seem
  the brakes;
And with leaves the oaks envelop themselves;
Happy is he who sees the one he loves!

Glittering seems the top of the oak; coolly purls the
  stream;
I wish to obtain the top of the birchen grove;
Abruptly goes the arrow of the haughty to give pain.

Brightly glitters the top of the hard holly, that opens
  its golden leaves;
When all are asleep on the surrounding walls,
God slumbers not when He means to give deliverance.

Glittering are the tops of the willows, brittle and tender;
In the long day of summer the war-horse flags,
Those that have mutual friendships will not offend.

Glittering are the tops of rushes, the stems are full of
    prickles;
When drawn under the pillow;
The wanton mind will be haughty.

Bright is the top of the hawthorn; confident is the fight
    of the steed;
It behoves the dependant to be grateful;
May it be good what the speedy messenger brings.

Glittering are the tops of cresses; warlike is the steed;
Trees are fair ornaments of the ground;
Joyful is the soul with the one it loves.

Brightly glares the top of the bush, valuable is the
    steed;
Reason joined with strength is effectual;
Let the unskilful be void of strength.

Glittering are the tops of the brakes, birds are their fair
    jewels;
The long day is the gift of the radiant light,
Mercy was formed by God, the most beneficent.

Glittering are the elmwood tops, sweet the music of the
    grove;
Boisterous among the trees the wind doth whistle;
Interceding with the obdurate will not avail.

Glittering are the tops of elder-trees; bold is the solitary
    songster;
Accustomed is the violent to oppress;
By want of care the food in hand may be lost.

The Tercets of Llywarc'h.

Entangling is the snare, clustered is the ash;
The ducks are in the pond; white breaks the wave;
More powerful than a hundred is the counsel of the heart.

Long the night, boisterous is the sea-shore;
Usual a tumult in a congregation;
The vicious will not agree with the good.

Long the night, boisterous is the mountain,
The wind whistles over the tops of trees;
Ill-nature will not deceive the discreet.

The saplings of the green-topped birch
Will extricate my foot from the shackle;
Disclose not thy secret to a youth.

The saplings of oaks in the grove
Will extricate my foot from the chain;
Disclose no secret to a maid.

The saplings of the leafy oaks
Will extricate my foot from the prison;
Divulge no secret to a babbler.

The saplings of bramble have berries on them;
The thrush is on her nest;
The liar will never be silent.

Rain without, the fern is drenched;
White the gravel of the sea; there is spray on the margin;
Reason is the fairest lamp for man.

Rain without, near is the shelter,
The furze yellow; the cow-parsnip withered and dry;
God the Creator! why hast thou made me a coward?

Rain without, my hair is drenched;
Full of complaint is the feeble; steep the cliff;
Pale white is the sea; salt is the brine.

Rain without, the ocean is drenched;
The wind whistles over the tops of the reeds;
After every feat, still without the genius.

Song to the Wind.

Discover thou what is
The strong creature from before the flood,
Without flesh, without bone,
Without vein, without blood,
Without head, without feet;
It will neither be older nor younger
Than at the beginning;
For fear of a denial,
These are no rude wants
With creatures.
Great God! how the sea whitens
When first it comes!
Great are its gusts
When it comes from the south;
Great are its evaporations
When it strikes on coasts.
It is in the field, it is in the wood,
Without hand and without foot,
Without signs of old age,
Though it be co-eval
With the five ages or periods;
And older still,
Though they be numberless years.
It is also so wide;
As the surface of the earth;
And it was not born,
Nor was it seen.
It will cause consternation
Wherever God willeth.
On sea, and on land,
It neither sees, nor is seen.
Its course is devious,
And will not come when desired
On land and on sea
It is indispensable.

It is without an equal,
It is four-sided ;
It is not confined,
It is incomparable ;
It comes from four quarters ;
It will not be advised,
It will not be without advice.
It commences its journey
Above the marble rock.
It is sonorous, it is dumb,
It is mild,
It is strong, it is bold,
When it glances over the land.
It is silent, it is vocal,
It is clamorous,
It is the most noisy
On the face of the earth.
It is good, it is bad,
It is extremely injurious.
It is concealed,
Because sight cannot perceive it.
It is noxious, it is beneficial ;
It is yonder, it is here ;
It will discompose,
But will not repair the injury ;
It will not suffer for its doings,
Seeing it is blameless.
It is wet, it is dry,
It frequently comes,
Proceeding from the heat of the sun,
And the coldness of the moon.
The moon is less beneficial,
Inasmuch as her heat is less.
One Being has prepared it,
Out of all creatures,
By a tremendous blast,
To wreck vengeance
On Maelgwn Gwynedd.

Odes of the Months.

Month of January—smoky is the vale ;
Weary the wine-bearer ; strolling the minstrel ;
Lean the cow ; seldom the hum of the bee ;
Empty the milking fold ; void of meat the kiln ;
Slender the horse ; very silent the bird ;
Long to the early dawn ; short the afternoon ;
Justly spoke Cynfelyn,
"Prudence is the best guide for man."

Month of February—scarce are the dainties ;
Wakeful the adder to generate its poison ;
Habitual is reproach from frequent acknowledgment ;
The hired ox has not skill to complain ;
Three things produce dreadful evils,
A woman's counsel, murder, and way-laying ;
Best is the dog upon a morning in spring ;
Alas ! to him who murders his maid !

Month of March—great is the forwardness of the birds,
Severe is the cold wind upon the headlands ;
Serene weather will be longer than the crops ;
Longer continues anger than grief ;
Every one feels dread ;
Every bird wings to its mate.
Every thing springs through the earth ;
But the dead, strong is his prison !

Month of April--aerial is the horizon ;
Fatigued the oxen ; bare the land ;
Common is the visitor without an invitation ;
Poor the deer ; blithesome the hare ;
Everyone claims his labour ;
Happy his state who governs himself ;
Common is separation with virtuous children ;
Common, after presumption, is a long cessation.

Month of May—wanton is the lascivious ;
Sheltering the ditch to everyone who loves it ;
Joyous the aged in his robes ;
Loquacious the cuckoo in the rural vales ;
Easy is society where there is affection ;
Covered with foliage are the woods, sportive the
    amorous,
There comes as often to the market,
The skin of the lamb as the skin of the sheep.

Month of June—beautiful are the fields ;
Smooth the sea, pleasing the strand ;
Beautifully long the day, playful the ladies ;
Full the flocks, apt to be firm the bog ;
God loves all tranquillity ;
The devil loves all mischief ;
Every one covets honour ;
Every mighty one, feeble his end.

Month of July—the hay is apt to smoke ;
Ardent the heat, dissolved the snow ;
The vagrant does not love a long confederacy ;
There is no success to the progeny of an unchaste
    person ;
Bare the farm-yard—partly empty the circular eminence ;
Clean the perfect person, disgraceful the boasting word ;
Justly spoke the foster-son of Mary,
"God judges, though man may prate."

Month of August—covered with foam is the beach ;
Blithesome the bee, full the hive ;
Better the work of the sickle than the bow ;
Fuller the stack than the theatre.
He that will neither work nor pray,
Is not worthy to have bread ;
Justly spoke Saint Breda,
"Evil will not be approached less than good."

ANEURIN

Month of September—benign are the planets;
Tending to please, the sea and the hamlet;
Common is it for steeds and men to be fatigued;
Common is it to possess all kinds of fruit:—
A princely girl was born,
To be our leader from painful slavery;—
Justly spake Saint Berned,
"God does not sleep when he gives deliverance."

Month of October—penetrable is the shelter;
Yellow the tops of the birch, solitary the summer
    dwelling;
Full of fat the birds and the fish;
Less and less the milk of the cow and the goat;
Alas! to him who merits disgrace by sin!
Death is better than frequent extravagance;
Three things follow every crime,
Fasting, prayer, and charity.

Month of November—very fat are the swine;
Let the shepherd go; let the minstrel come;
Bloody the blade, full the barn;
Pleased the sea, tasteless the caldron;
Long the night, active the prisoner;
Respected is every one who possesses property;
For three things men are not often concerned,
Sorrow, angry look, and an illiberal miser.

Month of December—the shoe is covered with dirt:
Heavy the land, flagging the sun;
Bare are the trees, still is the muscle;
Cheerful the cock, and determined the thief;
Whilst the twelve months proceed so sprightly,
Round the youthful mind, is the spoiler Satan;
Justly spoke Yscolan,
"God is better than an evil prophecy."

The Summer.

Thou Summer! father of delight,
With thy dense spray and thickets deep;
Gemm'd monarch, with thy rapt'rous light.
Rousing thy subject glens from sleep!
Proud has thy march of triumph been,
Thou prophet, prince of forest green!
Artificer of wood and tree,
Thou painter of unrivalled skill,
Who ever scatters gems like thee,
And gorgeous webs on park and hill?
Till vale and hill with radiant dyes
Become another Paradise!
And thou hast sprinkled leaves and flow'rs,
And goodly chains of leafy bow'rs;
And bid thy youthful warblers sing
On oak and knoll, the song of spring,
And black-birds' note of ecstacy
Burst loudly from the woodbine tree,
Till all the world is thronged with gladness—
Her multitudes have done with sadness!
O Summer! do I ask in vain?
Thus in thy glory wilt thou deign
My messenger to be?
Hence from the bowels of the land
Of wild, wild Gwyneth to the strand
Of fair Glamorgan—ocean's band—
Sweet margin of the sea!
To dear Glamorgan, when we part,
Oh bear a thousand times my heart!
My blessing give a thousand times,
And crown with joy her glowing climes?
Take on her lovely vales thy stand,
And tread and trample round the land,
The beauteous shore whose harvest lies
All sheltered from inclement skies.

Radiant with corn and vineyards sweet,
The lakes of fish and mansions neat,
With halls of stone where kindness dwells,
And where each hospitable lord
Heaps for the stranger guest his board!
And where the generous wine cup swells;
With trees that bear a luscious pear,
So thickly clustering everywhere,
That the fair country of my love
Looks dense as one continuous grove!
Her lofty woods with warblers teem,
Her fields with flow'rs that love the stream;
Her valleys varied crops display,
Eight kinds of corn, and three of hay;
Bright parlour, with her trefoiled floor!
Sweet garden, spread on ocean's shore!
Glamorgan's bounteous knights award
Bright mead and burnished gold to me:
Glamorgan boasts of many a bard,
Well skilled in harp and vocal glee:
The districts round her border spread
From her have drawn their daily bread—
Her milk, her meat, her varied stores,
Have been the life of distant shores!
And court and hamlet food have found
From the rich soil of Britain's southern bound.
And wilt thou then obey my power,
Thou Summer, in thy brightest hour?
To her thy glorious hues unfold
In one rich embassy of gold!
Her morns with bliss and splendour light,
And fondly kiss her mansions white;
Fling wealth and verdure o'er her bow'rs!
And for her gather all thy flow'rs!
Glance o'er her castles, white with lime,
With genial glimmerings sublime;
Plant on the verdant coast thy feet,

Her lofty hills, her woodlands greet.
Oh ! lavish blossoms with thy hand
O'er all the forests of the land ;
And let thy gifts like floods descending,
O'er every hill and glen be blending ;
Let orchard, garden, vine express
Thy fulness and thy fruitfulness—
O'er all the land of beauty fling
The costly traces of thy wing !
And thus 'mid all thy radiant flowers,
Thy thickening leaves and glossy bowers,
The poet's task shall be to glean
Roses and flowers that softly bloom
(The jewel of the forest's gloom !),
And trefoils wove in pavement green,
With sad humility to grace
His golden Ivor's resting-place.

To the Lark.

T'R Ehedydd.

Sentinel of the morning light!
Reveller of the spring!
How sweetly, nobly wild thy flight,
    Thy boundless journeying:
Far from thy brethren of the woods, alone,
A hermit chorister before God's throne!

Oh! wilt thou climb yon heavens for me,
Yon rampart's starry height,
Thou interlude of melody
    'Twixt darkness and the light,
And seek with heav'n's first dawn upon thy crest,
My lady love, the moonbeam of the west?

No woodland caroller art thou;
Far from the archer's eye,
Thy course is o'er the mountain's brow,
    Thy music in the sky:
Then fearless float thy path of cloud along,
Thou earthly denizen of angel song.

F

To the Fox.

The wretch my starry bird who slew,
Beast of the flameless ember hue,
Assassin, glutton of the night,
Mixed of all creatures that defile,
Land lobster, fugitive of light,
Thou coward mountain crocodile ;
With downcast eye and ragged tail,
That haunt'st the hollow rocks,
Thief, ever ready to assail
The undefended flocks,
Thy brass-hued breast and tattered locks
Shall not protect thee from the hound,
When with unbaffled eye he mocks
Thy mazy fortress underground,
Whilst o'er my peacock's shattered plumes shall shine
A pretty bower of faery eglantine.

The Song of the Thrush.

I was on the margin of a plain,
Under a wide spreading tree,
Hearing the song
Of the wild birds;
Listening to the language
Of the thrush cock,
Who from the wood of the valley
Composed a verse—
From the wood of the steep,
He sang exquisitely.
Speckled was his breast
Amongst the green leaves,
As upon branches
Of a thousand blossoms
On the bank of a brook,
All heard
With the dawn the song,
Like a silver bell;
Performing a sacrifice,
Until the hour of forenoon;
Upon the green altar
Ministering Bardism.
From the branches of the hazel
Of green broad leaves
He sings an ode
To God the Creator;
With a carol of love
From the green glade,
To all in the hollow
Of the glen, who love him;
Balm of the heart
To those who love.
I had from his beak
The voice of inspiration,
A song of metres

That gratified me;
Glad was I made
By his minstrelsy.
Then respectfully
Uttered I an address
From the stream of the valley
To the bird.
I requested urgently
His undertaking a message
To the fair one
Where dwells my affection.
Gone is the bard of the leaves
From the small twigs
To the second Lunet,
The sun of the maidens!
To the streams of the plain
St Mary prosper him,
To bring to me,
Under the green woods
The hue of the snow of one night,
Without delay.

PART II

I

IRISH

(Modern and Contemporary)

Sacrifice.

Those delicate wanderers,
The wind, the star, the cloud,
Ever before mine eyes,
As to an altar bowed,
Light and dew-laden airs
Offer in sacrifice.

The offerings arise:
Hazes of rainbow light,
Pure crystal, blue, and gold,
Through dreamland take their flight;
And 'mid the sacrifice
God moveth as of old.

In miracles of fire
He symbols forth His days;
In gleams of crystal light
Reveals what pure pathways
Lead to the soul's desire,
The silence of the height.

The Great Breath.

Its edges foamed with amethyst and rose,
Withers once more the old blue flower of day :
There where the ether like a diamond glows
    Its petals fade away.

A shadowy tumult stirs the dusky air ;
Sparkle the delicate dews, the distant snows ;
The great deep thrills, for through it everywhere
    The breath of Beauty blows.

I saw how all the trembling ages past,
Moulded to her by deep and deeper breath,
Neared to the hour when Beauty breathes her last
    And knows herself in death.

Mystery.

Why does this sudden passion smite me?
I stretch my hands all blind to see:
I need the lamp of the world to light me,
    Lead me and set me free.

Something a moment seemed to stoop from
The night with cool cool breath on my face:
Or did the hair of the twilight droop from
    Its silent wandering ways?

About me in the thick wood netted
The wizard glow looks human-wise;
And over the tree-tops barred and fretted
    Ponders with strange old eyes.

The tremulous lips of air blow by me
And hymn their time-old melody:
Its secret strain comes nigh and nigh me:
    "Ah, brother, come with me;

"For here the ancient mother lingers
To dip her hands in the diamond dew,
And lave thine ache with cloud-cool fingers
    Till sorrow die from you."

By the Margin of the Great Deep.

When the breath of twilight blows to flame the misty
  skies,
All its vaporous sapphire, violet glow and silver gleam,
With their magic flood me through the gateway of the
  eyes ;
  I am one with the twilight's dream.

When the trees and skies and fields are one in dusky
  mood,
Every heart of man is rapt within the mother's breast :
Full of peace and sleep and dreams in the vasty quietude,
  I am one with their hearts at rest.

From our immemorial joys of hearth and home and love
Strayed away along the margin of the unknown tide,
All its reach of soundless calm can thrill me far above
  Word or touch from the lips beside.

Aye, and deep and deep and deeper let me drink and
  draw
From the olden fountain more than light or peace or
  dream,
Such primeval being as o'erfills the heart with awe,
  Growing one with its silent stream.

The Breath of Light.

From the cool and dark-lipped furrows breathes a dim
delight
Through the woodland's purple plumage to the diamond
night.
Aureoles of joy encircle every blade of grass
Where the dew-fed creatures silent and enraptured pass:
And the restless ploughman pauses, turns, and wondering
Deep beneath his rustic habit finds himself a king;
For a fiery moment looking with the eyes of God
Over fields a slave at morning bowed him to the sod.
Blind and dense with revelation every moment flies,
And unto the Mighty Mother, gay, eternal, rise
All the hopes we hold, the gladness, dreams of things
to be.
One of all thy generations, Mother, hails to thee!
Hail! and hail! and hail for ever: though I turn again
From thy joy unto the human vesniture of pain.
I, thy child, who went forth radiant in the golden prime
Find thee still the mother-hearted through my night in
time;
Find in thee the old enchantment, there behind the veil
Where the Gods my brothers linger, Hail! for ever,
Hail!

Æolian Harp.

O pale green sea,
With long pale purple clouds above—
What lies in me like weight of love?
What dies in me
With utter grief, because there comes no sign
Through the sun-raying West, or the dim sea-line?

O salted air,
Blown round the rocky headlands chill—
What calls me there from cove and hill?
What calls me fair
From Thee, the first-born of the youthful night?
Or in the waves is coming through the dusk twilight?

O yellow Star,
Quivering upon the rippling tide—
Sendest so far to one that sigh'd?
Bendest thou, Star,
Above where shadows of the dead have rest
And constant silence, with a message from the blest?

The Fairies.

Up the airy mountain,
  Down the rushy glen,
We daren't go a-hunting
  For fear of little men ;
Wee folk, good folk,
  Trooping all together ;
Green jacket, red cap,
  And white owl's feather !

Down along the rocky shore
  Some make their home,
They live on crispy pancakes
  Of yellow tide-foam ;
Some in the reeds
  Of the black mountain lake,
With frogs for their watch-dogs,
  All night awake.

High on the hill-top
  The old king sits ;
He is now so old and gray
  He 's nigh lost his wits.
With a bridge of white mist
  Columbkill he crosses,
On his stately journeys
  From Slieveleague to Rosses ;
Or going up with music
  On cold starry nights,
To sup with the Queen
  Of the gay Northern Lights.

They stole little Bridget
  For seven years long ;
When she came down again
  Her friends were all gone.

They took her lightly back,
  Between the night and morrow,
They thought that she was fast asleep,
  But she was dead with sorrow.
They have kept her ever since
  Deep within the lake,
On a bed of flag-leaves,
  Watching till she wake.

By the craggy hill-side,
  Through the mosses bare,
They have planted thorn-trees
  For pleasure here and there.
Is any man so daring
  As dig up them in spite,
He shall find their sharpest thorns
  In his bed at night.

Up the airy mountain,
  Down the rushy glen,
We daren't go a-hunting
  For fear of little men ;
Wee folk, good folk,
  Trouping all together ;
Green jacket, red cap,
  And white owl's feather.

To the Lianhaun Shee.

Where is thy lovely perilous abode?
  In what strange phantom-land
Glimmer the fairy turrets whereto rode
  The ill-starred poet band?

Say, in the Isle of Youth hast thou thy home,
  The sweetest singer there,
Stealing on wingèd steed across the foam
  Thorough the moonlit air?

And by the gloomy peaks of Erigal,
  Haunted by storm and cloud,
Wing past, and to thy lover there let fall
  His singing robe and shroud?

Or, where the mists of bluebell float beneath
  The red stems of the pine,
And sunbeams strike thro' shadow, dost thou breathe
  The word that makes him thine?

Or, is thy palace entered thro' some cliff
  When radiant tides are full,
And round thy lover's wandering starlit skiff
  Coil in luxurious lull?

And would he, entering on the brimming flood,
  See caverns vast in height,
And diamond columns, crowned with leaf and bud,
  Glow in long lanes of light.

And there the pearl of that great glittering shell
  Trembling, behold thee lone,
Now weaving in slow dance an awful spell,
  Now still upon thy throne?

Thy beauty! ah, the eyes that pierce him thro'
  Then melt as in a dream;
The voice that sings the mysteries of the blue
  And all that Be and Seem!

Thy lovely motions answering to the rhyme
  That ancient Nature sings,
That keeps the stars in cadence for all time,
  And echoes through all things!

Whether he sees thee thus, or in his dreams,
  Thy light makes all lights dim;
An aching solitude from henceforth seems
  The world of men to him.

Thy luring song, above the sensuous roar,
  He follows with delight,
Shutting behind him Life's last gloomy door,
  And fares into the Night.

Remembrance.

Cold in the earth—and the deep snow piled above thee,
  Far, far removed, cold in the dreary grave!
Have I forgot, my only Love, to love thee,
  Severed at last by Time's all-severing wave?

Now, when alone, my thoughts no longer hover
  Over the mountains, on that northern shore,
Resting their wings where heath and fern-leaves cover
  Thy noble heart for ever, ever more.

Cold in the earth—and fifteen wild Decembers,
  From these brown hills, have melted into Spring!
Faithful, indeed, is the spirit that remembers
  After such years of change and suffering!

Sweet Love of youth, forgive, if I forget thee,
  While the world's tide is bearing me along;
Other desires and other hopes beset me,
  Hopes which obscure, but cannot do thee wrong.

No later light has lighted up my heaven,
  No second morn has ever shone for me;
All my life's bliss from thy dear life was given,
  All my life's bliss is in the grave with thee.

But, when the days of golden dreams had perished,
  And even despair was powerless to destroy;
Then did I learn how existence could be cherished,
  Strengthened, and fed without the aid of joy.

Then did I check the tears of useless passion—
  Weaned my young soul from yearning after thine;
Sternly denied its burning wish to hasten
  Down to that tomb already more than mine.

And, even yet, I dare not let it languish,
  Dare not indulge in memory's rapturous pain;
Once drinking deep of that divinest anguish,
  How could I seek the empty world again?

The Earth and Man.

A little sun, a little rain,
  A soft wind blowing from the west—
And woods and fields are sweet again,
  And warmth within the mountain's breast.

So simple is the earth we tread,
  So quick with love and life her frame,
Ten thousand years have dawned and fled,
  And still her magic is the same.

A little love, a little trust,
  A soft impulse, a sudden dream—
And life as dry as desert dust
  Is fresher than a mountain stream.

So simple is the heart of man
  So ready for new hope and joy ;
Ten thousand years since it began
  Have left it younger than a boy.

Song.

(From "Six Days.")

Come, where on the moorland steep
Silent sunlight dreams of sleep,
And in this high morning air
Love me, my companion fair!
All the clouds that high in Heaven
Rest and rove from morn to even,
All the beauty that doth live
By the winds—to thee I give.

See below deep meadow lands,
Misty moors and shining sands,
And blue hills so far and dim
They melt on the horizon's rim.
O how fresh the air, and sweet,
And with what a footfall fleet
O'er the grasses' ebb and flow
The light winds to the eastward go.

Noon is now with us.   Farewell
To this mountain citadel.
Come, and with your footing fine
Thread the scented paths of pine,
Till we see the Druid carn
Shadowed in the haunted tarn.
There the water blue and deep
Lies, like wearied thought, asleep.

While we watch, the storm awakes ;
Flash on flash the ripple breaks,
Purple, with a snow-white crest,
On the meadow's golden breast.
Roods of tinkling sedge are kissed
By the waves of amethyst :
Trouble knows the place, they say,
But we laugh at that to-day.

Onward to the glen below ;
Every nook and turn we know
Where the passion-haunted stream
Laughs and lingers in its dream,
Making where its pebbles shine
Naiad music, clear and fine,
But not sweeter than the song
Love sings as we rove along.

At the last the grassy seat,
Where of old we used to meet,
Holds us in its close embrace.
Hallowed ever be the place !
Here we kissed our hearts away
In a lovers' holiday !
Shall I dream a greater bliss
Than the memory of this ?

Maire, my Girl.

Over the dim blue hills
  Strays a wild river,
Over the dim blue hills
  Rests my heart ever.
Dearer and brighter than
  Jewels and pearl,
Dwells she in beauty there,
  Maire, my girl.

Down upon Claris heath
  Shines the soft berry,
On the brown harvest tree
  Droops the red cherry.
Sweeter thy honey lips,
  Softer the curl
Straying adown thy cheeks,
  Maire, my girl.

'Twas on an April eve
  That I first met her ;
Many an eve shall pass
  Ere I forget her.
Since, my young heart has been
  Wrapped in a whirl,
Thinking and dreaming of
  Maire, my girl.

She is too kind and fond
  Ever to grieve me,
She has too pure a heart
  E'er to deceive me.
Were I Tryconnell's chief
  Or Desmond's earl,
Life would be dark, wanting
  Maire, my girl !

Over the dim blue hills
  Strays a wild river,
Over the dim blue hills
  Rests my heart ever.
Dearer and brighter than
  Jewels or pearl,
Dwells she in beauty there,
  Maire, my girl.

Gracie Og Machree.*

(Song of the "Wild Geese.")

I placed the silver in her palm,
  By Inny's smiling tide,
And vowed, ere summer time came on,
  To claim her as a bride.
But when the summer time came on
  I dwelt beyond the sea;
Yet still my heart is ever true
  To Gracie Og Machree.

O bonnie are the woods of Targ,
  And green thy hills, Rathmore,
And soft the sunlight ever falls
  On Darre's sloping shore;
And there the eyes I love—in tears
  Shine ever mournfully,
While I am far, and far away
  From Gracie Og Machree.

When battle-steeds were neighing loud,
  With bright blades in the air,
Next to my inmost heart I wore
  A bright tress of her hair.
When stirrup-cups were lifted up
  To lips, with soldier glee,
One toast I always fondly pledged,
  'Twas Gracie Og Machree.

---

* Gracie óg mo-chridhe — " Young Gracie, my heart."

Dirge.
(From "The Sea Bride.")

Prayer unsaid, and mass unsung,
Deadman's dirge must still be rung :
    Dingle-dong, the dead-bells sound !
    Mermen chant his dirge around !

Wash him bloodless, smooth him fair,
Stretch his limbs, and sleek his hair :
    Dingle-dong, the dead-bells go !
    Mermen swing them to and fro !

In the wormless sand shall he
Feast for no foul glutton be :
    Dingle-dong, the dead-bells chime !
    Mermen keep the tone and time !

We must with a tombstone brave
Shut the shark out from his grave :
    Dingle-dong, the dead-bells toll !
    Mermen dirgers ring his knoll !

Such a slab will we lay o'er him
All the dead shall rise before him !
    Dingle-dong, the dead-bells boom !
    Mermen lay him in his tomb !

The Little Black Rose.

The Little Black Rose shall be red at last;
   What made it black but the March wind dry,
And the tear of the widow that fell on it fast?
   It shall redden the hills when June is nigh.

The Silk of the Kine shall rest at last;
   What drove her forth but the dragon-fly?
In the golden vale she shall feed full fast,
   With her mild gold horn and slow, dark eye.

The wounded wood-dove lies dead at last!
   The pine long bleeding, it shall not die!
This song is secret.   Mine ear it passed
   In a wind o'er the plains at Athenry.

Epitaph.

He roamed half round the world of woe,
  Where toil and labour never cease ;
Then dropped one little span below
  In search of peace.

And now to him mild beams and showers,
  All that he needs to grace his tomb,
From loneliest regions at all hours,
  Unsought for come.

Killiney Far Away.

To Killiney far away flies my fond heart night and day,
  To ramble light and happy through its fields and dells;
For here life smiles in vain, and earth's a land of pain,
  While all that's bright in Erin in Killiney dwells.

In Killiney in the West has a linnet sweet her nest,
  And her song makes all the wild birds in the green
    wood dumb;
To the captive without cheer, it were freedom but to hear
Such sorrow-soothing music from her fair throat come.

In Killiney's bower blows a blushing, budding rose,
  With perfume of the rarest that the June day yields;
And none who pass the way, but sighing wish that they
Might cull that fragrant flower of the dewy fields.

Through Killiney's meadows pass, on their way to early
    Mass,
  Like twin-stars 'mid the grass, two small feet bare;
And angel-pure the heart, where the murmured Aves start
On their wingèd way to Heaven from the chapel there.

And the pride of Irish girls is the dear brown head of
    curls,
  The pearl white of pearls, stoirin bàn mo chridhe;
As bright-browed as the dawn, and as meek-eyed as the
    fawn,
  And as graceful as the swan gliding on to sea.

Not for jewels nor for gold, nor for hoarded wealth
    untold,
  Not for all that mortals hold most desired and dear,
Would I my share forego in the loving heart aglow,
  That beats beneath the snow of her bosom fair.

Soon Killiney will you weep—for I know not rest nor
　sleep,
Till swiftly o'er the deep I with white sails come,
To win the linnet sweet, and the two white twinkling
　feet,
And the heart with true love beating, to my far-off
　home.

And O! farewell to care, when the rose of perfume rare,
　And the dear brown curling hair on my proud breast lie;
Then Killiney far away, never more by night or day,
　To thy skies, or dark or grey, shall my fond heart fly.

Cean Dubh Deelish.*

Put your head, darling, darling, darling,
  Your darling black head my heart above ;
Oh, mouth of honey, with thyme for fragrance,
  Who, with heart in breast, could deny you love ?

Oh, many and many a young girl for me is pining,
  Letting her locks of gold to the cold wind free,
For me, the foremost of our gay young fellows ;
  But I'd leave a hundred, pure love, for thee !

Then put your head, darling, darling, darling,
  Your darling black head my heart above ;
Oh, mouth of honey, with thyme for fragrance,
  Who, with heart in breast, could deny you love ?

---

* Pron. Cawn dhu dee-lish—i.e. "darling black head."

Molly Asthore.

O Mary dear! O Mary fair!
  O branch of generous stem!
White blossom of the banks of Nair,
  Though lilies grow on them;
You've left me sick at heart for love,
  So faint I cannot see;
The candle swims the board above,
  I'm drunk for love of thee!
O stately stem of maiden pride,
  My woe it is and pain
That I thus severed from thy side
  The long night must remain.

Through all the towns of Innisfail
  I've wandered far and wide,
But from Downpatrick to Kinsale,
  From Carlow to Kilbride,
Many lords and dames of high degree
  Where'er my feet have gone,
My Mary, one to equal thee
  I never looked upon:
I live in darkness and in doubt
  When'er my love's away;
But were the gracious sun put out,
  Her shadow would make day.

'Tis she, indeed, young bud of bliss,
  As gentle as she's fair.
Though lily-white her bosom is,
  And sunny bright her hair,
And dewy azure her blue eye,
  And rosy red her cheek,
Yet brighter she in modesty,
  Most beautifully meek:

The world's wise men from north to south
  Can never cure my pain ;
But one kiss from her honey mouth
  Would make me well again.

The Fair Hills of Ireland.

(From the Irish.)

A plenteous place is Ireland for hospitable cheer,
    Uileacan dubh O!
Where, the wholesome fruit is bursting from the yellow
    barley ear;
        Uileacan dubh O!
There is honey in the trees where her misty vales
    expand,
And her forest paths in summer are by falling waters
    fanned;
There is dew at high noontide there, and springs i' the
    yellow sand,
On the fair hills of holy Ireland.

Curled is he and ringleted, and plaited to the knee,
    Uileacan dubh O!
Each captain who comes sailing across the Irish Sea;
        Uileacan dubh O!
And I will make my journey, if life and health but stand,
Unto that pleasant country, that fresh and fragrant
    strand,
And leave your boasted braveries, your wealth and high
    command,
For the fair hills of holy Ireland.

Large and profitable are the stacks upon the ground;
    Uileacan dubh O!
The butter and the cream do wondrously abound,
    Uileacan dubh O!
The cresses on the water and the sorrels are at hand,
And the cuckoo's calling daily his note of music bland,
And the bold thrush sings so bravely his song i' the
    forest grand,
On the fair hills of holy Ireland.

Herring is King.

Let all the fish that swim the sea,
Salmon and turbot, cod and ling,
Bow down the head and bend the knee
To herring, their king! to herring, their king!

Sing, Hugamar féin an sowra lin',
'Tis we have brought the summer in.*

The sun sank down so round and red
Upon the bay, upon the bay;
The sails shook idly overhead,
Becalmed we lay, becalmed we lay;

Sing, Hugamar, etc.

Till Shawn the eagle dropped on deck,
The bright-eyed boy, the bright-eyed boy;
'Tis he has spied your silver track,
Herring, our joy, herring, our joy;

Sing, Hugamar, etc.

It is in with the sails and away to shore,
With the rise and swing, the rise and swing
Of two stout lads at each smoking oar,
After herring, our king! herring, our king.

Sing, Hugamar, etc.

The Manx and Cornish raised the shout,
And joined the chase, and joined the chase;
But their fleets they fouled as they went about,
And we won the race, we won the race;

Sing, Hugamar, etc.

---

* The second line to the refrain translates the first.

H

For we turned and faced you full to land,
  Down the góleen* long, the góleen long,
And after you slipped from strand to strand
  Our nets so strong, our nets so strong;

    Sing, Hugamar, etc.

Then we called to our sweethearts and our wives,
"Come welcome us home, welcome us home,"
Till they ran to meet us for their lives
  Into the foam, into the foam;

    Sing, Hugamar, etc.

O kissing of hands and waving of caps
  From girl and boy, from girl and boy,
While you leapt by scores in the lasses' laps,
  Herring our joy, herring our joy!

    Sing, Hugamar féin an sowra lin',
    'Tis we have brought the summer in!

---

* Creek.

The Rose of Kenmare.

I've been soft in a small way
On the girleens of Galway,
And the Limerick lasses have made me feel quare;
But there's no use denyin',
No girl I've set eye on
Could compate wid Rose Ryan of the town of Kenmare.

     O, where
   Can her like be found?
    No where,
   The country round,
   Spins at her wheel
     Daughter as true,
   Sets in the reel,
     Wid a slide of the shoe
      a slinderer,
      tinderer,
      purtier,
      wittier colleen than you,
    Rose, aroo!

Her hair mocks the sunshine,
And the soft, silver moonshine
Neck and arm of the colleen completely eclipse;
Whilst the nose of the jewel
Slants straight as Carran Tual
From the heaven in her eye to her heather-sweet lip.

    O, where, etc.

Did your eyes ever follow
The wings of the swallow
Here and there, light as air, o'er the meadow field glance?
For if not you've no notion
Of the exquisite motion
Of her sweet little feet as they dart in the dance.

    O, where, etc.

If y' inquire why the nightingale
Still shuns th' invitin' gale
That wafts every song-bird but her to the West,
Faix she knows, I suppose,
Ould Kenmare has a Rose
That would sing any Bulbul to sleep in her nest.

O, where, etc.

When her voice gives the warnin'
For the milkin' in the mornin'
Ev'n the cow known for hornin', comes runnin' to her
pail;
The lambs play about her
And the small bonneens* snout her
Whilst their parints salute her wid a twisht of the tail.

O, where, etc.

When at noon from our labour
We draw neighbour wid neighbour
From the heat of the sun to the shelter of the tree,
Wid spuds† fresh from the bilin',
And new milk, you come smilin',
All the boys' hearts beguilin', alannah machree!‡

O, where, etc.

But there's one sweeter hour
When the hot day is o'er,
And we rest at the door wid the bright moon above,
And she's sittin' in the middle,
When she's guessed Larry's riddle,
Cries, "Now for your fiddle, Shiel Dhuv, Shiel Dhuv."

---

* Piglings.
† Potatoes.
‡ My heart's delight.

O, where
Can her like be found?
No where,
The country round,
Spins at her wheel
    Daughter as true,
Sets in the reel,
    Wid a slide of the shoe
        a slinderer,
        tinderer,
        purtier,
        wittier colleen than you,
    Rose, aroo!

The Song of the Pratee.

When after the Winter alarmin',
The Spring steps in so charmin',
    So fresh and arch
    In the middle of March,
Wid her hand St Patrick's arm on,
Let us all, let us all be goin',
Agra, to assist at your sowin',
    The girls to spread
    Your iligant bed,
And the boys to set the hoe in.

Chorus—

Then good speed to your seed! God's grace and increase.
    Never more in our need may you blacken wid the blight;
But when summer is o'er, in our gardens, asthore,
    May the fruit at your root fill our bosoms wid delight.

So rest and sleep, my jewel,
Safe from the tempest cruel ;
    Till violets spring
    And skylarks sing
From Mourne to Carran Tual.
Then wake and build your bower,
Through April sun and shower,
    To bless the earth
    That gave you birth,
Through many a sultry hour.

Chorus—

Then good luck to your leaf. And ochone, ologone,
    Never more to our grief may it blacken wid the blight;
But when summer is o'er, in our gardens, asthore,
    May the fruit at your root fill our bosoms wid delight.

Thus smile with glad increasin',
Till to St John we 're raisin',
Through Erin's isle
The pleasant pile
That sets the bonfire blazin'.
O 'tis then that the midsummer fairy,
Abroad on his sly vagary,
Wid purple and white,
As he passes by night,
Your emerald leaf shall vary.

Chorus—

Then more power to your flower, and your merry green
leaf!
Never more to our grief may they blacken wid the
blight;
But when summer is o'er, in our gardens, asthore,
May the fruit at your root fill our bosoms wid delight.

And once again Mavourneen,
Some yellow autumn mornin',
At red sunrise
Both girls and boys
To your garden ridge we 're turnin',
Then under your foliage fadin'
Each man of us sets his spade in,
While the colleen bawn
Her brown kishane*
Full up wid your fruit is ladin'.

Chorus—

Then good luck to your leaf! more power to your flower!
Never more to our grief may they blacken wid the
blight;
But when summer is o'er, in our gardens, asthore,
May the fruit at your root fill our bosoms wid delight.

---

* A large basket carried on the back.

Irish Lullaby.

I'd rock my own sweet childie to rest in a cradle of
gold on a bough of the willow,
To the shoheen ho of the wind of the west and the
lulla lo of the soft sea billow.
      Sleep, baby dear,
      Sleep without fear,
      Mother is here beside your pillow.

I'd put my own sweet childie to sleep in a silver boat
on the beautiful river,
Where a shoheen whisper the white cascades, and a
lulla lo the green flags shiver.
      Sleep, baby dear,
      Sleep without fear,
      Mother is here with you for ever.

Lulla lo! to the rise and fall of mother's bosom 'tis
sleep has bound you,
And O, my child, what cosier nest for rosier rest could
love have found you?
      Sleep, baby dear,
      Sleep without fear,
      Mother's two arms are clasped around you.

Eileen Aroon.

When, like the early rose,
   Eileen Aroon!
Beauty in childhood blows,
   Eileen Aroon!
When, like a diadem,
Buds blush around the stem,
Which is the fairest gem?
   Eileen Aroon!

Is it the laughing eye,
   Eileen Aroon!
Is it the timid sigh,
   Eileen Aroon!
Is it the tender tone,
Soft as the stringed harp's moan?
Oh! it is truth alone,
   Eileen Aroon!

When, like the rising day,
   Eileen Aroon!
Love sends his early ray,
   Eileen Aroon!
What makes his dawning glow,
Changeless through joy or woe?
Only the constant know—
   Eileen Aroon!

I know a valley fair,
   Eileen Aroon!
I knew a cottage there,
   Eileen Aroon!
Far in that valley's shade
I knew a gentle maid,
Flower of a hazel glade,
   Eileen Aroon!

Who in the song so sweet?
    Eileen Aroon!
Who in the dance so fleet?
    Eileen Aroon!
Dear were her charms to me,
Dearer her laughter free,
Dearest her constancy,
    Eileen Aroon!

Were she no longer true,
    Eileen Aroon!
What should her lover do?
    Eileen Aroon!
Fly with his broken chain
Far o'er the sounding main,
Never to love again,
    Eileen Aroon!

Youth must with time decay,
    Eileen Aroon!
Beauty must fade away,
    Eileen Aroon!
Castles are sacked in war,
Chieftains are scattered far,
Truth is a fixèd star,
    Eileen Aroon!

The Dark Man.

Rose o' the world, she came to my bed
And changed the dreams of my heart and head:
For joy of mine she left grief of hers
And garlanded me with the prickly furze.

Rose o' the world, they go out and in,
And watch me dream and my mother spin:
And they pity the tears on my sleeping face
While my soul's away in a fairy place.

Rose o' the world, they have words galore,
For wide's the swing of my mother's door:
And soft they speak of my darkened brain,
But what do they know of my heart's dear pain?

Rose o' the world, the grief you give
Is worth all days that a man may live:
Is worth all prayers that the colleens say
On the night that darkens the wedding-day.

Rose o' the world, what man would wed
When he might remember your face instead?
Might go to his grave with the blessed pain
Of hungering after your face again?

Rose o' the world, they may talk their fill,
But dreams are good, and my life stands still
While the neighbours talk by their fires astir:
But my fiddle knows: and *I* talk to her.

April in Ireland.

She hath a woven garland all of the sighing sedge,
And all her flowers are snowdrops grown on the winter's
edge :
The golden looms of Tir na n' Og wove all the winter
through
Her gown of mist and raindrops shot with a cloudy blue.

Sunlight she holds in one hand, and rain she scatters
after,
And through the rainy twilight we hear her fitful laughter.
She shakes down on her flowers the snows less white
than they,
Then quicken with her kisses the folded "knots o' May."

She seeks the summer-lover that never shall be hers,
Fain for gold leaves of autumn she passes by the furze,
Though buried gold it hideth : she scorns her sedgy crown,
And pressing blindly sunwards she treads her snowdrops
down.

Her gifts are all a fardel of wayward smiles and tears,
Yet hope she also holdeth, this daughter of the years—
A hope that blossoms faintly set upon sorrow's edge :
She hath a woven garland of all the sighing sedge.

The Wind Among the Reeds.

Mavrone, Mavrone ! the wind among the reeds.
It calls and cries, and will not let me be ;
And all its cry is of forgotten deeds
When men were loved of all the Daoine-Sidhe.

O Shee that have forgotten how to love,
And Shee that have forgotten how to hate,
Asleep 'neath quicken boughs that no winds move,
Come back to us ere yet it be too late.

Pipe to us once again, lest we forget
What piping means, till all the Silver Spears
Be wild with gusty music, such as met
Carolan once, amid the dusty years.

Dance in your rings again : the yellow weeds
You used to ride so far, mount as of old—
Play hide-and-seek with wind among the reeds,
And pay your scores again with fairy gold.

My Grief on the Sea.

My grief on the sea,
  How the waves of it roll !
For they heave between me
  And the love of my soul !

Abandoned, forsaken,
  To grief and to care,
Will the sea ever waken
  Relief from despair ?

My grief, and my trouble !
  Would he and I wear,
In the province of Leinster,
  Or County of Clare.

Were I and my darling—
  O, heart-bitter wound !—
On the board of the ship
  For America bound.

On a green bed of rushes
  All last night I lay,
And I flung it abroad
  With the heat of the day.

And my love came behind me—
  He came from the South ;
His breast to my bosom
  His mouth to my mouth.

The Cooleen.

A honey mist on a day of frost, in a dark oak wood,
And love for thee in my heart in me, thou bright, white,
and good ;
Thy slender form, soft and warm, thy red lips apart,
Thou hast found me, and hast bound me, and put grief
in my heart.

In fair-green and market, men mark thee, bright, young,
and merry,
Though thou hurt them like foes with the rose of thy
blush of the berry :
Her cheeks are a poppy, her eye it is Cupid's helper,
But each foolish man dreams that its beams for himself are.

Whoe'er saw the Cooleen in a cool, dewy meadow
On a morning in summer in sunshine and shadow ;
All the young men go wild for her, my childeen, my
treasure,
But now let them go mope, they've no hope to possess
her.

Let us roam, O my darling, afar through the mountains,
Drink milk of the goat, wine and bulcaun in fountains ;
With music and play every day from my lyre,
And leave to come rest on my breast when you tire.

The Breedyeen.

'Tis the Breedyeen I love,
All dear ones above,
    Like a star from the start
    Round my heart she did move.
Her breast like a dove,
Or the foam in the cove,
    With her gold locks apart,
    In my heart she put love.

'Tis not Venus, I say,
Who grieved me this day,
    But the white one, the bright one,
    Who slighted my stay.
For her I shall pray—
I confess it—for aye,
    She's my sister, I missed her,
    When all men were gay.

To the hills let us go,
Where the raven and crow
    In dark dismal valleys
    Croak death-like and low;
By this volume I swear,
O bright Cool of fair hair,
    That though solitude shrieked
    I should seek for thee there.

To the hills let us go,
Where the raven and crow
    In the dark dismal valleys
    Wing silent and slow.
There's no Joy in men's fate
But Grief grins in the gate;
    There's no Fair without Foul,
    Without Crooked no Straight.

Her neck like the lime
And her breath like the thyme,
    And her bosom untroubled
    By care or by time.
Like a bird in the night,
At a great blaze of light,
    Astounded and wounded
    I swoon at her sight.

Since I gave thee my love,
I gave thee my love,
    I gave thee my love,
    O thou berry so bright ;
The sun in her height
Looked on with delight,
    And between thy two arms, may
    I die on the night.

And I would that I were
In the glens of the air,
    Or in dark dismal valleys
    Where the wildwood is bare,
What a kiss from her there
I should coax without care,
    From my star of the morning,
    My fairer than fair !

Like a Phœnix of flame,
Or like Helen of fame,
    Is the pearl of all pearls
    Of girls who came,
And who kindled a flame,
In my bosom. Thy name
    I shall rhyme thee in Irish
    And heighten thy fame.

Nelly of the Top-Knots.

Dear God! were I fisher and
  Back in Binédar,
And Nelly a fish who
  Would swim in the bay there,
I would privately set there
  My net there to catch her,
In Erin no maiden
  Is able to match her.

And Nelly, dear God!
  Why! you should not thus flee me,
I long to be near thee
  And hear thee and see thee,
My hand on the Bible
  And I swearing and kneeling
And giving thee part
  Of the heart you are stealing.

I 've a fair yellow casket
  And it fastened with crystal,
And the lock opens not
  To the shot of a pistol.
To Jesus I pray
  And to Columbkill's Master,
That Mary may guide thee
  Aside from disaster.

We may be, O maiden
  Whom none may disparage,
Some morning a-hearing
  The sweet mass of marriage,
But if fate be against us,
  To rend us and push us,
I shall mourn as the blackbird
  At eve in the bushes.

O God, were she with me
  Where the gull flits and tern,
Or in Paris the smiling,
  Or an Isle in Loch Erne,
I would coax her so well,
  I would tell her my story,
And talk till I won her,
  My sunshine of glory.

I shall not Die for Thee.

For thee I shall not die,
  Woman high of fame and name;
Foolish men thou mayest slay
  I and they are not the same.

Why should I expire
  For the fire of any eye,
Slender waist or swan-like limb,
  Is 't for them that I should die?

The round breasts, the fresh skin,
  Cheeks crimson, hair so long and rich;
Indeed, indeed, I shall not die,
  Please God, not I, for any such.

The golden hair, the forehead thin,
  The chaste mien, the gracious ease,
The rounded heel, the languid tone,
  Fools alone find death from these.

Thy sharp wit, thy perfect calm,
  Thy thin palm like foam o' the sea;
Thy white neck, thy blue eye,
  I shall not die for thee.

Woman, graceful as the swan,
  A wise man did nurture me,
Little palm, white neck, bright eye,
  I shall not die for ye.

The Red Wind.

Red Wind from out the East :
Red Wind of blight and blood !
Ah, when wilt thou have ceased
Thy bitter, stormy flood ?

Red Wind from over sea,
Scourging our holy land !
What angel loosened thee
Out of his iron hand ?

Red Wind ! whose word of might
Winged thee with wings of flame ?
O fire of mournful night !
What is thy Master's name ?

Red Wind ! who bade thee burn,
Branding our hearts ? Who bade
Thee on and never turn
Till waste our souls were laid ?

Red Wind ! from out the West
Pour Winds of Paradise :
Winds of eternal rest,
That weary souls entice.

Wind of the East ! Red Wind !
Thou scorchest the soft breath
Of Paradise the kind :
Red Wind of burning death !

O Red Wind ! hear God's voice :
Hear thou, and fall, and cease.
Let Innisfail rejoice
In her Hesperian peace.

To Morfydd.

A voice on the winds,
A voice on the waters,
    Wanders and cries:
O what are the winds?
And what are the waters?
    Mine are your eyes.

Western the winds are,
And western the waters,
    Where the light lies:
O what are the winds?
And what are the waters?
    Mine are your eyes.

Cold, cold grow the winds,
And dark grow the waters,
    Where the sun dies:
O what are the winds?
And what are the waters?
    Mine are your eyes.

And down the night winds,
And down the night waters
    The music flies:
O what are the winds?
And what are the waters?
Cold be the winds,
And wild be the waters,
    So mine be your eyes.

A Lament.

Youth's bright palace
Is overthrown,
With its diamond sceptre
And golden throne ;
As a time-worn stone
Its turrets are humbled,—
All hath crumbled
But grief alone !

Whither, oh ! whither
Have fled away
The dreams and hopes
Of my early day ?
Ruined and grey
Are the towers I builded ;
And the beams that gilded—
Ah ! where are they ?

Once this world
Was fresh and bright,
With its golden noon
And its starry night ;
Glad and light,
By mountain and river,
Have I blessed the Giver
With hushed delight.

Youth's illusions,
One by one,
Have passed like clouds
That the sun looked on.
While morning shone,
How purple their fringes !
How ashy their tinges
When that was gone !

As fire-flies fade
When the nights are damp—
As meteors are quenched
In a stagnant swamp—
Thus Charlemagne's camp,
Where the Paladins rally,
And the Diamond Valley,
And the Wonderful Lamp,

And all the wonders
Of Ganges and Nile,
And Haroun's rambles,
And Crusoe's isle,
And Princes who smile
On the Genii's daughters
'Neath the Orient waters
Full many a mile,

And all that the pen
Of Fancy can write,
Must vanish
In manhood's misty light—
Squire and Knight,
And damosels' glances,
Sunny romances
So pure and bright!

These have vanished,
And what remains?
Life's budding garlands
Have turned to chains—
Its beams and rains
Feed but docks and thistles,
And sorrow whistles
O'er desert plains!

The Fair Hills of Eiré, O!

(After the Irish of DONOGH MAC CON-MARA.)

Take a blessing from my heart to the land of my birth,
And the fair Hills of Eiré, O !
And to all that yet survive of Eibhear's tribe on earth,
On the fair Hills of Eiré, O !
In that land so delightful the wild thrush's lay—
Seems to pour a lament forth for Eiré's delay—
Alas ! alas ! why pine I a thousand miles away
From the fair Hills of Eiré, O !

The soil is rich and soft—the air is mild and bland,
Of the fair Hills of Eiré, O !
Her barest rock is greener to me than this rude land—
O ! the fair Hills of Eiré, O !
Her woods are tall and straight, grove rising over grove;
Trees flourish in her glens below, and on her heights
above ;
O, in heart and in soul, I shall ever, ever love
The fair Hills of Eiré, O !

A noble tribe, moreover, are the now hapless Gael,
On the fair Hills of Eiré, O !
A tribe in Battle's hour unused to shrink or fail
On the fair Hills of Eiré, O !
For this is my lament in bitterness outpoured,
To see them slain or scattered by the Saxon sword.
Oh, woe of woes, to see a foreign spoiler horde
On the fair Hills of Eiré, O ! .

Broad and tall rise the cruachs in the golden morning's
glow
On the fair Hills of Eiré, O !
O'er her smooth grass for ever sweet cream and honey
flow
On the fair Hills of Eiré, O !

O, I long, I am pining, again to behold
The land that belongs to the brave Gael of old ;
Far dearer to my heart than a gift of gems or gold
    Are the fair Hills of Eiré, O !

The dewdrops lie bright 'mid the grass and yellow corn
    On the fair Hills of Eiré, O !
And the sweet-scented apples blush redly in the morn
    On the fair Hills of Eiré, O !
The water-cress and sorrel fill the vales below ;
The streamlets are hushed, till the evening breezes blow;
While the waves of the Suir, noble river ! ever flow
    Near the fair Hills of Eiré, O !

A fruitful clime is Eiré's, through valley, meadow, plain,
    And the fair land of Eiré, O !
The very " Bread of Life " is in the yellow grain
    On the fair Hills of Eiré, O !
Far dearer unto me than the tones music yields,
Is the lowing of her kine and the calves in her fields,
And the sunlight that shone long ago on the shields
    Of the Gaels, on the fair Hills of Eiré, O !

Dark Rosaleen.

O my dark Rosaleen,
  Do not sigh, do not weep!
The priests are on the ocean green,
  They march along the Deep.
There 's wine . . . . from the royal Pope,
  Upon the ocean green ;
And Spanish ale shall give you hope,
  My dark Rosaleen !
  My own Rosaleen !
Shall glad your heart, shall give you hope,
Shall give you health, and help, and hope,
  My dark Rosaleen.

Over hills, and through dales,
  Have I roamed for your sake ;
All yesterday I sailed with sails
  On river and on lake.
The Erne . . . . at its highest flood,
  I dashed across unseen,
For there was lightning in my blood,
  My dark Rosaleen !
  My own Rosaleen !
Oh ! there was lightning in my blood,
Red lightning lightened through my blood,
  My dark Rosaleen !

All day long in unrest,
  To and fro do I move,
The very soul within my breast
  Is wasted for you, love !
The heart . . . . in my bosom faints
  To think of you my Queen,
My life of life, my saint of saints,
  My dark Rosaleen !
  My own Rosaleen !

To hear your sweet and sad complaints,
My life, my love, my saint of saints,
My dark Rosaleen !

Woe and pain, pain and woe,
Are my lot, night and noon,
To see your bright face clouded so,
Like to the mournful moon.
But yet . . . . will I rear your throne
Again in golden sheen ;
'Tis you shall reign, shall reign alone,
My dark Rosaleen !
My own Rosaleen !
'Tis you shall have the golden throne,
'Tis you shall reign, shall reign alone,
My dark Rosaleen !

Over dews, over sands,
Will I fly, for your weal :
Your holy delicate white hands
Shall girdle me with steel.
At home . . . . in your emerald bowers,
From morning's dawn till e'en,
You 'll pray for me, my flower of flowers,
My dark Rosaleen !
My fond Rosaleen !
You 'll think of me through Daylight's hours,
My virgin flower, my flower of flowers,
My dark Rosaleen !

I could scale the blue air,
I could plough the high hills,
Oh, I could kneel all night in prayer,
To heal your many ills !
And one . . . . beamy smile from you
Would float the light between
My toils and me, my own, my true,
My dark Rosaleen !
My fond Rosaleen !

Would give me life and soul anew,
A second life, a soul anew,
  My dark Rosaleen !

O ! the Erne shall run red
  With redundance of blood,
The earth shall rock beneath our tread,
  And flames wrap hill and wood,
And gun-peal, and slogan cry,
  Wake many a glen serene,
Ere you shall fade, ere you can die,
  My dark Rosaleen !
  My own Rosaleen !
The Judgment Hour must first be nigh
Ere you can fade, ere you can die,
  My dark Rosaleen !

The One Mystery.

'Tis idle! we exhaust and squander
  The glittering mine of thought in vain
All-baffled reason cannot wander,
      Beyond her chain.
The flood of life runs dark—dark clouds
  Make lampless night around its shore:
The dead, where are they? In their shrouds—
      Man knows no more.

Evoke the ancient and the past,
  Will one illumining star arise?
Or must the film, from first to last,
      O'erspread thine eyes?
When life, love, glory, beauty, wither,
  Will wisdom's page, or science chart,
Map out for thee the region whither
      Their shades depart?

Supposest thou the wondrous powers,
  To high imagination given,
Pale types of what shall yet be ours,
      When earth is heaven?
When this decaying shell is cold,
  Oh! sayest thou the soul shall climb
What magic mount she trod of old,
      Ere childhood's time?

And shall the sacred pulse that thrilled,
  Thrill once again to glory's name?
And shall the conquering love that filled
      All earth with flame,
Re-born, revived, renewed, immortal,
  Resume his reign in prouder might,
A sun beyond the ebon portal,
      Of death and night?

No more, no more—with aching brow,
And restless heart, and burning brain,
We ask the When, the Where, the How,
And ask in vain.
And all philosophy, all faith,
All earthly—all celestial lore,
Have but one voice, which only saith
Endure—adore !

The Wild Geese.

I had no sail to cross the sea,
A brave white bird went forth from me,
My heart was hid beneath his wing :
O strong white bird, come back in spring !

I watched the Wild Geese rise and cry
Across the flaring western sky ;
Their winnowing pinions clove the light,
Then vanished, and came down the night.

I laid me low, my day was done,
I longed not for the morrow's sun,
But closely swathed in swoon of sleep,
Forgot to hope, forgot to weep.

The moon, through veils of gloomy red,
A warm yet dusky radiance shed
All down our valley's golden stream
And flushed my slumber with a dream.

Her mystic torch lit up my brain ;
My spirit rose and lived amain,
And follow through the windy spray
That bird upon its watery way.

"O wild white bird, O wail for me !
My soul hath wings to fly with thee :
On foam waves, lengthening out afar,
We 'll ride toward the western star.

"O'er glimmering plains, through forest gloom,
To track a wanderer's feet I come ;
'Mid lonely swamp, by haunted brake,
I 'll pass unfrighted for his sake.

"Alone, afar, his footsteps roam,
The stars his roof, the tent his home.
Saw'st thou what way the Wild Geese flew
To sunward through the thick night dew ?

"Carry my soul where he abides,
And pierce the mystery that hides
His presence, and through time and space
Look with mine eyes upon his face."

"Beside his prairie fire he rests,
All feathered things are in their nests:
'What strange wild bird is this,' he saith,
'Still fragrant with the ocean's breath?

"'Perch on my hand, thou briny thing,
And let me stroke thy shy wet wing;
What message in thy soft eye thrills?
I see again my native hills

"'And vale, the river's silver streak,
The mist upon the blue, blue peak,
The shadows grey, the golden sheaves,
The mossy walls, the russet eaves.

"'I greet the friends I've loved and lost,
Do all forget? No, tempest-tost,
That braved for me the ocean's foam,
Some heart remembers me at home.

"'Ere spring's return I will be there,
Thou strange sea-fragrant messenger!
I wake and weep; the moon shines sweet,
O dream too short! O bird too fleet!'"

Lament for a Little Child.

I am lying in the tomb, love,
Lying in the tomb,
Tho' I move within the gloom, love,
Breathe within the gloom!
Men deem life not fled, dear,
Deem my life not fled,
Tho' I with thee am dead, dear,
I with thee am dead,
O my little child!

What is the grey world, darling,
What is the grey world,
Where the worm lies curled, darling,
The death-worm lies curled?
They tell me of the spring, dear!
Do I want the spring?
Will she waft upon her wing, dear,
The joy-pulse of her wing,
Thy songs, thy blossoming,
O my little child!

For the hallowing of thy smile, love,
The rainbow of thy smile,
Gleaming for a while, love,
Gleaming to beguile,
Re-plunged me in the cold, dear,
Leaves me in the cold,
And I feel so very old, dear,
Very, very old!

Would they put me out of pain, dear,
Out of all my pain,
Since I may not live again, dear,
Never live again!

I am lying in the grave, love,
In thy little grave,
Yet I hear the wind rave, love,
And the wild wave!
I would lie asleep, darling,
With thee lie asleep,
Unhearing the world weep, darling,
Little children weep!
O my little child!

The Swimmer.

Yonder, lo! the tide is flowing;
Clamber, while the breeze is blowing,
Down to where a soft foam flusters
Dulse and fairy feathery clusters!
While it fills the shelly hollows,
A swift sister-billow follows,
Leaps in hurrying with the tide,
Seems the lingering wave to chide;
Both push on with eager life,
And a gurgling show of strife.
O the salt, refreshing air
Shrilly blowing in the hair!
A keen, healthful savour haunts
Sea-shell, sea-flower, and sea-plants.
Innocent billows on the strand
Leave a crystal over sand,
Whose thin ebbing soon is crossed
By a crystal foam-enmossed,
Variegating silver-grey
Shell-empetalled sand in play:
When from sand dries off the brine,
Vanishes swift shadow fine;
But a wet sand is a glass
Where the plumy cloudlets pass,
Floating islands of the blue,
Tender, shining, fair, and true.

Who would linger idle,
Dallying would lie,
When wind and wave, a bridal
Celebrating, fly?
Let him plunge among them,
Who hath wooed enough,
Flirted with them, sung them,
In the salt sea-trough

He may win them, onward
On a buoyant crest,
Far to seaward, sunward,
Ocean-borne to rest!
Wild wind will sing over him,
And the free foam cover him,
Swimming seaward, sunward,
On a blithe sea-breast!
On a blithe sea-bosom
Swims another too,
Swims a live sea-blossom,
A grey-winged sea-mew!
Grape-green all the waves are,
By whose hurrying line
Half of ships and caves are
Buried under brine;
Supple, shifting ranges
Lucent at the crest,
With pearly surface-changes
Never laid to rest:
Now a dipping gunwale
Momently he sees,
Now a fuming funnel,
Or red flag in the breeze;
Arms flung open wide,
Lip the laughing sea;
For playfellow, for bride,
Claim her impetuously!
Triumphantly exult with all the free,
Buoyant, bounding splendour of the sea!
And if while on the billow
Wearily he lay,
His awful wild playfellow
Filled his mouth with spray,
Reft him of his breath,
To some far realms away
He would float with Death;

Wild wind would sing over him,
And the free foam cover him,
Waft him sleeping onward,
Floating seaward, sunward,
All alone with Death ;
In a realm of wondrous dreams,
And shadow-haunted ocean gleams !

The Dance.

The dance! the dance!
Maidens advance
Your undulating charm!
A line deploys
Of gentle boys,
Waving the light arm,
Bronze, alive and warm;
Reed flute and drum
Sound as they come,
Under your eyelight warm!

Many a boy,
A dancing joy,
Many a mellow maid,
With fireflies in the shade,
Mingle and glide,
Appear and hide,
Here in a fairy glade:
Ebb and flow
To a music low,
Viol, and flute and lyre,
As melody mounts higher:
With a merry will,
They touch and thrill,
Beautiful limbs of fire!

Red berries, shells,
Over bosom-dells,
And girdles of light grass,
May never hide
The youthful pride
Of beauty, ere it pass:
Yet, ah! sweet boy and lass,
Refrain, retire!
Love is a fire!
Night will pass!

From "The Water-Nymph and the Boy."

I flung me round him,
I drew him under;
I clung, I drowned him,
My own white wonder . .

Father and mother,
Weeping and wild,
Came to the forest,
Calling the child,
Came from the palace,
Down to the pool,
Calling my darling,
My beautiful!

Under the water,
Cold and so pale!
Could it be love made
Beauty to fail?

Ah me! for mortals:
In a few moons,
If I had left him,
After some Junes
He would have faded,
Faded away,
He, the young monarch, whom
All would obey,
Fairer than day;
Alien to springtime,
Joyless and grey,
He would have faded,
Faded away,
Moving a mockery,
Scorned of the day!

Now I have taken him
All in his prime,
Saved from slow poisoning
Pitiless Time,
Filled with his happiness,
One with the prime,
Saved from the cruel
Dishonour of Time,
Laid him, my beautiful,
Laid him to rest,
Loving, adorable,
Softly to rest,
Here in my crystalline,
Here in my breast!

A Casual Song.

She sang of lovers met to play
"Under the may bloom, under the may,"
But when I sought her face so fair,
I found the set face of Despair.

She sang of woodland leaves in spring,
And joy of young love dallying;
But her young eyes were all one moan,
And Death weighed on her heart like stone.

I could not ask, I know not now,
The story of that mournful brow;
It haunts me as it haunted then,
A flash from fire of hell-bound men.

"The Pity of it."

If our love may fail, Lily,
If our love may fail,
What will mere life avail, Lily,
Mere life avail?

Seed that promised blossom,
Withered in the mould,
Pale petals overblowing,
Failing from the gold!

When the fervent fingers
Listlessly unclose,
May the life that lingers
Find repose, Lily,
Find repose!

Who may dream of all the music
Only a lover hears,
Hearkening to hearts triumphant
Bearing down the years?
Ah! may eternal anthems dwindle
To a low sound of tears?

Room in all the ages
For our love to grow,
Prayers of both demanded
A little while ago:

And now a few poor moments,
Between life and death,
May be proven all too ample
For love's breath!

Seed that promised blossom,
Withered in the mould!
Pale petals overblowing,
Failing from the gold!

I well believe the fault lay
More with me than you,
But I feel the shadow closing
Cold about us two.

An hour may yet be yielded us,
Or a very little more—
Then a few tears, and silence
For evermore, Lily,
For evermore !

The Old.

They are waiting on the shore
For the bark to take them home;
They will toil and grieve no more;
The hour for release hath come.

All their long life lies behind,
Like a dimly blending dream;
There is nothing left to bind
To the realms that only seem.

They are waiting for the boat,
There is nothing left to do;
What was near them grows remote,
Happy silence falls like dew;
Now the shadowy bark is come,
And the weary may go home.

By still water they would rest,
In the shadow of the tree;
After battle sleep is best,
After noise tranquillity.

Maura Du of Ballyshannon.

I.

Maura du* of Ballyshannon!
Maura du, my flower of flowers!
Can you hear me there out seaward,
Calling back the bygone hours?
Maura du, my own, my honey!
With wild passion still aglow,
I am singing you the old songs
That I sung you long ago.
And you mind, love, how it ran on—
        "In your eyes asthore machree!†
        All my Heaven there I see,
        And that's true!
        Maura du!
        Maura du of Ballyshannon!"

II.

Maura du of Ballyshannon!
Maura du, my soul's one queen!
Big with love my heart is flying,
Where the grass is growing green.
Maura du, my own, my honey!
That I love you, well you know,
And still sing for you the old song,
That I sung you long ago.
And you mind, love, how it ran on—
        "In your eyes asthore machree!
        All my Heaven there I see,
        And that's true!
        Maura du!
        Maura du of Ballyshannon!"

---

* Maura du, "Dear Mary."
† Asthore machree, "The darling of my heart."

III.

Maura du of Ballyshannon,
Maura du, the day is drear!
Ah, the night is long and weary,
Far away from you, my dear!
Maura du, my own, my honey!
Still let winds blow high or low,
I must sing to you the old song,
That I sung you long ago,
And you mind, love, how it ran on—
"In your eyes asthore machree!
All my Heaven there I see,
And that's true!
Maura du!
Maura du of Ballyshannon!

IV.

Maura du of Ballyshannon!
Maura du, when winds blow south,
I will with the birds fly homeward,
There to kiss your Irish mouth.
Maura du, my own, my honey!
When time is no longer foe,
By your side I'll sing the old song,
That I sung you long ago,
And you mind, love, how it ran on—
"In your eyes asthore machree!
All my Heaven there I see,
And that's true!
Maura du!
Maura du of Ballyshannon!"

A Spinning Song.

My love to fight the Saxon goes,
   And bravely shines his sword of steel,
A heron's feather decks his brows,
   And a spur on either heel ;
His steed is blacker than a sloe,
   And fleeter than the falling star ;
Amid the surging ranks he 'll go
   And shout for joy of war.

Twinkle, twinkle, pretty spindle, let the white wool
   drift and dwindle,
  Oh ! we weave a damask doublet for my love's coat
   of steel.
Hark ! the timid, turning treadle, crooning soft old-
   fashioned ditties
  To the low, slow murmur of the brown, round wheel.

My love is pledged to Ireland's fight ;
   My love would die for Ireland's weal,
To win her back her ancient right,
   And make her foemen reel.
Oh, close I 'll clasp him to my breast
   When homeward from the war he comes ;
The fires shall light the mountain's crest,
   The valley peal with drums.

Twinkle, twinkle, pretty spindle, let the white wool
   drift and dwindle,
  Oh ! we weave a damask doublet for my love's coat
   of steel.
Hark ! the timid, turning treadle, crooning soft old-
   fashioned ditties
  To the low, slow murmur of the brown, round wheel.

A White Rose.

The red rose whispers of passion,
  And the white rose breathes of love ;
Oh, the red rose is a falcon,
  And the white rose is a dove.

But I send you a cream-white rosebud
  With a flush on its petal tips ;
For the love that is purest and sweetest
  Has a kiss of desire on the lips.

The Fountain of Tears.

If you go over desert and mountain,
  Far into the country of Sorrow,
  To-day and to-night and to-morrow,
And maybe for months and for years ;
  You shall come with a heart that is bursting
  For trouble and toiling and thirsting,
You shall certainly come to the fountain
At length,—to the Fountain of Tears.

Very peaceful the place is, and solely
  For piteous lamenting and sighing,
  And those who come living or dying
Alike from their hopes and their fears ;
  Full of Cyprus-like shadows the place is,
  And statues that cover their faces :
But out of the gloom springs the holy
And beautiful Fountain of Tears.

And it flows and it flows with a motion,
  So gentle and lovely and listless,
  And murmurs a tune so resistless
To him who hath suffered and hears—
  You shall surely—without a word spoken,
  Kneel down there and know your heart broken,
And yield to the long-curb'd emotion
That day by the Fountain of Tears.

For it grows and it grows, as though leaping
  Up higher the more one is thinking ;
  And even its tunes go on sinking
More poignantly into the ears :
  Yea, so blessèd and good seems that fountain,
  Reached after dry desert and mountain,
You shall fall down at length in your weeping
And bathe your sad face in the tears.

Then, alas ! while you lie there a season,
And sob between living and dying,
And give up the land you were trying
To find 'mid your hopes and your fears ;
—O the world shall come up and pass o'er you,
Strong men shall not stay to care for you,
Nor wonder indeed for what reason
Your way should seem harder than theirs.

But perhaps, while you lie, never lifting
Your cheek from the wet leaves it presses,
Nor caring to raise your wet tresses
And look how the cold world appears,—
O perhaps the mere silences round you
All things in that place grief hath found you,
Yea, e'en to the clouds o'er you drifting
May soothe you somewhat through your tears.

You may feel, when a falling leaf brushes
Your face, as though someone had kissed you ;
Or think at least some one who missed you
Hath sent you a thought,—if that cheers ;
Or a bird's little song faint and broken,
May pass for a tender word spoken :
—Enough, while around you there rushes
That life-drowning torrent of tears.

And the tears shall flow faster and faster,
Brim over, and baffle resistance,
And roll down bleared roads to each distance
Of past desolation and years ;
Till they cover the place of each sorrow,
And leave you no Past and no Morrow :
For what man is able to master
And stem the great Fountain of Tears ?

But the floods of the tears meet and gather;
The sound of them all grows like thunder:
—O into what bosom, I wonder,
Is poured the whole sorrow of years?
For Eternity only seems keeping
Account of the great human weeping:
May God then, the Maker and Father—
May he find a place for the tears!

After Death.

Shall mine eyes behold thy glory, O my country? Shall
mine eyes behold thy glory?
Or shall the darkness close around them, ere the sun-blaze
break at last upon thy story?

When the nations ope for thee their queenly circle, as a
sweet new sister hail thee,
Shall these lips be sealed in callous death and silence,
that have known but to bewail thee?

Shall the ear be deaf that only loved thy praises, when
all men their tribute bring thee?
Shall the mouth be clay that sang thee in thy squalor,
when all poets' mouths shall sing thee?

Ah! the harpings and the salvos and the shouting of thy
exiled sons returning!
I should hear, tho' dead and mouldered, and the grave-
damps should not chill my bosom's burning.

Ah! the tramp of feet victorious! I should hear them
'mid the shamrocks and the mosses,
And my heart should toss within the shroud and quiver
as a captive dreamer tosses.

I should turn and rend the cere-clothes round me, giant
sinews I should borrow—
Crying, "O my brothers, I have also loved her in her
loneliness and sorrow.

"Let me join with you the jubilant procession: let me
chant with you her story;
Then contented I shall go back to the shamrocks, now
mine eyes have seen her glory!"

The Dead at Clonmacnois.

(From the Irish of Enoch o' Gillan.)

In a quiet watered land, a land of roses,
   Stands Saint Kieran's City fair ;
And the warriors of Erin in their famous generations
   Slumber there.

There beneath the dewy hillside sleep the noblest of the
   Clan of Conn,
Each below his stone with name in branching Ogham
   And the sacred knot thereon.

There they laid to rest the seven Kings of Tara,
   There the sons of Cairbrè sleep—
Battle banners of the Gael, that in Kieran's plain of
   crosses
   Now their final posting keep.

And in Clonmacnois they laid the men of Teffia,
   And right many a lord of Breagh ;
Deep the sod above Clan Creidè and Clan Conaill,
   Kind in hall and fierce in fray.

Many and many a son of Conn the Hundred-Fighter
   In the red earth lies at rest ;
Many a blue eye of Clan Colman the turf covers,
   Many a swan-white breast.

Unknown Ideal.

Whose is the voice that will not let me rest?
I hear it speak.   `
Where is the shore will gratify my quest,
Show what I seek?
Not yours, weak Muse, to mimic that far voice,
With halting tongue;
No peace, sweet land, to bid my heart rejoice
Your groves among.

Whose is the loveliness I know is by,
Yet cannot place?
Is it perfection of the sea or sky,
Or human face?
Not yours, my pencil, to delineate
The splendid smile!
Blind in the sun, we struggle on with Fate
That glows the while.

Whose are the feet that pass me, echoing
On unknown ways?
Whose are the lips that only part to sing
Through all my days?
Not yours, fond youth, to fill mine eager eyes
That still adore
Beauty that tarries not, nor satisfies
For evermore.

Mo Cáilin Donn.

The blush is on the flower, and the bloom is on the
tree,
And the bonnie, bonnie sweet birds are carolling their
glee;
And the dews upon the grass are made diamonds by the
sun,
All to deck a path of glory for my own Cáilin
Donn!*

O, fair she is! O, rare she is! O, dearer still to me!
More welcome than the green leaf to winter-stricken
tree,
More welcome than the blossom to the weary, dusty
bee,
Is the coming of my true love—my own Cáilin Donn!

O Sycamore! O Sycamore! wave, wave your banners
green—
Let all your pennons flutter, O Beech! before my queen!
Ye fleet and honied breezes, to kiss her hand ye run;
But my heart has passed before ye to my own Cáilin
Donn!

O, fair she is! O, rare she is! O, dearer still to me!

Ring out, ring out, O Linden! your merry leafy bells!
Unveil your brilliant torches, O Chestnut! to the dells;
Strew, strew the glade with splendour, for morn it
cometh on!
Oh, the morn of all delight to me—my own Cáilin
Donn!

O, fair she is! O, rare she is! O, dearer still to me!

---

* Pron. Colleen Dhun—a "brown (haired) girl."

She is coming, where we parted, where she wanders
  every day ;
There's a gay surprise before her who thinks me far
  away ;
O, like hearing bugles triumph when the fight of Free-
  dom's won,
Is the joy around your footsteps, my own Cáilin
  Donn !

O, fair she is ! O, rare she is ! O, dearer still to me !
More welcome than the green leaf to winter-stricken
  tree,
More welcome than the blossom to the weary, dusty
  bee,
Is your coming, O my true love—my own Cáilin
  Donn !

An Irish Love Song.

O, you plant the pain in my heart with your wistful
    eyes,
    Girl of my choice, Maureen!
Will you drive me mad for the kisses your shy sweet
    mouth denies,
    Maureen!

Like a walking ghost I am, and no words to woo,
    White rose of the West, Maureen;
For it's pale you are, and the fear that's on you is over
    me too,
    Maureen!

Sure it's our complaint that's on us, asthore, this day,
    Bride of my dreams, Maureen;
The smart of the bee that stung us, his honey must cure,
    they say,
    Maureen!

I'll coax the light to your eyes, and the rose to your
    face,
    Mavourneen, my own Maureen,
When I feel the warmth of your breast, and your nest
    is my arms' embrace,
    Maureen!

O where was the King o' the World that day—only me,
    My one true love, Maureen,
And you the Queen with me there, and your throne in
    my heart, machree,
    Maureen!

The Sunburst.

Through the midnight of despair, I heard one making
  moan
For her dead, her victors fall'n to gain all battles but
  her own ;
I heard the voice of Ireland, wailing for her dead
  With wailing unavailing, and sobbing as she said :
" In vain in many a battle have my heroes fought and
  bled,
Like water, in vain slaughter, my sons' best blood been
  shed,
For my house is desolate, discrowned my head !

" In vain my daughters bear their babes—babes with
  the mournful eyes
Of children without father that hear strange lullabies,
Rocked in their lonely cradles by mothers crooning low,
And weeping o'er their sleeping, sad songs of long ago ;
Whose eyes, as they remember, while the wailing night-
  winds blow,
Their nation's desolation, in their singing overflow
With the overflowing of an ancient woe !"

O Mother, mournful Mother, turn from wailing for thy
  dead,
Grey Sibyl, still unvanquished, lift up thy dauntless
  head,
O thou Swan among the nations, enchanted long, so
  long
That the story of thy glory is a half-forgotten song,
Lift thy voice and bless the living, thy sons who round
  thee throng !
In the hour of their power they shall right thine ancient
  wrong ;
In thyself is thy salvation, let thy heart be strong !

The Leaf of many Sorrows, wet with thy tears for dew,
Emblem of thy long patience ; that hearts, as brave and
　true
As those united hearts of green, through infamy and
　scorn,
Through the nation's tribulations, like Saints the cross,
　have worn,
We'll blazon with the Sunburst, star of thy destined
　morn,
Set in hope's hue, our ancient blue on royal banners
　borne ;
And green the Shamrock long shall shine, no more for-
　lorn !

Song.

Bring from the craggy haunts of birch and pine,
    Thou wild wind, bring
Keen forest odours from that realm of thine,
    Upon thy wing!

O wind, O mighty, melancholy wind,
    Blow through me, blow!
Thou blowest forgotten things into my mind,
    From long ago.

Winter Sunset.

Roses in the sky,
  Roses in the sea ;
Bowers of scarlet sky-roses ;
  Take my heart and me.

God was good to make,
  This December weather,
All this sky a rose-garden,
  Rose and fire together.

To the East are burning
  Roses in a garden,
Roses in a rosy field,
  Hesper for their warden.

Yonder to the West
  Roses all afire,
Mirror now some rare splendid
  Rose of their desire.

Pulsing deeper, deeper,
  Waves of fire throb on,
Never were such red roses
  At sunset or dawn.

Roses on the hills,
  Roses in the hollow,
Roses on the wet hedges,
  In the shining fallow.

West wind, blow and blow !
  That has blown ajar
Gates of God's great rose-garden,
  Where His Angels are,

Gathering up the rose-leaves
  For a shower of roses
On the night the Lord Babe
  His sweet eye uncloses.

All the sky is scarlet
  Flaming on the azure.
O, there's fire in Heaven !
  My heart aches with pleasure.

Leagues of rose and scarlet,
  Roses red as blood :
All the world's a rose-garden.
  God is good, is good.

Shamrock Song.

O, the red rose may be fair,
And the lily statelier;
But my shamrock, one in three,
Takes the very heart of me!

Many a lover hath the rose
When June's musk-wind breathes and blows:
And in many a bower is heard
Her sweet praise from bee and bird.

Through the gold hours dreameth she,
In her warm heart passionately,
Her fair face hung languid-wise:
O, her breath of honey and spice!

Like a fair saint virginal
Stands your lily, silver and tall;
Over all the flowers that be
Is my shamrock dear to me.

Shines the lily like the sun,
Crystal-pure, a cold, sweet nun;
With her austere lip she sings
To her heart of heavenly things.

Gazeth through a night of June
To her sister-saint, the moon;
With the stars communeth long
Of the angels and their song.

But when summer died last year
Rose and lily died with her;
Shamrock stayeth every day,
Be the winds or gold or grey.

Irish hills, as grey as the dove,
Know the little plant I love;
Warm and fair .it mantles them
Stretching down from throat to hem.

And it laughs o'er many a vale,
Sheltered safe from storm and gale ;
Sky and sun and stars thereof
Love the gentle plant I love.

Soft it clothes the ruined floor
Of many an abbey, grey and hoar,
And the still home of the dead
With its green is carpeted.

Roses for an hour of love,
With the joy and pain thereof :
Stand my lilies white to see
All for prayer and purity.

These are white as the harvest moon,
Roses flush like the heart of June ;
But my shamrock, brave and gay,
Glads the tired eyes every day.

O, the red rose shineth rare,
And the lily saintly fair ;
But my shamrock, one in three,
Takes the inmost heart of me !

M

Wild Geese.

(A Lament for the Irish Jacobites.)

I have heard the curlew crying
  On a lonely moor and mere;
And the sea-gull's shriek in the gloaming
  Is a lonely sound in the ear:
And I've heard the brown thrush mourning
  For her children stolen away;—
But it's O for the homeless Wild Geese
  That sailed ere the dawn of day!

For the curlew out on the moorland
  Hath five fine eggs in the nest;
And the thrush will get her a new love
  And sing her song with the best.
As the swallow flies to the Summer
  Will the gull return to the sea:
But never the wings of the Wild Geese
  Will flash over seas to me.

And 'tis ill to be roaming, roaming
  With homesick heart in the breast!
And how long I've looked for your coming,
  And my heart is the empty nest!
O sore in the land of the stranger
  They'll pine for the land far away!
But day of Aughrim, my sorrow,
  It was you was the bitter day!

Dreams.

I troubled in my dream. I knew
  The silent gates and walls.
Around me out of shadow grew
  The steady waterfalls.
Afar the raven spot-like flew
  Where nothing wakes or calls.

I fell on deeper trance. I was
  Where all the dead are hid.
They dreamed. They did not sleep, because
  They saw with lifted lid.
They worked with neither word nor pause :
  I knew not what they did.

I stood there with the dead in hell
  Dreaming, and heard no moan.
The light died, and the darkness fell
  About me like a stone.
I woke upon the midnight bell
  In God's dream here alone.

Poppies.

The sudden night is here at once:
  The lost lamb cries and runs and stands,
  For all the poppy cups are hands
To seize and take him when he runs.

The dusky cups are blood colour;
  And like a cup of blood this one
  To drink, and be with Babylon,
And love and kiss the lips of her.—

Thy sins as snow!—just then it burned
  The dark—a flaming face and bust;
  And just beneath here in the dust
The Scarlet Woman laughed and turned.

They went forth to the Battle, but they always fell.

Rose of all Roses, Rose of all the World,
The tall thought-woven sails that flap unfurled
Above the tide of hours, rise on the air,
And God's bell buoyed to be the waters' care,
And pressing on, or lingering slow with fear,
The throngs with blown wet hair are gathering near.
" Turn if ye may," I call out to each one,
" From the grey ships and battles never won.
Danger no refuge holds, and war no peace,
For him who hears Love sing and never cease
Beside her clean swept hearth, her quiet shade ;
But gather all for whom no Love hath made
A woven silence, or but came to cast
A song into the air, and singing past
To smile upon her stars ; and gather you,
Who have sought more than is in rain or dew,
Or in the sun and moon, or on the earth,
Or sighs amid the wandering, starry mirth,
Or comes in laughter from the sea's sad lips,
And wage God's battles in the long grey ships.
The sad, the lonely, the insatiable,
To these Old Night shall all her mystery tell,
God's bell has claimed them by the little cry
Of their sad hearts that may not live nor die."

Rose of all Roses, Rose of all the World,
You, too, have come where the dim tides are hurled
Upon the wharves of sorrow, and heard ring
The bell that calls us on—the sweet far thing.
Beauty grown sad with its eternity,
Made you of us and of the dim grey sea.
Our long ships loose thought-woven sails and wait,
For God has bid them share an equal fate ;

And when at last defeated in His wars,
They have gone down under the same white stars,
We shall no longer hear the little cry
Of our sad hearts that may not live nor die.

The White Birds.

I would that we were, my beloved, white birds on the
    foam of the sea,
We tire of the flame of the meteor, before it can pass
    by and flee ;
And the flame of the blue star of twilight, hung low on
    the rim of the sky,
Has awaked in our hearts, my beloved, a sadness that
    never may die.

A weariness comes from those dreamers, dew dabbled,
    the lily and rose,
Ah, dream not of them, my beloved, the flame of the
    meteor that goes,
Or the flame of the blue star that lingers hung low in
    the fall of the dew :
For I would we were changed to white birds on the
    wandering foam—I and you.

I am haunted by numberless islands, and many a Danaan
    shore,
Where Time would surely forget us, and Sorrow come
    near us no more,
Soon far from the rose and the lily, and the fret of the
    flames would we be,
Were we only white birds, my beloved, buoyed out on
    the foam of the sea.

The Lake of Innisfree.

I will arise and go now, and go to Innisfree,
  And a small cabin build there, of clay and wattles
    made ;
Nine bean rows will I have there, a hive for the honey
  bee,
  And live alone in the bee-loud glade.

And I shall have some peace there, for peace comes
  dropping slow,
  Dropping from the veils of the morning to where the
    cricket sings ;
There midnight 's all a glimmer, and noon a purple glow,
  And evening full of the linnet's wings.

I will arise and go now, for always night and day
  I hear lake water lapping with low sounds by the
    shore ;
While I stand on the roadway or on the pavements
  gray,
  I hear it in the deep heart's core.

II

SCOTO-CELTIC
(Middle Period)

From the "Sean Dana."

Prologue to Gaul.

How mournful is the silence of Night
When she pours her dark clouds over the valleys!
Sleep has overcome the youth of the chase:
He slumbers on the heath, and his dog at his knee.
The children of the mountain he pursues
In his dream, while sleep forsakes him.

Slumber, ye children of fatigue;
Star after star is now ascending the height.
Slumber! thou swift dog and nimble,—
Ossian will arouse thee not from thy repose.
Lonely I keep watch,—
And dear to me is the gloom of night
When I travel from glen to glen,
With no hope to behold a morning or brightness.

Spare thy light, O Sun!
Waste not thy lamps so fast.
Generous is thy soul, as the King of Morven's:
But thy renown shall yet fade;—
Spare thy lamps of a thousand flames
In thy blue hall, when thou retirest
Under thy dark-blue gates to sleep,
Beneath the dark embraces of the storm.
Spare them, ere thou art forsaken for ever,
As I am, without one whom I may love!
Spare them,—for there is not a hero now
To behold the blue flame of the beautiful lamps!

Ah, Cona of the precious lights,
Thy lamps burn dimly now:
Thou art like a blasted oak:
Thy dwellings and thy people are gone
East or west, on the face of thy mountain,
There shall no more be found of them but the trace!

In Selma, Tara, or Temora
There is not a song, a shell, or a harp;
They have all become green mounds;
Their stones have fallen into their own meadows;
The stranger from the deep or the desert
Will never behold them rise above the clouds.

And, O Selma! home of my delight,
Is this heap my ruin,
Where grows the thistle, the heather, and the wild
   grass?

In Hebrid Seas.

We turned her prow into the sea,
  Her stern into the shore,
And first we raised the tall tough masts,
  And then the canvas hoar;

Fast filled our towering cloud-like sails,
  For the wind came from the land,
And such a wind as we might choose
  Were the winds at our command:

A breeze that rushing down the hill
  Would strip the blooming heather,
Or, rustling through the green-clad grove,
  Would whirl its leaves together.

But when it seized the aged saugh,
  With the light locks of grey,
It tore away its ancient root,
  And there the old trunk lay!

It raised the thatch too from the roof,
  And scattered it along;
Then tossed and whirled it through the air,
  Singing a pleasant song.

It heaped the ruins on the land:
  Though sire and son stood by
They could no help afford, but gaze
  With wan and troubled eye!

A flap, a flash, the green roll dashed,
  And laughed against the red;
Upon our boards, now here, now there,
  It knocked its foamy head.

The dun bowed whelk in the abyss,
  As on the galley bore,
Gave a tap upon her gunwale
  And a slap upon her floor.

She could have split a slender straw—
So clean and well she went—
As still obedient to the helm
  Her stately course she bent.

We watched the big beast eat the small—
The small beast nimbly fly,
And listened to the plunging eels—
  The sea-gull's clang on high.

We had no other music
  To cheer us on our way :
Till round those sheltering hills we passed
And anchored in this bay.

Cumha Ghriogair Mhic Griogair.

(The Lament of Gregor MacGregor.)

Early on a Lammas morning,
  With my husband was I gay;
But my heart got sorely wounded
  Ere the middle of the day.

> Ochan, ochan, ochan uiri
>   Though I cry, my child, with thee—
> Ochan, ochan, ochan uiri,
>   Now he hears not thee nor me!

Malison on judge and kindred,
  They have wrought me mickle woe;
With deceit they came about us,—
  Through deceit they laid him low.

> Ochan, ochan, ochan uiri, etc.

Had they met but twelve MacGregors,
  With my Gregor at their head;
Now my child had not been orphaned,
  Nor these bitter tears been shed.

> Ochan, ochan, ochan uiri, etc.

On an oaken block they laid him,
  And they spilt his blood around;
I'd have drunk it in a goblet
  Largely, ere it reached the ground.

> Ochan, ochan, ochan uiri, etc.

Would my father then had sickened—
  Colin, with the plague been ill;
Though Rory's daughter, in her anguish,
  Smote her palms, and cried her fill.

> Ochan, ochan, ochan uiri, etc.

I could Colin shut in prison,
    And black Duncan put in ward,—
Every Campbell now in Bealach,
    Bind with handcuffs, close and hard.

        Ochan, ochan, ochan uiri, etc.

When I reached the plain of Bealach,
    I got there no rest, nor calm ;
But my hair I tore in pieces,—
    Wore the skin from off each palm !

        Ochan, ochan, ochan uiri, etc.

Oh ! could I fly up with the skylark—
    Had I Gregor's strength in hand ;
The highest stone that's in yon castle
    Should lie lowest on the land.

        Ochan, ochan, ochan uiri, etc.

Would I saw Finlarig blazing,
    And the smoke of Bealach smelled,
So that fair, soft-handed Gregor
    In these arms once more I held.

        Ochan, ochan, ochan uiri, etc.

While the rest have all got lovers
    Now a lover have I none ;
My fair blossom, fresh and fragrant,
    Withers on the ground alone.

        Ochan, ochan, ochan uiri, etc.

While all other wives the night-time
    Pass in slumber's balmy bands,
I upon my bedside weary,
    Never cease to wring my hands.

        Ochan, ochan, ochan uiri, etc.

For, far better be with Gregor
Where the heather's in its prime,
Than with mean and Lowland barons
In a house of stone and lime.

   Ochan, ochan, ochan uiri, etc.

Greatly better be with Gregor
In a mantle rude and torn,
Than with little Lowland barons
Where fine silk and lace are worn.

   Ochan, ochan, ochan uiri, etc.

Though it rained and roared together,
All throughout the stormy day,
Gregor, in a crag, could find me
A kind shelter where to stay.

   Ochan, ochan, ochan uiri, etc.

Bahu, bahu, little nursling—
Oh! so tender now and weak ;
I fear the day will never brighten
When revenge for him you'll seek.

   Ochan, ochan, ochan uiri,
    Though I cry, my child, with thee—
   Ochan, ochan, ochan uiri,
    Yet he hears not thee nor me!

Drowned.

No wonder my heart it is sore,
  No wonder the tears that I weep;
My true love I'll see him no more,
  He lies fathoms down in the deep.

He lies fathoms down in the deep,
  Where the cold clammy seaweeds abound.
How cruel thy wild waves to me,
  O sea that my true love hast drowned!

O sea that my true love hast drowned,
  Thou hast reft me of joy evermore;
Thy waves make me shudder with fear
  As I listen and hear their wild roar.

My true love and I, hand in hand,
  Often wandered the uplands among,
Where the wild flowers are freshest to see,
  And the wild birds are freest of song;

But alas for the days that are gone,
  Alas for my sorrow and me!
Alas that my true love is drowned
  Fathoms down in the depths of the sea!

The Manning of the Birlinn.

The Sailing. .

The sun had opened golden yellow,
From his case,
Though still the sky wore dark and drumly
A scarr'd and frowning face :
Then troubled, tawny, dense, dun-bellied,
Scowling and sea-blue,
Every dye that's in the tartan
O'er it grew.
Far away to the wild westward
Grim it lowered,
Where rain-charged clouds on thick squalls wandering
Loomed and towered.
Up they raised the speckled sails through
Cloud-like light,
And stretched them on the mighty halyards,
Tense and tight.
High on the mast so tall and stately—
Dark-red in hue—
They set them firmly, set them surely,
Set them true.
Round the iron pegs the ropes ran,
Each its right ring through ;
Thus having ranged the tackle rarely,
Well and carefully,
Every man sat waiting bravely,
Where he ought to be.
For now the airy windows opened,
And from spots of bluish grey
Let loose the keen and crabbed wild winds—
A fierce band were they—
'Twas then his dark cloak the ocean
Round him drew.
Dusky, livid, ruffling, whirling,
Round at first it flew,

Till up he swell'd to mountains, or to glens,
    Dishevelled, rough, sank down—
While the kicking, tossing waters
    All in hills had grown.
Its blue depth opened in huge maws,
    Wild and devouring,
Down which, clasped in deadly struggles,
    Fierce strong waves were pouring.
It took a man to look the storm-winds
    Right in the face—
As they lit up the sparkling spray on every surge-hill,
    In their fiery race.
The waves before us, shrilly yelling,
    Raised their high heads hoar,
While those behind, with moaning trumpets,
    Gave a bellowing roar.
When we rose up aloft, majestic,
    On the heaving swell,
Need was to pull in our canvas
    Smart and well :
When she sank down with one huge swallow
    In the hollow glen,
Every sail she bore aloft
    Was given to her then.
The drizzling surges high and roaring
    Rush'd on us louting,
Long ere they were near us come,
    We heard their shouting :—
They roll'd sweeping up the little waves
    Scourging them bare,
Till all became one threatening swell,
    Our steersman's care.
When down we fell from off the billows'
    Towering shaggy edge,
Our keel was well-nigh hurled against
    The shells and sedge ;

The whole sea was lashing, dashing,
    All through other :
It kept the seals and mightiest monsters
    In a pother !
The fury and the surging of the water,
    And our good ship's swift way
Spatter'd their white brains on each billow,
    Livid and grey.
With piteous wailing and complaining
    All the storm-tossed horde,
Shouted out "We're now your subjects ;
    Drag us on board."
And the small fish of the ocean
    Turn'd over their white breast—
Dead, innumerable, with the raging
    Of the furious sea's unrest.
The stones and shells of the deep channel
    Were in motion ;
Swept from out their lowly bed
    By the tumult of the ocean ;
Till the sea, like a great mess of pottage,
    Troubled, muddy grew
With the blood of many mangled creatures,
    Dirty red in hue—
When the horn'd and clawy wild beasts,
    Short-footed, splay,
With great wailing gumless mouths
    Huge and wide open lay.
But the whole deep was full of spectres,
    Loose and sprawling
With the claws and with the tails of monsters,
    Pawing, squalling.
It was frightful even to hear them
    Screech so loudly ;
The sound might move full fifty heroes
    Stepping proudly.

Our whole crew grew dull of hearing
  In the tempest's scowl,
So sharp the quavering cries of demons
  And the wild beasts' howl.
With the oaken planks the weltering waves were wrestling
  In their noisy splashing;
While the sharp beak of our swift ship
  On the sea-pigs came dashing.
The wind kept still renewing all its wildness
  In the far West,
Till with every kind of strain and trouble
  We were sore distress'd.
We were blinded with the water
  Showering o'er us ever;
And the awful night like thunder,
  And the lightning ceasing never.
The bright fireballs in our tackling
  Flamed and smoked;
With the smell of burning brimstone
  We were well-nigh choked.
All the elements above, below,
  Against us wrought;
Earth and wind and fire and water,
  With us fought.
But when the evil one defied the sea
  To make us yield,
At last, with one bright smile of pity,
  Peace with us she seal'd:
Yet not before our yards were injured,
  And our sails were rent,
Our poops were strained, our oars were weaken'd,
  All our masts were bent.
Not a stay but we had started,
  Our tackling all was wet and splashy,
Nails and couplings, twisted, broken.
  Feeshie, fashie,

All the thwarts and all the gunwale
    Everywhere confess'd,
And all above and all below,
    How sore they had been press'd.
Not a bracket, not a rib,
    But the storm had loosed ;
Fore and aft from stem to stern,
    All had got confused.
Not a tiller but was split,
    And the helm was wounded ;
Every board its own complaint
    Sadly sounded.
Every trennel, every fastening
    Had been giving way ;
Not a board remain'd as firm
    As at the break of day.
Not a bolt in her but started,
    Not a rope the wind that bore,
Not a part of the whole vessel
    But was weaker than before.
The sea spoke to us its peace prattle
    At the cross of Islay's Kyle,
And the rough wind, bitter boaster !
    Was restrained for one good while.
The tempest rose from off us into places
    Lofty in the upper air,
And after all its noisy barking
    Ruffled round us fair.
Then we gave thanks to the High King,
    Who rein'd the wind's rude breath,
And saved our good Clan Ranald
    From a bad and brutal death.
Then we furl'd up the fine and speckled sails
    Of linen wide,
And we took down the smooth red dainty masts,
    And laid them by the side—

On our long and slender polish'd oars
   Together leaning—
They were all made of the fir cut by Mac Barais
   In Eilean Fionain—
We went with our smooth, dashing rowing,
   And steady shock,
Till we reach'd the good port round the point
   Of Fergus' Rock.
There casting anchor peacefully
   We calmly rode;
We got meat and drink in plenty,
   And there we abode.

The Lament of the Deer.

(Cumha nam Fiadh.)

O for my strength! once more to see the hills!
The wilds of Strath-Farar of stags,
The blue streams, and winding vales,
Where the flowering tree sends forth its sweet perfume.

My thoughts are sad and dark!—
I lament the forest where I loved to roam,
The secret corries, the haunt of hinds,
Where often I watched them on the hill!

Corrie-Garave! O that I was within thy bosom
Scuir-na-Làpaich of steeps, with thy shelter,
Where feed the herds which never seek for stalls,
But whose skin gleams red in the sunshine of the hills.

Great was my love in youth, and strong my desire,
Towards the bounding herds;
But now, broken, and weak, and hopeless,
Their remembrance wounds my heart.

To linger in the laich * I mourn,
My thoughts are ever in the hills;
For there my childhood and my youth was nursed—
The moss and the craig in the morning breeze was my
    delight.

Then was I happy in my life,
When the voices of the hill sung sweetly;
More sweet to me, than any string,
It soothed my sorrow or rejoiced my heart.

My thoughts wandered to no other land
Beyond the hill of the forest, the shealings of the deer,
Where the nimble herds ascended the hill,—
As I lay in my plaid on the dewy bed.

---

* Low Country.

The sheltering hollows, where I crept towards the hart,
On the pastures of the glen, or in the forest wilds—
And if once more I may see them as of old,
How will my heart bound to watch again the pass!

Great was my joy to ascend the hills
In the cause of the noble chief,
Mac Shimé of the piercing eye—never to fail at need,
With all his brave Frasers, gathered beneath his banner.

When they told of his approach, with all his ready arms,
My heart bounded for the chase—
On the rugged steep, on the broken hill,
By hollow, and ridge, many were the red stags which
    he laid low.

He is the pride of hunters; my trust was in his gun,
When the sound of its shot rung in my ear,
The grey ball launched in flashing fire,
And the dun stag fell in the rushing speed of his course.

When evening came down on the hill,
The time for return to the star of the glen,
The kindly lodge where the noble gathered,
The sons of the tartan and the plaid,

With joy and triumph they returned
To the dwelling of plenty and repose;
The bright blazing hearth—the circling wine—
The welcome of the noble chief!

Ben Dorain.

The honour o'er each hill
  Hath Ben Dorain;
Scene, to me, the sweetest still
  That day dawns upon:
Its long moor's level way,
  And its nooks whence wild deer stray,
To the lustre on the brae
  Oft I 've lauded them.

Dear to me its dusky boughs,
  In the wood where green grass grows,
And the stately herd repose,
  Or there wander slow;
But the troops with bellies white,
  When the chase comes into sight,
Then I love to watch their flight,
  Going nosily.

The stag is airy, brisk, and light,
  And no pomp has he;
Though his garb 's the fashion quite,
  Never haughty he:
Yet a mantle 's round him spread,
  Not soon threadbare, then shed,
And its hue as wax is red—
  Fairly clothing him.

The delight I felt to rise
  At the morning's call!
And to see the troops I prize
  The hills thronging all:
Ten score with stately tread,
  And with light uplifted head,
Quite unpampered there that fed,
  Fond and fawning all.

Lightsomely there came
From each clean and shapely frame,
Through their murmuring lips, a tame
Chant, with drawling fall.
In the pool one rolled a low—
With the hind one played the beau,
As she trotted to and fro,
Looking saucily.

I would rather have the deer
Gasping moaningly,
Than all Erin's songs to hear
Sung melodiously ;
For above the finest bass
Hath the stag's sweet voice a grace,
As he bellows on the face
Of Ben Dorain.

Loud and long he gives a roar
From his very inmost core,
Which is heard behind, before,
Far and fallingly ;
But the hind of softer notes,
With her calf that near her trots,
Match each other's tuneful throats,
Crying longingly.

Her eye's soft and tender ray
With no flaw in it,
O'er whose lid the brow is gray,
Guides her wandering feet :
Very well she walks, and bold,
Lively o'er the russet wold,
Tripping from her desert hold
Most undauntingly.

Faultless is her pace,
And her leap is full of grace—
Ha! the last when in the race
Never saw I her :

When she takes yon startled stride,
  Nor once turns her head aside,
Aught to match her hasty pride
  Is not known to me.

But now she's on the heath,
  As she ought to be,
Where the tender grass she seeth,
  Growing dawtily;
The dry bent, the moor grass bare,
  With the sappy herbs are there,
That make fat, and full, and fair,
  Her plump quarters all.

And those little wells are nigh,
  Where the water-cresses lie,
Above wine she likes to try
  Their waves' solacing;
Of the rye-grass, twisted rows,
  On the rude hill side it grows,
Than of rarest festal shows,
  Is she fonder far.

The choice increase of the earth
  Forms her joyous treat;
The primrose, St John's wort,
  Tops of gowans sweet,
The new buds of the groves,
  The soft heath o'er which she roves,
Are the tit-bits that she loves,
  With good cause too.

For speckled, spotted, rare,
  Tall, and fine, and fair,
From such food before her there
  She grows sonsily;
And it is still the surest mean
  To cure the weak ones and the lean,
Who for any time have been
  Wasted, wan, and low.

Soon it would clothe their back
  With the garb which most they lack—
That rich fat, which they can pack
  Most commodiously.

She's a flighty young hind
  When leaves ward her,
Nearer her haunts where they bind
  The brae border:
Lightsome and urbane
  Is her gay heart, free of stain,
Tho' rash head and somewhat vain—
  Somewhat thoughtless.

Yet her form, so full of grace,
  She keeps hiding in a place,
Where the green glen shows no trace
  Of a falling off;
But she's so healthy, and so clean—
  So chaste where'er she's seen—
Should you kiss her lips, I ween
  'Twould not cause you shame.

Greatly prized is she, I know,
  By the stag with crested brow,
Whose thundering hoofs around him throw
  Such a saucy sound;
When with him she meets the view
  Red and yellow in her hue,
And of virtues not a few
  That belong to her,
Then too is she free of fear,
  And in speed without a peer,
And the primest ear to hear
  In all Europe's hers.

Oh! how sweetly they embrace,
  Young and fawning,
When they gather to their place
  In the gloaming;

There, till silent night is by,
Never terror comes them nigh,
While beneath the bush they lie—
Their known haunt of old.

Let the wild herd seek their bed,
Let them slumber, free of dread,
Where yon mighty moor is spread,
Broad and brawly ;
Where, with joy, I 've often spied
The sun colour their red hide,
As they wandered in their pride
O'er Ben Dorain.

The Hill-Water.

From the rim it trickles down
Of the mountain's granite crown
    Clear and cool ;
Keen and eager though it go
Through your veins with lively flow,
Yet it knoweth not to reign
In the chambers of the brain
    With misrule ;

Where dark water-cresses grow
You will trace its quiet flow,
With mossy border yellow,
So mild, and soft, and mellow,
    In its pouring.
With no shiny dregs to trouble
The brightness of its bubble
As it threads its silver way
From the granite shoulders grey
    Of Ben Dorain.

Then down the sloping side
It will slip with glassy slide
    Gently welling,
Till it gather strength to leap,
With a light and foamy sweep,
To the corrie broad and deep
    Proudly swelling ;

Then bends amid the boulders,
'Neath the shadow of the shoulders
    Of the Ben,
Through a country rough and shaggy,
So jaggy and so knaggy,

Full of hummocks and of hunches,
Full of stumps and tufts and bunches,
Full of bushes and of rushes,
  In the glen,

Through rich green solitudes,
And wildly hanging woods
With blossom and with bell,
In rich redundant swell,
  And the pride
Of the mountain daisy there,
And the forest everywhere,
With the dress and with the air
  Of a bride.

Song for Macleod of Macleod.

Alone on the hill-top,
  Sadly and silently,
Downward on Islay
  And over the sea—
I look and I wonder
  How time hath deceived me :
A stranger in Muile*
  Who ne'er thought to be.

Ne'er thought it, my island !
  Where rests the deep dark shade
Thy grand mossy mountains
  For ages have made—
God bless thee, and prosper !
  Thy chief of the sharp blade,
All over these islands,
  His fame never fade !

Never fade it, Sir Norman !
  For well 'tis the right
Of thy name to win credit
  In council or fight ;
By wisdom, by shrewdness,
  By spirit, by might,
By manliness, courage,
  By daring, by sleight.

In council or fight, thy kindred
  Know these should be thine—
Branch of Lochlin's wide-ruling
  And king-bearing line !
And in Erin they know it—
  Far over the brine :
No Earl would in Albin
  Thy friendship decline.

---

*   ull.

Yes ! the nobles of Erin
  Thy titles well know,
To the honour and friendship
  Of high and of low.
Born the deed-marks to follow,
  Thy father did show,—
That friend of the noble—
  That manliest foe.

That friend of the noble—
  From him art thou heir
To virtues which Albin
  Was proud to declare :
Crown'd the best of her chieftains
  Long, long may'st thou wear
The blossoms paternal
  His broad branches bare !

O banner'd Clan Ruari !
  Whose loss is my woe,
Of this chief who survives
  May I ne'er hear he 's low ;
But, darling of mortals !
  From him though I go,
Long the shapeliest, comeliest
  Form may he show !

The shapeliest, comeliest,
  Faultless in bearing—
Cheerful, cordial, and kind,
  The red and white wearing,
Well looks the blue-eyed chief ;
  Blue, bright, and daring,
His eye o'er his red cheek shines,
  Blue, bright, calmly daring.

His red cheek shines,
  Like hip on the brier-tree,
'Neath the choicest of curly hair
  Waving and free.

A warm hearth, a drinking cup,
    Meet shall he see,
And a choice of good armour
    Whoe'er visits thee.

Drinking-horns, trenchers bright,
    And arms old and new ;
Long, narrow-bladed swords,
    Cold, clear, and blue—
These are seen in thy mansion,
    With rifles and carbines, too ;
And hempen-strung long-bows,
    Of hard, healthy yew.

Long-bows and cross-bows,
    With strings that well wear ;
Arrows, with polish'd heads,
    In quivers full and fair,
From the eagle's wing feather'd,
    With silk fine and rare ;
And guns dear to purchase—
    Long slender—are there.

My heart 's with thee, hero !
    May Mary's son keep
My stripling who loves
    The lone forest to sweep ;
Rejoicing to feel there
    The solitude deep
Of the long moor and valley,
    And rough mountain steep.

The mountain steep searching
    And rough rocky chains ;
The old dogs he caresses,
    The young dogs he restrains :
Then, soon from my chieftain's spear
    The life-blood rains
Of the red-hided deer or doe
    And the green heather stains.

Fall the red stag, the white-bellied doe ;
  Then stand on the heather,
Thy gentle companions,
  Well arm'd altogether,
Well taught on the hunter's craft,
  Well skill'd in the weather ;
They know the rough sea as well
  As the green heather !

III

MODERN AND
CONTEMPORARY
SCOTO-CELTIC

Monaltri.

There 's a sound on the hill,
  Not of joy but of ailing ;
Dark-hair'd women mourn—
  Beat their hands, with loud wailing.

They cry out, Ochon !
  For the young Monaltri,
Who went to the hill ;
  But home came not he.

Without snood, without plaid
  Katrina 's gone roaming.
O Katrina, my dear !
  Homeward be coming.

Och ! hear, on the castle
  Yon pretty bird singing,
"Snoodless and plaidless,
  Her hands she is ringing."

An Coineachan—A Highland Lullaby.

Hó-bhan, hó-bhan, Goiridh òg O,
Goiridh òg O, Goiridh òg O ;
Hó-bhan, hó-bhan, Goiridh òg O,
I 've lost my darling baby O !

I left my darling lying here,
A-lying here, a-lying here ;
I left my darling lying here,
    To go and gather blaeberries.

I 've found the wee brown otter's track,
The otter's track, the otter's track ;
I 've found the wee brown otter's track,
    But ne'er a trace of baby O !

I found the track of the swan on the lake,
The swan on the lake, the swan on the lake ;
I found the track of the swan on the lake,
    But not the track of baby O !

I found the track of the yellow fawn,
The yellow fawn, the yellow fawn ;
I found the track of the yellow fawn,
    But could not trace my baby O !

I 've found the trail of the mountain mist,
The mountain mist, the mountain mist ;
I 've found the trail of the mountain mist,
    But ne'er a trace of baby O !

A Boat Song.

Ho, my bonnie boatie,
Thou bonnie boatie mine !
So trim and tight a boatie
Was never launched on brine.
Ho, my bonnie boatie,
My praise is justly thine
Above all bonnie boaties
Were builded on Loch Fyne !

> *Hò mo bhàta laghach,*
> *'S tu mo bhàta grinn ;*
> *Hò mo bhàta laghach,*
> *'S tu mo bhàta grinn.*
> *Hò mo bhàta laghach,*
> *'S tu mo bhàta grinn :*
> *Mo bhàta boidheach laghach,*
> *Thogadh taobh Loch Fin.*

To build thee up so firmly,
I knew the stuff was good ;
Thy keel of stoutest elm-tree,
Well fixed in oaken wood ;
Thy timbers ripely seasoned
Of cleanest Norway pine
Well cased in ruddy copper,
To plough the deep were thine !

> *Hò mo bhàta, etc.*

How lovely was my boatie
At rest upon the shore,
Before my bonnie boatie
Had known wild ocean's roar.
Thy deck so smooth and stainless,
With such fine bend thy rim,
Thy seams that know no gaping,
Thy masts so tall and trim.

> *Hò mo bhàta, etc.*

And bonnie was my boatie
Afloat upon the bay,
When smooth as mirror round her
The heaving ocean lay;
While round the cradled boatie
Light troops of plumy things
To praise the bonnie boatie
Made music with their wings.
          Hò mo bhàta, etc.

How eager was my boatie
To plough the swelling seas,
When o'er the curling waters
Full sharply blew the breeze!
O, 'twas she that stood to windward,
The first among her peers,
When shrill the blasty music
Came piping round her ears!
          Hò mo bhàta, etc.

And where the sea came surging
In mountains from the west,
And reared the racing billow
Its high and hissing crest;
She turned her head so deftly,
With skill so firmly shown,
The billows they went their way
The boatie went her own.
          Hò mo bhàta, etc.

And when the sudden squall came
Black swooping from the Ben,
And white the foam was spinning
Around thy topmast then,
O never knew my boatie
A thought of ugly dread,
But dashed right through the billow,
With the spray-shower round her head!
          Hò mo bhàta, etc.

Yet wert thou never headstrong
To stand with forward will,
When yielding was thy wisdom
And caution was my skill.
How neatly and how nimbly
Thou turned thee to the wind,
With thy leeside in the water
And a swirling trail behind!

Hò mo bhàta, etc.

What though a lonely dwelling
On barren shore I own,
My kingdom is the blue wave,
My boatie is my throne!
I 'll never want a dainty dish
To breakfast or to dine,
While men may man my boatie
And fish swim in Loch Fyne!

Hò mo bhàta laghach,
'S tu mo bhàta grinn.
Hò mo bhàta laghach,
'S tu mo bhàta grinn.
Hò mo bhàta laghach,
'S tu mo bhàta grinn:
Mo bhàta boidheach laghach,
Thogadh taobh Loch Fin.

The Old Soldier of the Gareloch Head.

I 've wander'd east and west,
  And a soldier I hae been ;
The scars upon my breast
  Tell the wars that I have seen.
But now I 'm old and worn,
  And my locks are thinly spread,
And I 'm come to die in peace,
  By the Gareloch Head.

When I was young and strong,
  Oft a wandering I would go,
By the rough shores of Loch Long,
  Up to lone Glencroe.
But now I 'm fain to rest,
  And my resting-place I 've made,
On the green and gentle bosom
  Of the Gareloch Head.

'Twas here my Jeanie grew,
  Like a lamb amid the flocks,
With her eyes of bonnie blue,
  And her gowden locks.
And here we often met,
  When with lightsome foot we sped,
O'er the green and grassy knolls
  At the Gareloch Head.

'Twas here she pined and died—
  O! the salt tear in my e'e
Forbids my heart to hide
  What Jeanie was to me!
'Twas here my Jeanie died,
  And they scoop'd her lowly bed,
'Neath the green and grassy turf
  At the Gareloch Head.

Like a leaf in leafy June,
    From the leafy forest torn,
She fell, and I 'll fall soon
    Like a sheaf of yellow corn.
For I 'm sere and weary now,
    And I soon shall make my bed
With my Jeanie 'neath the turf
    At the Gareloch Head.

Flower of the World.

Wherever men sinned and wept,
I wandered in my quest;
At last in a Garden of God
I saw the Flower of the World.

This Flower had human eyes,
Its breath was the breath of the mouth;
Sunlight and starlight came,
And the Flower drank bliss from both.

Whatever was base and unclean,
Whatever was sad and strange,
Was piled around its roots;
It drew its strength from the same.

Whatever was formless and base
Pass'd into fineness and form;
Whatever was lifeless and mean
Grew into beautiful bloom.

Then I thought "O Flower of the World,
Miraculous Blossom of things,
Light as a faint wreath of snow
Thou tremblest to fall in the wind:

"O beautiful Flower of the World,
Fall not nor wither away;
He is coming—He cannot be far—
The Lord of the Flow'rs and the Stars."

And I cried, "O Spirit divine!
That walkest the Garden unseen,
Come hither, and bless, ere it dies,
The beautiful Flower of the World."

The Strange Country.

I have come from a mystical Land of Light
  To a Strange Country;
The Land I have left is forgotten quite
  In the Land I see.

The round Earth rolls beneath my feet,
  And the still Stars glow,
The murmuring Waters rise and retreat,
  The Winds come and go.

Sure as a heart-beat all things seem
  In this Strange Country;
So sure, so still, in a dazzle of dream,
  All things flow free.

'Tis life, all life, be it pleasure or pain,
  In the Field and the Flood,
In the beating Heart, in the burning Brain,
  In the Flesh and the Blood.

Deep as Death is the daily strife
  Of this Strange Country:
All things thrill up till they blossom in Life,
  And flutter and flee.

Nothing is stranger than the rest,
  From the pole to the pole,
The weed by the way, the eggs in the nest,
  The Flesh and the Soul.

Look in mine eyes, O Man I meet
  In this Strange Country!
Lie in my arms, O Maiden sweet,
  With thy mouth kiss me!

P

Go by, O King, with thy crownèd brow
And thy sceptred hand—
Thou art a straggler too, I vow,
From the same strange Land.

O wondrous Faces that upstart
In this Strange Country!
O Souls, O Shades, that become a part
Of my Soul and me!

What are ye working so fast and fleet,
O Humankind?
"We are building Cities for those whose feet
Are coming behind;

"Our stay is short, we must fly again
From this Strange Country;
But others are growing, women and men,
Eternally!"

Child, what art thou? and what am *I*?
But a breaking wave!
Rising and rolling on, we hie
To the shore of the grave.

I have come from a mystical Land of Light
To this Strange Country;
This dawn I came, I shall go to-night,
Ay me! ay me!

I hold my hand to my head and stand
'Neath the air's blue arc,
I try to remember the mystical Land,
But all is dark.

And all around me swim Shapes like mine
In this Strange Country;—
They break in the glamour of gleams divine,
And they moan "Ay me!"

Like waves in the cold Moon's silvern breath
  They gather and roll,
Each crest of white is a birth or a death,
  Each sound is a Soul.

Oh, whose is the Eye that gleams so bright
  O'er this Strange Country?
It draws us along with a chain of light,
  As the Moon the Sea!

The Dream of the World without Death.

Now, sitting by her side, worn out with weeping,
Behold, I fell to sleep, and had a vision,
Wherein I heard a wondrous Voice intoning :

Crying aloud, "The Master on His throne
Openeth now the seventh seal of wonder,
And beckoneth back the angel men name Death.

And at His feet the mighty Angel kneeleth,
Breathing not ; and the Lord doth look upon him,
Saying, 'Thy wanderings on earth are ended.'"

And lo ! the mighty Shadow sitteth idle
Even at the silver gates of heaven,
Drowsily looking in on quiet waters,
And puts his silence among men no longer.

*

The world was very quiet. Men in traffic
Cast looks over their shoulders ; pallid seamen
Shivered to walk upon the decks alone ;

And women barred their doors with bars of iron,
In the silence of the night ; and at the sunrise
Trembled behind the husbandmen afield.

I could not see a kirkyard near or far ;
I thirsted for a green grave, and my vision
Was weary for the white gleam of a tombstone.

But hearkening dumbly, ever and anon
I heard a cry out of a human dwelling,
And felt the cold wind of a lost one's going.

One struck a brother fiercely, and he fell,
And faded in a darkness ; and that other
Tore his hair, and was afraid, and could not perish.

One struck his aged mother on the mouth,
And she vanished with a gray grief from his hearth-
stone.
One melted from her bairn, and on the ground

With sweet unconscious eyes the bairn lay smiling.
And many made a weeping among mountains,
And hid themselves in caverns, and were drunken.

I heard a voice from out the beauteous earth,
Whose side rolled up from winter into summer,
Crying, "I am grievous for my children."

I heard a voice from out the hoary ocean,
Crying, "Burial in the breast of me were better,—
Yea, burial in the salt flags and green crystals."

I heard a voice from out the hollow ether,
Saying, "The thing ye cursed hath been abolished—
Corruption, and decay, and dissolution!"

And the world shrieked, and the summer-time was
bitter,
And men and women feared the air behind them;
And for lack of its green graves the world was hateful.

*

Now at the bottom of a snowy mountain
I came upon a woman thin with sorrow,
Whose voice was like the crying of a sea-gull:

Saying, "O Angel of the Lord, come hither,
And bring me him I seek for on thy bosom,
That I may close his eyelids and embrace him.

"I curse thee that I cannot look upon him!
I curse thee that I know not he is sleeping!
Yet know that he has vanished upon God!

" I laid my little girl upon a wood-bier,
And very sweet she seemed, and near unto me ;
And slipping flowers into her shroud was comfort.

" I put my silver mother in the darkness,
And kissed her, and was solaced by her kisses,
And set a stone, to mark the place, above her.

" And green, green were their quiet sleeping places,
So green that it was pleasant to remember
That I and my tall man would sleep beside them.

" The closing of dead eyelids is not dreadful,
For comfort comes upon us when we close them,
And tears fall, and our sorrow grows familiar ;

" And we can sit above them where they slumber,
And spin a dreamy pain into a sweetness,
And know indeed that we are very near them.

" But to reach out empty arms is surely dreadful,
And to feel the hollow empty world is awful,
And bitter grow the silence and the distance.

" There is no space for grieving or for weeping ;
No touch, no cold, no agony to strive with,
And nothing but a horror and a blankness ! "

*

Now behold I saw a woman in a mud-hut
Raking the white spent embers with her fingers,
And fouling her bright hair with the white ashes.

Her mouth was very bitter with the ashes ;
Her eyes with dust were blinded ; and her sorrow
Sobbed in the throat of her like gurgling water.

And, all around, the voiceless hills were hoary,
But red light scorched their edges ; and above her
There was a soundless trouble of the vapours.

" Whither, and O whither," said the woman,
" O Spirit of the Lord, hast Thou conveyed them,
My little ones, my little son and daughter?

" For, lo ! we wandered forth at early morning,
And winds were blowing round us, and their mouths
Blew rose-buds to the rose-buds, and their eyes

" Looked violets at the violets, and their hair
Made sunshine in the sunshine, and their passing
Left a pleasure in the dewy leaves behind them ;

" And suddenly my little son looked upward,
And his eyes were dried like dew-drops ; and his going
Was like a blow of fire upon my face.

" And my little son was gone. My little daughter
Looked round me for him, clinging to my vesture ;
But the Lord had drawn him from me, and I knew it

" By the sign He gives the stricken, that the lost one
Lingers nowhere on the earth, on hill or valley,
Neither underneath the grasses nor the tree-roots.

" And my shriek was like the splitting of an ice-reef,
And I sank among my hair, and all my palm
Was moist and warm where the little hand had filled it.

" Then I fled and sought him wildly, hither and thither—
Though I knew that he was stricken from me wholly
By the token that the Spirit gives the stricken.

" I sought him in the sunlight and the starlight,
I sought him in great forests, and in waters
Where I saw mine own pale image looking at me.

" And I forgot my little bright-haired daughter,
Though her voice was like a wild-bird's far behind me,
Till the voice ceased, and the universe was silent.

" And stilly, in the starlight, came I backward
  To the forest where I missed him; and no voices
  Brake the stillness as I stooped down in the starlight,

" And saw two little shoes filled up with dew,
  And no mark of little footsteps any farther,
  And knew my little daughter had gone also."

*

But beasts died; yea, the cattle in the yoke,
The milk-cow in the meadow, and the sheep,
And the dog upon the doorstep: and men envied.

And birds died; yea, the eagle at the sun-gate,
The swan upon the waters, and the farm-fowl,
And the swallows on the housetops: and men envied.

And reptiles; yea, the toad upon the roadside,
The slimy, speckled snake among the grass,
The lizard on the ruin: and men envied.

The dog in lonely places cried not over
The body of his master; but it missed him,
And whined into the air, and died, and rotted.

The traveller's horse lay swollen in the pathway,
And the blue fly fed upon it; but no traveller
Was there; nay, not his footprint on the ground.

The cat mewed in the midnight, and the blind
Gave a rustle, and the lamp burned blue and faint,
And the father's bed was empty in the morning.

The mother fell to sleep beside the cradle,
Rocking it, while she slumbered, with her foot,
And wakened,—and the cradle there was empty.

I saw a two-years' child, and he was playing;
And he found a dead white bird upon the doorway,
And laughed, and ran to show it to his mother.

The mother moaned, and clutched him, and was bitter,
And flung the dead white bird across the threshold;
And another white bird flitted round and round it,

And uttered a sharp cry, and twittered and twittered,
And lit beside its dead mate, and grew busy,
Strewing it over with green leaves and yellow.

✻

So far, so far to seek for were the limits
Of affliction; and men's terror grew a homeless
Terror, yea, and a fatal sense of blankness.

There was no little token of distraction,
There was no visible presence of bereavement,
Such as the mourner easeth out his heart on.

There was no comfort in the slow farewell,
Nor gentle shutting of belovèd eyes,
Nor beautiful broodings over sleeping features.

There were no kisses on familiar faces,
No weaving of white grave-clothes, no last pondering
Over the still wax cheeks and folded fingers.

There was no putting tokens under pillows,
There was no dreadful beauty slowly fading,
Fading like moonlight softly into darkness.

There were no churchyard paths to walk on, thinking
How near the well-beloved ones are lying.
There were no sweet green graves to sit and muse on,

Till grief should grow a summer meditation,
The shadow of the passing of an angel,
And sleeping should seem easy, and not cruel.

Nothing but wondrous parting and a blankness.

✻

※

But I woke,
And, lo! the burthen was uplifted,
And I prayed within the chamber where she slumbered,
And my tears flowed fast and free, but were not bitter.

I eased my heart three days by watching near her,
And made her pillow sweet with scent and flowers,
And could bear at last to put her in the darkness.

And I heard the kirk-bells ringing very slowly,
And the priests were in their vestments, and the earth
Dripped awful on the hard wood, yet I bore it.

And I cried, "O unseen Sender of Corruption,
I bless Thee for the wonder of Thy mercy,
Which softeneth the mystery and the parting.

"I bless Thee for the change and for the comfort,
The bloomless face, shut eyes, and waxen fingers,—
For Sleeping, and for Silence, and Corruption."

The Faëry Foster-Mother.

Bright Eyes, Light Eyes! Daughter of a Fay!
I had not been a wedded wife a twelvemonth and a
day,
I had not nurs'd my little one a month upon my knee,
When down among the blue-bell banks rose elfins three
times three,
They gripp'd me by the raven hair, I could not cry for
fear,
They put a hempen rope around my waist and dragg'd
me here,
They made me sit and give thee suck as mortal mothers
can,
Bright Eyes, Light Eyes! strange and weak and wan!

Dim Face, Grim Face! lie ye there so still?
Thy red, red lips are at my breast, and thou may'st
suck thy fill;
But know ye, tho' I hold thee firm, and rock thee to
and fro,
'Tis not to soothe thee into sleep, but just to still my
woe?
And know ye, when I lean so calm against the wall of
stone,
'Tis when I shut my eyes and try to think thou art
mine own?
And know ye, tho' my milk be here, my heart is far
away,
Dim Face, Grim Face! Daughter of a Fay!

Gold Hair, Cold Hair! Daughter to a King!
Wrapp'd in bands of snow-white silk with jewels
glittering,
Tiny slippers of the gold upon thy feet so thin,
Silver cradle velvet-lin'd for thee to slumber in,

Pygmy pages, crimson-hair'd, to serve thee on their
    knees,
To fan thy face with ferns and bring thee honey bags
    of bees,—
I was but a peasant lass, my babe had but the milk,
Gold Hair, Cold Hair! raimented in silk!

Pale Thing, Frail Thing! dumb and weak and thin,
Altho' thou ne'er dost utter sigh thou 'rt shadow'd with
    a sin;
Thy minnie scorns to suckle thee, thy minnie is an elf,
Upon a bed of rose's-leaves she lies and fans herself;
And though my heart is aching so for one afar from
    me,
I often look into thy face and drop a tear for thee,
And I am but a peasant born, a lowly cottar's wife,
Pale Thing, Frail Thing! sucking at my life!

Weak Thing, Meek Thing! take no blame from me,
Altho' my babe may moan for lack of what I give to
    thee;
For though thou art a faëry child, and though thou art
    my woe,
To feel thee sucking at my breast is all the bliss I
    know;
It soothes me, though afar away I hear my daughter
    call,
My heart were broken if I felt no little lips at all!
If I had none to tend at all, to be its nurse and slave,
Weak Thing, Meek Thing! I should shriek and rave!

Bright Eyes, Light Eyes! lying on my knee!
If soon I be not taken back unto mine own countree,
To feel my own babe's little lips, as I am feeling thine,
To smooth the golden threads of hair, to see the blue
    eyes shine,—

I 'll lean my head against the wall and close my weary
  eyes,
And think my own babe draws the milk with balmy
  pants and sighs,
And smile and bless my little one and sweetly pass
  away,
Bright Eyes, Light Eyes! Daughter of a Fay!

When we Two parted.

When we two parted
　In silence and tears,
Half-broken-hearted
　To sever for years,
Pale grew thy cheek and cold,
　Colder thy kiss ;
Truly that hour foretold
　Sorrow to this.

The dew of the morning
　Sank chill on my brow—
It felt like the warning
　Of what I feel now.
Thy vows are all broken,
　And light is thy fame ;
I hear thy name spoken,
　And share in its shame.

They name thee before me,
　A knell to mine ear ;
A shudder comes o'er me—
　Why wert thou so dear?
They know not I knew thee,
　Who knew thee too well :—
Long, long shall I rue thee,
　Too deeply to tell.

In secret we met—
　In silence I grieve,
That thy heart could forget,
　Thy spirit deceive.
If I should meet thee
　After long years,
How shall I greet thee ?—
　With silence and tears.

Stanzas for Music.

There be none of Beauty's daughters
    With a magic like thee ;
And like music on the waters
    Is thy sweet voice to me :
When, as if its sound were causing
The charmed ocean's pausing,
The waves lie still and gleaming,
And the lull'd winds seem dreaming.

And the midnight moon is weaving
    Her bright chain o'er the deep ;
Whose breast is gently heaving,
    As an infant's asleep :
So the spirit bows before thee,
To listen and adore thee ;
With a full but soft emotion,
Like the swell of Summer's ocean.

Colin's Cattle.

(Crodh Chaillean.)

A maiden sang sweetly
As a bird on a tree,
Cro' Chaillean, Cro' Chaillean,
Cro' Chaillean for me !

My own Colin's cattle,
Dappled, dun, brown, and grey,
They return to the milking
At the close of the day.

In the morning they wander
To their pastures afar,
Where the grass grows the greenest
By corrie and scaur.

They wander the uplands
Where the soft breezes blow,
And they drink from the fountain
Where the sweet cresses grow.

But so far as they wander,
Dappled, dun, brown, and grey,
They return to the milking
At the close of the day.

My bed 's in the Shian
On the canach's soft down,
But I 'd sleep best with Colin
In our shieling alone.

Thus a maiden sang sweetly
As a bird on a tree,
Cro' Chaillean, Cro' Chaillean,
Cro' Chaillean for me.

MacCrimmon's Lament.

Round Coolin's peak the mist is sailing,
The banshee croons her note of wailing,
Mild blue eyne with sorrow are streaming
For him that shall never return, MacCrimmon!

The breeze on the brae is mournfully blowing!
The brook in the hollow is plaintively flowing,
The warblers, the soul of the groves, are moaning,
For MacCrimmon that's gone, with no hope of returning!

The tearful clouds the stars are veiling,
The sails are spread, but the boat is not sailing,
The waves of the sea are moaning and mourning
For MacCrimmon that's gone to find no returning!

No more on the hill at the festal meeting
The pipe shall sound with echo repeating,
And lads and lasses change mirth to mourning
For him that is gone to know no returning!

No more, no more, no more for ever,
In war or peace, shall return MacCrimmon;
No more, no more, no more for ever
Shall love or gold bring back MacCrimmon!

Q

242 IAN CAMERON
("Ian Mòr")

Song.

Thy dark eyes to mine, Aithne,
Lamps of desire!
O how my soul leaps
Leaps to their fire!

Sure, now, if I in heaven
Dreaming in bliss,
Heard but the whisper,
But the lost echo even
Of one such kiss—

All of the Soul of me
Would leap afar—
If that called me to thee,
Aye, I would leap afar
A falling star!

A Loafer.

I hang about the streets all day,
　At night I hang about ;
I sleep a little when I may,
　But rise betimes the morning's scout ;
For through the year I always hear
　Afar, aloft, a ghostly shout.

My clothes are worn to threads and loops ;
　My skin shows here and there ;
About my face like seaweed droops
　My tangled beard, my tangled hair ;
From cavernous and shaggy brows
　My stony eyes untroubled stare.

I move from eastern wretchedness
　Through Fleet Street and the Strand ;
And as the pleasant people press
　I touch them softly with my hand,
Perhaps I know that still I go
　Alive about a living land.

For, far in front the clouds are riven ;
　I hear the ghostly cry,
As if a still voice fell from heaven
　To where sea-whelmed the drowned folk lie
In sepulchres no tempest stirs
　And only eyeless things pass by.

In Piccadilly spirits pass :
　Oh, eyes and cheeks that glow !
Oh, strength and comeliness ! Alas,
　The lustrous health is earth I know
From shrinking eyes that recognise
　No brother in my rags and woe.

I know no handicraft, no art,
　But I have conquered fate ;

For I have chosen the better part,
　And neither hope, nor fear, nor hate.
With placid breath on pain and death,
　My certain alms, alone I wait.

And daily, nightly comes the call,
　The pale unechoing note,
The faint "Aha!" sent from the wall
　Of heaven, but from no ruddy throat
Of human breed or seraph's seed,
　A phantom voice that cries by rote.

In Romney Marsh.

As I went down to Dymchurch Wall,
  I heard the South sing o'er the land ;
I saw the yellow sunlight fall
  On knolls where Norman churches stand.

And ringing shrilly, taut and lithe,
  Within the wind a core of sound,
The wire from Romney town to Hythe
  Along its airy journey wound.

A veil of purple vapour flowed
  And trailed its fringe along the Straits ;
The upper air like sapphire glowed :
  And roses filled Heaven's central gates.

Masts in the offing wagged their tops ;
  The swinging waves pealed on the shore ;
The saffron beach, all diamond drops
  And beads of surge, prolonged the roar.

As I came up from Dymchurch Wall,
  I saw above the Downs' low crest
The crimson brands of sunset fall,
  Flicker and fade from out the West.

Night sank : like flakes of silver fire
  The stars in one great shower came down ;
Shrill blew the wind ; and shrill the wire
  Rang out from Hythe to Romney town.

The darkly shining salt sea drops
  Streamed as the waves clashed on the shore ;
The beach, with all its organ stops
  Pealing again, prolonged the roar.

O'er the Muir amang the Heather.

Comin' through the craigs o' Kyle,
  Amang the bonnie bloomin' heather,
There I met a bonnie lassie,
  Keepin' a' her ewes thegither.

> O'er the muir amang the heather,
> O'er the muir amang the heather,
> There I met a bonnie lassie
> Keepin' a' her ewes thegither.

Says I, My dear, where is thy hame?
  In muir or dale, pray tell me whether?
Says she, I tent the fleecy flocks
  That feed amang the bloomin' heather.
    O'er the muir, etc.

We laid us down upon a bank,
  Sae warm and sunnie was the weather;
She left her flocks at large to rove
  Amang the bonnie bloomin' heather.
    O'er the muir, etc.

While thus we lay, she sang a sang,
  Till echo rang a mile and further;
And aye the burden of the sang
  Was, O'er the muir amang the heather.
    O'er the muir, etc.

She charmed my heart, and aye sin syne
  I couldna' think on ony ither;
By sea and sky! she shall be mine,
  The bonnie lass amang the heather.

> O'er the muir amang the heather,
> O'er the muir amang the heather,
> There I met a bonnie lassie
> Keepin' a' her flocks thegither.

Song.

Once I was a child,
    Oimè!
Full of frolic wild;
    Oimè!
All the stars for glancing,
All the earth for dancing;
    Oimè! Oimè!

When I ran about,
    Oimè!
All the flowers came out,
    Oimè!
Here and there like stray things,
Just to be my playthings.
    Oimè! Oimè!

Mother's eyes were deep,
    Oimè!
Never needing sleep.
    Oimè!
Morning—they're above me!
Eventide—they love me!
    Oimè! Oimè!

Father was so tall!
    Oimè!
Stronger he than all!
    Oimè!
On his arm he bore me,
Queen of all before me.
    Oimè! Oimè!

Mother is asleep!
    Oimè!
For her eyes so deep,
    Oimè!

Grew so tired and aching,
They could not keep waking,
        Oimè ! Oimè !

Father though so strong
        Oimè !
Laid him down along—
        Oimè !
By my mother sleeping ;
And they left me weeping,
        Oimè ! Oimè !

Now nor bird, nor bee,
        Oimè !
Ever sings to me !
        Oimè !
Since they left me crying,
All things have been dying.
        Oimè ! Oimè !

Song.

Alas, alas, eheu!
That the sky is only blue,
  To gather from the grass
The rain and dew!

Alas! that eyes are fair:
That tears may gather there
  Mist and the breath of sighs
From the marsh of care!

Alas, alas, eheu!
That we meet but to bid adieu:
  That the sands in Time's ancient glass
Are so swift and few!

Alas, alas, eheu!
That the heart is only true
  To gather, where false feet pass,
The thorn and rue!

A Spring Trouble.

All the meadowlands were gay
Once upon a morn of May ;
All the tree of life was dight
With the blossoms of delight.

And my whole heart was a-tune
With the songs of long ere noon—
Dew-bedecked and fresh and free,
As the unsunned meadows be.

"Lo!" I said unto my spirit,
"Earth and sky thou dost inherit."
Forth I wandered, void of care,
In the largesse of the air.

By there came a damosel,
At a look I loved her well :
But she passed and would not stay—
And all the rest has gone away.

And now no fields are fair to see,
Nor any bud on any tree ;
Nor have I share in earth or sky—
All for a maiden's passing by !

Culloden Moor.

(Seen in Autumn Rain.)

Full of grief, the low winds sweep
O'er the sorrow-haunted ground ;
Dark the woods where night rains weep,
Dark the hills that watch around.

Tell me, can the joy of spring
Ever make this sadness flee,
Make the woods with music ring,
And the streamlet laugh for glee?

When the summer moor is lit
With the pale fire of the broom,
And through green the shadows flit,
Still shall mirth give place to gloom?

Sad shall it be, though sun be shed
Golden bright on field and flood ;
E'en the heather's crimson red
Holds the memory of blood.

Here that broken, weary band
Met the ruthless foe's array,
Where those moss-grown boulders stand,
On that dark and fatal day.

Like a phantom hope had fled,
Love to death was all in vain,
Vain, though heroes' blood was shed,
And though hearts were broke in twain.

Many a voice has cursed the name
Time has into darkness thrust,
Cruelty his only fame
In forgetfulness and dust,

Noble dead that sleep below,
We your valour ne'er forget ;
Soft the heroes' rest who know
Hearts like theirs are beating yet.

The Weaving of the Tartan.

I saw an old Dame weaving,
Weaving, weaving,
I saw an old Dame weaving,
    A web of tartan fine.
"Sing high," she said, "sing low," she said,
"Wild torrent to the sea,
    That saw my exiled bairnies torn,
    In sorrow far frae me.
    And warp well the long threads,
    The bright threads, the strong threads ;
    Woof well the cross threads,
        To make the colours shine."

    She wove in red for every deed,
    Of valour done for Scotia's need :
    She wove in green, the laurel's sheen,
    In memory of her glorious dead.
    She spake of Alma's steep incline,
    The desert march, the "thin red line,"
    Of how it fired the blood and stirred the heart,
    Where'er a bairn of hers took part.
"'Tis for the gallant lads," she said,
"Who wear the kilt and tartan plaid :
    'Tis for the winsome lasses too,
    Just like my dainty bells of blue.
    So weave well the bright threads,
    The red threads, the green threads ;
    Woof well the strong threads
    That bind their hearts to mine."

    I saw an old Dame sighing,
    Sighing, sighing ;
    I saw an old Dame sighing,
        Beside a lonely glen.

"Sing high," she said, "sing low," she said,
"Wild tempests to the sea,
The wailing of the pibroch's note,
That bade farewell to me.
And wae fa' the red deer,
The swift deer, the strong deer,
Wae fa' the cursed deer,
    That take the place o' men."

Where'er a noble deed is wrought,
Where'er the brightest realms of thought,
The artists' skill, the martial thrill,
Be sure to Scotia's land is wed.
She casts the glamour of her name,
O'er Britain's throne and statesman's fame;
From distant lands 'neath foreign names,
Some brilliant son his birthright claims.
For ah!—she has reared them amid tempests,
And cradled them in snow,
To give the Scottish arms their strength,
Their hearts a kindly glow.
So weave well the bright threads,
The red threads, the green threads,
Woof well the strong threads
That bind their hearts to thine.

The Thrush's Song.

(From the Gaelic.)

Dear, dear, dear,
In the rocky glen,
Far away, far away, far away
The haunts of men ;
There shall we dwell in love
With the lark and the dove,
Cuckoo and corn-rail,
Feast on the bearded snail,
Worm and gilded fly,
Drink of the crystal rill
Winding adown the hill
Never to dry.
With glee, with glee, with glee
Cheer up, cheer up, cheer up here ;
Nothing to harm us, then sing merrily,
Sing to the loved one whose nest is near.

Qui, qui, queen, quip ;
Tiurru, tiurru, chipïwi,
Too-tee, too-tee, chin-choo,
Chirri, chirri, chooee
Quin, qui, qui !

The Prayer of Women.

O Spirit, that broods upon the hills
And moves upon the face of the deep,
And is heard in the wind,
Save us from the desire of men's eyes,
And the cruel lust of them,
And the springing of the cruel seed
In that narrow house which is as the grave
For darkness and loneliness . . .
That women carry with them with shame, and weariness,
    and long pain,
Only for the laughter of man's heart,
And the joy that triumphs therein,
And the sport that is in his heart,
Wherewith he mocketh us,
Wherewith he playeth with us,
Wherewith he trampleth upon us . . .
Us, who conceive and bear him;
Us, who bring him forth;
Who feed him in the womb, and at the breast, and at
    the knee:
Whom he calleth mother and wife,
And mother again of his children and his children's
    children.
Ah, hour of the hours,
When he looks at our hair and sees it is grey;
And at our eyes and sees they are dim;
And at our lips straightened out with long pain;
And at our breasts, fallen and seared as a barren hill;
And at our hands, worn with toil!
Ah, hour of the hours,
When, seeing, he seeth all the bitter ruin and wreck of
    us—
All save the violated womb that curses him—
All save the heart that forbeareth . . . for pity—
All save the living brain that condemneth him—

All save the spirit that shall not mate with him
All save the soul he shall never see
Till he be one with it, and equal ;
He who hath the bridle, but guideth not ;
He who hath the whip, yet is driven ;
He who as a shepherd calleth upon us,
But is himself a lost sheep, crying among the hills !
O Spirit, and the Nine Angels who watch us,
And Thy Son, and Mary Virgin,
Heal us of the wrong of man :
We, whose breasts are weary with milk,
Cry, cry to Thee, O Compassionate !

The Rune of Age.

O Thou that on the hills and wastes of Night art
  Shepherd,
Whose folds are flameless moons and icy planets,
Whose darkling way is gloomed with ancient sorrows :
Whose breath lies white as snow upon the olden,
Whose sigh it is that furrows breasts grown milkless,
Whose weariness is in the loins of man
And is the barren stillness of the woman :
O thou whom all would 'scape, and all must meet,
Thou that the Shadow art of Youth Eternal,
The gloom that is the hush'd air of the Grave,
The sigh that is between last parted love,
The light for aye withdrawing from weary eyes,
The tide from stricken hearts forever ebbing !

O thou the Elder Brother whom none loveth,
Whom all men hail with reverence or mocking,
Who broodest on the brows of frozen summits
Yet dreamest in the eyes of babes and children :
Thou, Shadow of the Heart, the Brain, the Life,
Who art that dusk What-is that is already Has-Been,
To thee this rune of the fathers-to-the-sons
And of the sons to the sons, and mothers to new
  mothers—
To thee who art Aois,
To thee who art Age !

Breathe thy frosty breath upon my hair, for I am weary !
Lay thy frozen hand upon my bones that they support
  not,
Put thy chill upon the blood that it sustain not ;
Place the crown of thy fulfilling on my forehead ;
Throw the silence of thy spirit on my spirit,
Lay the balm and benediction of thy mercy
On the brain-throb and the heart-pulse and the life-
  spring—

R

For thy child that bows his head is weary,
For thy child that bows his head is weary.
I the shadow am that seeks the Darkness.
Age, that hath the face of Night unstarr'd and moonless,
Age, that doth extinguish star and planet,
Moon and sun and all the fiery worlds,
Give me now thy darkness and thy silence!

A Milking Song.

O sweet St Bride of the
    Yellow, yellow hair:
Paul said, and Peter said,
And all the saints alive or dead
Vowed she had the sweetest head,
Bonnie, sweet St Bride of the
    Yellow, yellow hair.

White may my milking be,
    White as thee:
Thy face is white, thy neck is white,
Thy hands are white, thy feet are white,
For thy sweet soul is shining bright—
    O dear to me,
    O dear to see
    St Bridget white!

Yellow may my butter be,
    Soft, and round:
Thy breasts are sweet,
Soft, round and sweet,
So may my butter be:
So may my butter be O
    Bridget sweet!

Safe thy way is, safe, O
    Safe, St Bride:
May my kye come home at even,
None be fallin' none be leavin',
Dusky even, breath-sweet even,
Here, as there, where O
    St Bride thou
Keepest tryst with God in heav'n,
Seest the angels bow

And souls be shriven—
Here, as there, 'tis breath-sweet even
    Far and wide—
Singeth thy little maid
Safe in thy shade
    Bridget, Bride!

Lullaby.

Lennavan-mo,
Lennavan-mo,
Who is it swinging you to and fro,
With a long low swing and a sweet low croon,
And the loving words of the mother's rune?

Lennavan-mo,
Lennavan-mo,
Who is it swinging you to and fro?
I 'm thinking it is an angel fair,
The Angel that looks on the gulf from the lowest stair
And swings the green world upward by its leagues of
    sunshine hair.

Lennavan-mo,
Lennavan-mo,
Who is it swings you and the Angel to and fro?
It is He whose faintest thought is a world afar,
It is He whose wish is a leaping seven-moon'd star,
It is He, Lennavan-mo,
To whom you and I and all things flow.

Lennavan-mo,
Lennavan-mo,
It is only a little wee lass you are, Eilidh-mo-chree,
But as this wee blossom has roots in the depths of the
    sky,
So you are at one with the Lord of Eternity—
Bonnie wee lass that you are,
My morning-star,
Eilidh-mo-chree, Lennavan-mo,
        Lennavan-mo.

The Songs of Ethlenn Stuart.

I.

His face was glad as dawn to me,
His breath was sweet as dusk to me,
His eyes were burning flames to me,
  Shule, Shule, Shule, agràh!

The broad noon-day was night to me,
The full-moon night was dark to me,
The stars whirled and the poles span
The hour God took him far from me.

Perhaps he dreams in heaven now,
Perhaps he doth in worship bow,
A white flame round his foam-white brow,
  Shule, Shule, Shule, agràh!

I laugh to think of him like this,
Who once found all his joy and bliss
Against my heart, against my kiss,
  Shule, Shule, Shule, agràh!

Star of my joy, art still the same
Now thou hast gotten a new name,
Pulse of my heart, my Blood, my Flame,
  Shule, Shule, Shule, agràh!

II.

He laid his dear face next to mine,
His eyes aflame burned close to mine,
His heart to mine, his lips to mine,
O he was mine, all mine, all mine.

Drunk with old wine of love I was,
Drunk as the wild-bee in the grass
Singing his honey-mad sweet bass,
Drunk, drunk with wine of love I was!

His lips of life to me were fief,
Before him I was but a leaf
Blown by the wind, a shaken leaf,
Yea, as the sickle reaps the sheaf,
                    My Grief!
He reaped me as a gathered sheaf!

His to be gathered, his the bliss,
But not a greater bliss than this!
All of the empty world to miss
For wild redemption of his kiss!
                    My Grief!

For hell was lost, though heaven was brief
Sphered in the universe of thy kiss—
So cries to thee thy fallen leaf,
Thy gathered sheaf,
Lord of my life, my Pride, my Chief,
                    My Grief!

The Closing Doors.

Eilidh,* Eilidh, Eilidh, heart of me, dear and sweet!
In dreams I am hearing the whisper, the sound of your
  coming feet:
The sound of your coming feet that like the sea-hoofs
  beat
A music by day and night, Eilidh, on the sands of my
  heart, my sweet!

O sands of my heart what wind moans low along thy
  shadowy shore?
Is that the deep sea-heart I hear with the dying sob at
  its core?
Each dim lost wave that lapses is like a closing door:
'Tis closing doors they hear at last who soon shall hear
  no more,
        Who soon shall hear no more.

Eilidh, Eilidh, Eilidh, come home, come home to the
  heart o' me:
It is pain I am having ever, Eilidh, a pain that will
  not be:
Come home, come home, for closing doors are as the
  waves o' the sea,
Once closed they are closed for ever, Eilidh, lost, lost,
  for thee and me,
        Lost, lost, for thee and me.

---

* Eilidh is pronounced Eily (liq.).

The Sorrow of Delight.

Till death be filled with darkness
  And life be filled with light,
The sorrow of ancient sorrows
  Shall be the Sorrow of Night:
But then the sorrow of sorrows
  Shall be the Sorrow of Delight.

Heart's-joy must fade with sorrow,
  For both are sprung from clay:
But the Joy that is one with Sorrow,
  Treads an immortal way:
Each hath in fee To-morrow,
  And their soul is Yesterday.

Joy that is clothed with shadow
  Is the Joy that is not dead:
For the joy that is clothed with the rainbow
  Shall with the bow be sped:
Where the Sun spends his fires is she,
  And where the Stars are led.

Farewell to Fiunary.

The wind is fair, the day is fine,
And swiftly, swiftly runs the time,
The boat is floating on the tide
That wafts me off from Fiunary.

> Eirigh agus tingainn O!
> Eirigh agus tingainn O!
> Erigh agus tingainn O!
> Farewell, farewell to Fiunary!

A thousand, thousand tender ties
Awake this day my plaintive sighs,
My heart within me almost dies
To think of leaving Fiunary.

> Eirigh agus tingainn O! etc.

With pensive steps I often strolled
Where Fingal's castle stood of old,
And listened while the shepherd told
The legend tales of Fiunary.

> Eirigh agus tingainn O! etc.

I 'll often pause at close of day
Where Ossian sang his martial lay,
And viewed the sun's departing ray
Wandering o'er Dun Fiunary.

> Eirigh agus tingainn O! etc.

A Kiss of the King's Hand.

It wasna from a golden throne,
Or a bower with milk-white roses blown,
But mid the kelp on northern sand
That I got a kiss of the king's hand.

I durstna raise my een tae see
If he even cared to glance at me ;
His princely brow with care was crossed
For his true men slain and kingdom lost.

Think not his hand was soft and white,
Or his fingers a' with jewels dight,
Or round his wrists were jewels grand
When I got a kiss of the king's hand.

But dearer far tae my twa een
Was the ragged sleeve of red and green
O'er that young weary hand that fain,
With the guid broadsword, had found its ain.

Farewell for ever, the distance gray
And the lapping ocean seemed to say—
For him a home in a foreign land.
And for me one kiss of the king's hand.

The First Ship.

The sky in beauty arch'd
　　The wide and weltering flood,
While the winds in triumph march'd
　　Through their pathless solitude—
Rousing up the plume on ocean's hoary crest,
　　That like space in darkness slept,
　　When his watch old Silence kept,
　　Ere the earliest planet leapt
　　　　From its breast.

A speck is on the deeps,
　　Like a spirit in her flight ;
How beautiful she keeps
　　Her stately path in light !
She sweeps the shining wilderness in glee—
　　The sun has on her smiled,
　　And the waves, no longer wild,
　　Sing in glory round that child
　　　　Of the sea.

'Twas at the set of sun
　　That she tilted o'er the flood,
Moving like God alone
　　O'er the glorious solitude—
The billows crouch around her as her slaves.
　　How exulting are her crew !—
　　Each sight to them is new,
　　As they sweep along the blue
　　　　Of the waves.

Fair herald of the fleets
　　That yet shall cross the waves,
Till the earth with ocean meets
　　One universal grave,
What armaments shall follow thee in joy !
　　Linking each distant land
　　With trade's harmonious band,
　　Or bearing havoc's brand
　　　　To destroy !

The Land o' the Leal.

I 'm wearin' awa, John,
Like snaw-wreaths in thaw, John,
I 'm wearin' awa
    To the land o' the leal.

There 's nae sorrow there, John,
There 's neither cauld nor care, John,
The day is aye fair
    In the land o' the leal.

Our bonnie bairn 's there, John,
She was baith gude and fair, John,
And, oh, we grudged her sair
    To the land o' the leal.

But sorrow's sel' wears past, John,
And joy 's a-comin' fast, John,
The joy that 's aye to last,
    In the land o' the leal.

Oh, dry your glist'ning ee, John,
My saul langs to be free, John,
And Angels beckon me
    To the land o' the leal.

O haud ye leal and true, John,
Your day it 's wearin' through, John,
And I 'll welcome you
    To the land o' the leal.

Now fare-ye-weel, my ain John,
The warld's cares are vain, John,
We 'll meet and we 'll be fain
    In the land o' the leal.

Skye.

My heart is yearning to thee, O Skye!
    Dearest of Islands!
There first the sunshine gladdened my eye,
    On the sea sparkling;
There doth the dust of my dear ones lie,
    In the old graveyard.

Bright are the golden green fields to me,
    Here in the Lowlands;
Sweet sings the mavis in the thorn-tree,
    Snowy with fragrance:
But oh for a breath of the great North Sea,
    Girdling the mountains!

Good is the smell of the brine that laves
    Black rock and skerry,
Where the great palm-leaved tangle waves
    Down in the green depths,
And round the craggy bluff pierced with caves
    Sea-gulls are screaming.

Where the sun sinks beyond Humish Head,
    Crowning in glory,
As he goes down to his ocean bed
    Studded with islands,
Flushing the Coolin with royal red,
    Would I were sailing!

Many a hearth round that friendly shore
    Giveth warm welcome;
Charms still are there, as in days of yore,
    More than of mountains;
But hearths and faces are seen no more,
    Once of the brightest.

Many a poor black cottage is there,
    Grimy with peat smoke,

Sending up in the soft evening air
    Purest blue incense,
While the low music of psalm and prayer
    Rises to Heaven.

Kind were the voices I used to hear
    Round such a fireside,
Speaking the mother tongue old and dear,
    Making the heart beat
With sudden tales of wonder and fear,
    Or plaintive singing.

Great were the marvellous stories told
    Of Ossian's heroes,
Giants, and witches, and young men bold,
    Seeking adventures,
Winning kings' daughters and guarded gold,
    Only with valour.

Reared in those dwellings have brave ones been ;
    Brave ones are still there ;
Forth from their darkness on Sunday I 've seen
    Coming pure linen,
And like the linen the souls were clean
    Of them that wore it.

See that thou kindly use them, O man !
    To whom God giveth
Stewardship over them, in thy short span
    Not for thy pleasure ;
Woe be to them who choose for a clan
    Four-footed people !

Blessings be with ye, both now and aye,
    Dear human creatures !
Yours is the love that no gold can buy !
    Nor time can wither,
Peace be to thee and thy children, O Skye !
    Dearest of islands.

Midnight by the Sea.

(Autumn.)

Waves of the wild North Sea,
  Breaking—breaking—breaking!
From the dumb agony
  Of dreams awaking,
How sweet within the loosened arms of sleep
  To lie in silence deep,
Lone listening to your many-throated roar
  Along the caverned shore,
In midnight darkness breaking—breaking—breaking!

Wind of the wild North Sea,
  Calling—calling—calling!
What may your message be,
  Rising and falling?
From out the infinite ye make reply:
"Whither? and whence? and why?"
And my soul echoes the despairing moan—
  Which none can answer—none!—
From out its depths abysmal calling—calling—calling.

In Shadowland.

Between the moaning of the mountain stream
  And the hoarse thunder of the Atlantic deep,
  An outcast from the peaceful realms of sleep
I lie, and hear as in a fever-dream
The homeless night-wind in the darkness scream
  And wail around the inaccessible steep
  Down whose gaunt sides the spectral torrents leap
From crag to crag,—till almost I could deem
The plaided ghosts of buried centuries
  Were mustering in the glen with bow and spear
  And shadowy hounds to hunt the shadowy deer,
Mix in phantasmal sword-play, or, with eyes
  Of wrath and pain immortal, wander o'er
  Loved scenes where human footstep comes no more.

Mountain Twilight.

The hills slipped over each on each
  Till all their changing shadows died.
Now in the open skyward reach
  The lights grow solemn side by side.
While of these hills the westermost
Rears high his majesty of coast
  In shifting waste of dim-blue brine
  And fading olive hyaline;
Till all the distance overflows,
  The green in watchet and the blue
In purple.   Now they fuse and close—
A darkling violet, fringed anew
With light that on the mountain soars,
A dusky flame on tranquil shores;
  Kindling the summits as they grow
In audience to the skies that call,
Ineffable in rest and all
  The pathos of the afterglow.

Durisdeer.

We 'll meet nae mair at sunset when the weary day is
dune,
Nor wander hame thegither by the lee licht o' the mune.
I 'll hear your steps nae langer amang the dewy corn,
For we 'll meet nae mair, my bonniest, either at e'en or
morn.

The yellow broom is waving abune the sunny brae,
And the rowan berries dancing where the sparkling
waters play ;
Tho' a' is bright and bonnie it 's an eerie place to me,
For we 'll meet nae mair, my dearest, either by burn or
tree.

Far up into the wild hills there 's a kirkyard lone and
still,
Where the frosts lie ilka morning and the mists hang
low and chill.
And there ye sleep in silence while I wander here my
lane
Till we meet ance mair in Heaven never to part again !

November's Cadence.

The bees about the Linden-tree,
When blithely summer blooms were springing,
Would hum a heartsome melody,
The simple baby-soul of singing ;
And thus my spirit sang to me
When youth its wanton way was winging :
  "Be glad, be sad—thou hast the choice—
  But mingle music with thy voice."

The linnets on the Linden-tree,
Among the leaves in autumn dying,
Are making gentle melody,
A mild, mysterious, mournful sighing ;
And thus my spirit sings to me
While years are flying, flying, flying :
  "Be sad, be sad, thou hast no choice,
  But mourn with music in thy voice."

Cailleach Bein-y-Vreich.

Weird wife of Bein-y-Vreich! horo! horo!
  Aloft in the mist she dwells;
Vreich horo! Vreich horo! Vreich horo!
  All alone by the lofty wells.

Weird, weird wife! with the long gray locks,
  She follows her fleet-foot stags,
Noisily moving through splinter'd rocks,
  And crashing the grisly crags.

Tall wife, with the long gray hose! in haste
  The rough stony beach she walks;
But dulse or seaweed she will not taste,
  Nor yet the green kail stalks.

*

O I will not let my herd of deer,
  My bonny red deer go down;
I will not let them go down to the shore,
  To feed on the sea-shells brown.

Oh, better they love in the corrie's recess,
  Or on mountain top to dwell,
And feed by my side on the green, green cress,
  That grows by the lofty well.

Broad Bein-y-Vreich is grisly and drear,
  But wherever my feet have been
The well-springs start for my darling deer,
  And the grass grows tender and green.

And there high up on the calm nights clear,
  Beside the lofty spring,
They come to my call, and I milk them there,
  And a weird wild song I sing.

But when hunter men round my dun deer prowl,
  I will not let them nigh;
Through the rended cloud I cast one scowl,
  They faint on the heath and die.

And when the north wind o'er the desert bare
  Drives loud, to the corries below
I drive my herds down, and bield them there
  From the drifts of the blinding snow.

Then I mount the blast, and we ride full fast,
  And laugh as we stride the storm,
I, and the witch of the Cruachan Ben,
  And the scowling-eyed Seul-Gorm.

An Old Tale of Three.

Ah bonnie darling, lift your dark eyes dreaming!
See, the firelight fills the gloaming, though deep darkness
grows without—

Hush, dear, hush, I hear the sea-birds screaming,
And down beyond the haven the tide comes with a shout!

Ah, birdeen, sweetheart, sure he is not coming,
He who has your hand in fee, while I have all your
heart—

Hush, dear, hush, I hear the wild bees humming
Far away in the underworld where true love shall not part!

Darling, darling, darling, all the world is singing,
Singing, singing, singing a song of joy for me!

Hush, dear, hush, what wild sea-wind is bringing
Gloom o' the sea about thy brow, athwart the eyes of thee?

Ah, heart o' me, darling, darling, all my heart's aflame!
Sure, at the last we are all in all, all in all we two!

At the Door,

A VOICE.

This is the way I take my own, this is the boon I
claim!

(Later, in the dark, the living brooding beside the dead:—)

Sure, at the last, ye are all in all, all in all, ye two—
Ah, hell of my heart! Ye are dust to me—and dust
with dust may woo!

UNKNOWN
(From the Gaelic,
Western Isles.)

Lost Love.

My heart ! my pulse ! my flame !
 O the gloom, O the pain !
He has no wish to save me
 Who will not come again.

Love ! Love ! Love !
 The fair cheek, the dark hair,
The promise forgotten ;
 'Twill go with me there.

False ! false ! false !
 O, youth is false for ever :
He loves far more than living me—
 The lifeless heather.

The hunting field,
 The greenwood tree,
The trout, the running deer, he loves,
 Far more than me.

He loves—loves—loves
 To stalk the frightened doe ;
He never heeds the pain he gives,
 His skill to show.

O, the dark blue eye—
 A flower wet with dew ;
O, the fair false face—
 Too sweet to view !

Love ! Love ! Love !
 The fair cheek, the dark hair !
For him I 'd scale the walls of hell
 Gin he were there !

IV
CONTEMPORARY
ANGLO-CELTIC POETS
(Wales)

Dirge in Woods.

A wind sways the pines,
      And below
Not a breath of wild air ;
Still as the mosses that glow
On the flooring and over the lines
Of the roots here and there.
The pine-tree drops its dead ;
They are quiet, as under the sea.
Overhead, overhead
Rushes life in a race,
As the clouds the clouds chase ;
      And we go,
And we drop like the fruits of the tree,
      Even we,
      Even so.

Outer and Inner.

I.

From twig to twig the spider weaves
  At noon his webbing fine.
So near to mute the zephyr's flute
  That only leaflets dance.
The sun draws out of hazel leaves
  A smell of woodland wine.
I wake a swarm to sudden storm
  At any step's advance.

II.

Along my path is bugloss blue,
  The star with fruit in moss;
The foxgloves drop from throat to top
  A daily lesser bell.
The blackest shadow, nurse of dew,
  Has orange skeins across;
And keenly red is one thin thread
  That flashing seems to swell.

III.

My world I note ere fancy comes,
  Minutest hushed observe:
What busy bits of motioned wits
  Through antlered mosswork strive;
But now so low the stillness hums,
  My springs of seeing swerve,
For half a wink to thrill and think
  The woods with nymphs alive.

IV.

I neighbour the invisible
  So close that my consent
Is only asked for spirits masked
  To leap from trees and flowers.

And this because with them I dwell
  In thought, while calmly bent
To read the lines dear Earth designs
  Shall speak her life on ours.

V.

Accept, she says; it is not hard
  In woods; but she in towns
Repeats, accept; and have we wept,
  And have we quailed with fears,
Or shrunk with horrors, sure reward
  We have whom knowledge crowns;
Who see in mould the rose unfold,
  The soul through blood and tears.

Night of Frost in May.

With splendour of a silver day,
A frosted night had opened May :
And on that plumed and armoured night,
As one close temple hove our wood,
Its border leafage virgin white.
Remote down air an owl halloed.
The black twig dropped without a twirl ;
The bud in jewelled grasp was nipped ;
The brown leaf cracked with a scorching curl ;
A crystal off the green leaf slipped.
Across the tracks of rimy tan,
Some busy thread at whiles would shoot ;
A limping minnow-rillet ran,
To hang upon an icy foot.

In this shrill hush of quietude,
The ear conceived a severing cry.
Almost it let the sound elude,
When chuckles three, a warble shy,
From hazels of the garden came,
Near by the crimson-windowed farm.
They laid the trance on breath and frame,
A prelude of the passion-charm.

Then soon was heard, not sooner heard
Than answered, doubled, trebled, more,
Voice of an Eden in the bird
Renewing with his pipe of four
The sob : a troubled Eden, rich
In throb of heart : unnumbered throats
Flung upward at a fountain's pitch,
The fervour of the four long notes,
That on the fountain's pool subside ;
Exult and ruffle and upspring :
Endless the crossing multiplied
Of silver and of golden string.

There chimed a bubbled underbrew
With witch-wild spray of vocal dew.

It seemed a single harper swept
Our wild wood's inner chords and waked
A spirit that for yearning ached
Ere men desired and joyed or wept.
Or now a legion ravishing
Musician rivals did unite
In love of sweetness high to sing
The subtle song that rivals light ;
From breast of earth to breast of sky :
And they were secret, they were nigh :
A hand the magic might disperse ;
The magic swung my universe.

Yet sharpened breath forbade to dream,
Where all was visionary gleam ;
Where Seasons, as with cymbals, clashed ;
And feelings, passing joy and woe,
Churned, gurgled, spouted, interflashed,
Nor either was the one we know :
Nor pregnant of the heart contained
In us were they, that griefless plained,
That plaining soared ; and through the heart
Struck to one note the wide apart :—
A passion surgent from despair ;
A paining bliss in fervid cold ;
Off the last vital edge of air,
Leaping heavenward of the lofty-souled,
For rapture of a wine of tears ;
As had a star among the spheres
Caught up our earth to some mid-height
Of double life to ear and sight,
She giving voice to thought that shines
Keen-brilliant of her deepest mines ;
While steely drips the rillet clinked,
And hoar with crust the cowslips swelled.

Then was the lyre of Earth beheld,
Then heard by me : it holds me linked ;
Across the years to dead-ebb shores
I stand on, my blood-thrill restores.
But would I conjure into me
Those issue notes, I must review
What serious breath the woodland drew ;
The low throb of expectancy ;
How the white mother-muteness pressed
On leaf and meadow-herb ; how shook,
Nigh speech of mouth, the sparkle-crest
Seen spinning on the bracken crook.

Hymn to Colour.

I.

With Life and Death I walked when Love appeared,
And made them on each side a shadow seem.
Through wooded vales the land of dawn we neared,
Where down smooth rapids whirls the helmless dream
To fall on daylight ; and night puts away
> Her darker veil for grey.

II.

In that grey veil green grassblades brushed we by ;
We came where woods breathed sharp, and overhead
Rocks raised clear horns on a transforming sky :
Around, save for those shapes, with him who led
And linked them, desert varied by no sign
> Of other life than mine.

III.

By this the dark-winged planet, raying wide,
From the mild pearl-glow to the rose upborne,
Drew in his fires, less faint than far descried,
Pure-fronted on a stronger wave of morn :
And those two shapes the splendour interweaved,
> Hung web-like, sank and heaved.

IV.

Love took my hand when hidden stood the sun
To fling his robe on shoulder-heights of snow.
Then said : There lie they, Life and Death in one.
Whichever is, the other is : but know,
It is thy craving self that thou dost see,
> Not in them seeing me.

V.

Shall man into the mystery of breath,
From his quick breathing pulse a pathway spy ?
Or learn the secret of the shrouded death,
By lifting up the lid of a white eye ?
Cleave thou thy way with fathering desire
> Of fire to reach to fire.

T

VI.

Look now where Colour, the soul's bridegroom, makes
The house of heaven splendid for the bride.
To him as leaps a fountain she awakes,
In knotting arms, yet boundless : him beside,
She holds the flower to heaven, and by his power
      Brings heaven to the flower.

VII.

He gives her homeliness in desert air,
And sovereignty in spaciousness; he leads
Through widening chambers of surprise to where
Throbs rapture near an end that aye recedes,
Because his touch is infinite and lends
      A yonder to all ends.

VIII.

Death begs of Life his blush ; Life Death persuades
To keep long day with his caresses graced.
He is the heart of light, the wing of shades,
The crown of beauty ; never soul embraced
Of him can harbour unfaith ; soul of him
      Possessed walks never dim.

IX.

Love eyed his rosy memories : he sang :
O bloom of dawn, breathed up from the gold sheaf
Held springing beneath Orient ! that dost hang
The space of dewdrops running over leaf ;
Thy fleetingness is bigger in the ghost
      Than Time with all his host !

X.

Of thee to say behold, has said adieu :
But love remembers how the sky was green,
And how the grasses glimmered lightest blue ;
How saint-like grey took fervour : how the screen
Of cloud grew violet ; how thy moment came
      Between a blush and flame.

XI.

Love saw the emissary eglantine
Break wave round thy white feet above the gloom ;
Lay finger on thy star ; thy raiment line
With cherub wing and limb ; wed thy soft bloom,
Gold-quivering like sunrays in thistle-down,
      Earth under rolling brown.

XII.

They do not look through love to look on thee,
Grave heavenliness ! nor know they joy of sight,
Who deem the wave of rapt desire must be
Its wrecking and last issue of delight.
Dead seasons quicken in one petal-spot
      Of colour unforgot.

XIII.

This way have men come out of brutishness
To spell the letters of the sky and read
A reflex upon earth else meaningless.
With thee, O fount of the Untimed ! to lead ;
Drink they of thee, thee eyeing, they unaged
      Shall on through brave wars waged.

XIV.

More gardens will they win than any lost ;
The vile plucked out of them, the unlovely slain.
Not forfeiting the beast with which they are crossed,
To stature of the Gods will they attain.
They shall uplift their Earth to meet her Lord,
      Themselves the attuning chord !

XV.

The song had ceased ; my vision with the song.
Then of those Shadows, which one made descent
Beside me I knew not : but Life ere long
Came on me in the public ways and bent
Eyes deeper than of old : Death met I too,
      And saw the dawn glow through.

Shadows.

Lonely o'er the dying ember
    I the past recall,
And remember in December
April buds and August skies,
As the shadows fall and rise,
As the shadows rise and fall.

Quicker now they lift and flicker
    On the dreary wall ;
Aye, and quicker still and thicker
Throng the fitful fantasies,
As the shadows fall and rise,
As the shadows rise and fall.

Dimmer now they shoot and shimmer
    On the dreary wall,
Dimmer, dimmer, still they glimmer
Till the light in darkness dies,
And the other shadows rise,
And the other shadows fall.

When the World is Burning.

When the world is burning,
Fired within, yet turning
  Round with face unscathed ;
Ere fierce flames, uprushing,
O'er all lands leap, crushing,
  Till earth fall, fire-swathed ;
Up against the meadows,
Gently through the shadows,
  Gentle flames will glide,
Small, and blue, and golden.
Though by bard beholden,
When in calm dreams folden,—
  Calm his dreams will bide.

Where the dance is sweeping,
Through the greensward peeping,
  Shall the soft lights start;
Laughing maids, unstaying,
Deeming it trick-playing,
High their robes upswaying,
  O'er the lights shall dart;
And the woodland haunter
Shall not cease to saunter
  When, far down some glade,
Of the great world's burning,
One soft flame upturning
Seems, to his discerning,
  Crocus in the shade.

The Hand.

Lone o'er the moors I stray'd ;
With basely timid mind,
Because by some betray'd
Denouncing human-kind ;
I heard the lonely wind,
And wickedly did mourn
I could not share its loneliness,
And all things human scorn.

And bitter were the tears,
I cursed as they fell ;
And bitterer the sneers
I strove not to repel :
With blindly mutter'd yell,
I cried unto mine heart,—
" Thou shalt beat the world in falsehood
And stab it ere we part."

My hand I backward drave
As one who seeks a knife ;
When startlingly did crave
To quell that hand's wild strife
Some other hand ; all rife
With kindness, clasp'd it hard
On mine, quick frequent claspings
That would not be debarr'd.

I dared not turn my gaze
To the creature of the hand ;
And no sound did it raise,
Its nature to disband
Of mystery ; vast, and grand,
The moors around me spread,
And I thought, some angel message
Perchance their God may have sped.

But it press'd another press,
So full of earnest prayer,
While o'er it fell a tress
Of cool soft human hair,
I fear'd not;—I did dare
Turn round, 'twas Hannah there!
Oh! to no one out of heaven
Could I what pass'd declare.

We wander'd o'er the moor
Through all that blessed day;
And we drank its waters pure,
And felt the world away;
In many a dell we lay,
And we twined flower-crowns bright;
And I fed her with moor-berries
And bless'd her glad eye-light.

And still that earnest prayer
That saved me many stings,
Was oft a silent sayer
Of countless loving things;—
I'll ring it all with rings,
Each ring a jewell'd band;
For heaven shouldn't purchase
That little sister hand.

EMILY DAVIS
(Mrs Pfeiffer)

A Song of Winter.

Barb'd blossom of the guarded gorse,
  I love thee where I see thee shine:
Thou sweetener of our common-ways,
And brightener of our wintry days.

Flower of the gorse, the rose is dead,
  Thou art undying, O be mine!
Be mine with all thy thorns, and prest
Close on a heart that asks not rest.

I pluck thee and thy stigma set
  Upon my breast, and on my brow;
Blow, buds, and plenish so my wreath
That none may know the wounds beneath.

O crown of thorn that seem'st of gold,
  No festal coronal art thou;
Thy honey'd blossoms are but hives
That guard the growth of winged lives.

I saw thee in the time of flowers
  As sunshine spill'd upon the land,
Or burning bushes all ablaze
With sacred fire; but went my ways;

I went my ways, and as I went
  Pluck'd kindlier blooms on either hand;
Now of those blooms so passing sweet
None lives to stay my passing feet.

And still thy lamp upon the hill
  Feeds on the autumn's dying sigh,
And from thy midst comes murmuring
A music sweeter than in spring.

Barb'd blossoms of the guarded gorse,
  Be mine to wear until I die,
And mine the wounds of love which still
Bear witness to his human will.

The Night Ride.

To-night we rode beneath a moon
   That made the moorland pale ;
And our horses' feet kept well the tune
   And our pulses did not fail.

The moon shone clear ; the hoar-frost fell,
   The world slept, as it seemed ;
Sleep held the night, but we rode well,
   And as we rode we dreamed.

We dreamed of ghostly horse and hound,
   And flight at dead of night ;—
The more the fearful thoughts we found,
   The more was our delight.

And when we saw the white-owl fly,
   With hoot, how woebegone !
We thought to see dead men go by,
   And pressed our horses on.

The merrier then was Sylvia's song
   Upon the homeward road,—
Oh, whether the way be short or long
   Is all in the rider's mood !

And still our pulses kept the tale,
   Our gallop kept the tune,
As round and over hill and vale
   We rode beneath the moon.

The House of Hendra.

'S'ai Plas Hendre
Yn Nghaer Fyrddin :
Canu Brechfa,
Tithau Lywelyn'.

I.

The House of Hendra stood in Merlin's Town, and was sung by Brechva on his Harp of gold at the October Feasting of Ivor.

In the town where wondrous Merlin
    Lived, and still
In deep sleep, they say, lies dreaming
Near it, under Merlin's Hill,

In that town of pastoral Towy,
    Once of old
Stood the ancient House of Hendra,
Sung on Brechva's harp of gold.

With his harp to Ivor's feasting
    Brechva came,
There he sang and made this ballad,
While the last torch spent its flame.

Long they told,—the men of Ivor,
    Of the strain
At the heart of Brechva's harping
Heard that night, and not again.

II.

Incipit Brechva's Ballad of
the House of Hendra,
and of his deep sleep
there on Hallowmas
Night, and of his
strange awaking.

In yon town, he sang,—there Hendra
 Waits my feet,
In renownèd Merlin's town where
Clare's white castle keeps the street.

There, within that house of heroes,
 I drew breath ;
And 'tis there my feet must bear me,
For the darker grace of death.

There that last year's night I journeyed,—
 Hallowmas !
When the dead of Earth, unburied,
In the darkness rise and pass.

Then in Hendra (all his harp cried
 At the stroke),
Twelve moons gone, there came upon me
Sleep like death. At length I woke :

I awoke to utter darkness,
 Still and deep,
With the walls around me fallen
Of the sombre halls of sleep :

With my hall of dreams downfallen,
 Dark I lay,
Like one houseless, though about me
Hendra stood, more fast than they :

But what broke my sleep asunder,—
 Light or sound ?
There was shown no sound, where only
Night, and shadow's heart, were found.

III.

Anon he hears a voice in
the night, and rising
from sleep, looks out
upon the sleeping
town.

So it passed, till with a troubled
    Lonely noise,
Like a cry of men benighted,
Midnight made itself a voice.

Then I rose, and from the stairloop,
    Looking down,
Nothing saw, where far before me
Lay, one darkness, all the town.

In that grave day seemed for ever
    To lie dead,
Nevermore at wake of morning
To lift up its pleasant head:

All its friendly foolish clamour,
    Its delight,
Fast asleep, or dead, beneath me,
In that black descent of night:

But anon, like fitful harping,
    Hark, a noise!
As in dream, suppose your dreamer's
Men of shadow found a voice.

IV.

Hearing his name called,
Brechva descends to
the postern, and sees
thence a circle of
Shadows, in a solemn
dance of Death.

Night-wind never sang more strangely
    Song more strange ;
All confused, yet with a music
In confusion's interchange.

Now it cried, like harried night-birds,
    Flying near,
Now, more nigh, with multiplying
Voice on voice, "O Brechva, hear!"

I was filled with fearful pleasure
    At the call,
And I turned, and by the stairway
Gained the postern in the wall :

Deep as Annwn lay the darkness
    At my feet ;—
Like a yawning grave before me,
When I opened, lay the street.

Dark as death, and deep as Annwn,—
    But these eyes
Yet more deeply, strangely, seeing,
From that grave saw life arise.

And therewith a mist of shadows
    In a ring,
Like the sea-mist on the sea-wind,
Waxing, waning, vanishing.

Circling as the wheel of spirits
    Whirled and spun,
Spun and whirled, to forewarn Merlin
In the woods of Caledon.

V.

The spirits are no dream-
folk; but ancient in-
mates of the House
of Hendra.

Shades of men, ay, bards and warriors!—
      Wrought of air,
You may deem, but 'twas no dream-folk,
Born of night, that crossed me there.

And my heart cried out,—"O Vorwyn!
      They are those
Who of old-time lived to know here
Life's great sweetness in this house."

I had bid them kinsman's welcome,
      In a word,
For the ancient sake of Hendra,
Which they served with harp and sword.

But as still I watched them, wondering,
      Curiously,
Knowing all they should forewarn me,—
Of my death and destiny!

Ere I marked all in the silence,
      Ere I knew,
Swift as they had come, as strangely
Now their shadowy life withdrew.

The Spirits being gone,
Brechva hears aërial
VI.   music, and sees in
vision all the Bards in
the seventh Heaven.

They were gone ; but what sweet wonder
    Filled the air !—
With a thousand harping noises,—
Harping, chiming, crying there.

At that harping and that chiming,
    Straightway strong
Grew my heart, and in the darkness
Found great solace at that song.

Through the gate of night, its vision,
    Three times fine,
Saw the seventh heaven of heroes,
'Mid a thousand torches' shine :

All the bards and all the heroes
    Of old time
There with Arthur and with Merlin
Weave again the bardic rhyme.

There a seat is set and ready,
    And the name
There inscribed, and set on high there,—
Brechva of the Bards of Fame.

V

CONTEMPORARY
ANGLO-CELTIC POETS
(Manx)

U

The Childhood of Kitty of the Sherragh Vane.

Nice lookin', eh?
Aye, that's your way—
Well, I tell ye, the first time ever I seen her,
She wasn' much more till* a baby—
Six years, may be,
Would have been her
Age; at the little clogs at her,†
Clitter-clatter,
And her little hand
In mine, to show me the way, you'll understand,
Down yandher brew,
And me a stranger too,
That was lost on the mountain;
And the little sowl in the house all alone,
And for her to be goin'
The best part of a mile—
Bless the chile!
Till she got me right—
Not a bit shy, not her!
Nor freckened,‡ but talkin' as purty
As a woman of thirty—
And—"That's the way down to the School," says she,
"And Saul and me
Is goin' there every day;
You'll aisy find the way"—
And turns, and off like a bird on the wing,
Aw, a bright little thing!

Isn' it that way with these people of the mountain?
No accountin'
But seemin very fearless though—
Very—not for fightin', no!

---

* than.　　　† of hers.　　　‡ frightened.

Nor tearin', but just the used they are
Of fogs and bogs, and all the war
Of winds and clouds, and ghos'es creepin'
Unknownst upon them, and fairies cheepin'
Like birds, you'd think, and big bugganes *
In holes in rocks; lek makin' frens
With the like, that'll work like niggers, they will,
If you'll only let them; and paisible
Uncommon they are; and little scraps,
That's hardly off their mammies' laps
'll walk about there in the night
The same as the day, and all right—
Bless ye! ghos'es! ar'n' they half
Ghos'es themselves? Just hear them laugh,
Or hear them cry,
It's like up in the sky—
Aw, differin'
Total—aye; for the air is thin
And fine up there, and they ucks it in
Very strong,
Very long,
And mixes it in the mould
Of all their body and all their sowl—
So they're often seemin'
Like people dreamin',
With their eyes open like a surt of a trance.

---

* Hobgoblins.

Graih my Chree.

(Love of my Heart.)

I.

She was Joney, the rich man's only child,
    He was Juan, a son of the sea.
"Thy father hath cast me forth of his door,
But, poor as I am, to his teeth I swore
    I should wed thee, O graih my chree."

He broke a ring and gave her the half,
    And she buried it close at her heart.
"I must leave thee, love of my soul," he said,
"But I vow by our troth that living or dead,
I will come back rich to thine arms and thy bed,
    And fetch thee as sure as we part."

He sailed to the north, he sailed to the south,
    He sailed to the foreign strand,
But whether he touched on the icy cone
Or the coral reef of the Indian zone,
    It turned to a golden land.

And he cried to his crew, "Hoist sail and about,
    For no more do I need to roam;
I have silks and satins and lace and gold,
I have treasure as deep as my ship will hold
    To win me a wife at home."

They had not sailed but half of their course
    To the haven where they would be,
When the devil beguiled their barque on a rock,
And down it sank with a woeful shock
    On the banks of Italy.

Then over the roar of the clamorous waves
    The skipper his voice was heard,
"I vowed by our troth that dead or alive
I should come back yet to wed and to wive,
    And by t' Lady I keep my word.

"I will come to thee still, O love of my heart,
From the arms of the envious sea;
Though the tempest should swallow my choking
breath,
In the spite of hell and the devil and death
I will come to thee, graih my chree."

II.

"He will come no more to thine arms, my child,
He is false or lost and dead,
Now wherefore make ye these five years' moan,
And wherefore sit by the sea alone?"
"He will keep his vow," she said.

She climbed the brows of the cliffs at home,
She gazed on the false, false sea.
"It comes and it goes for ever," she cried,
"And tidings it brings to the wife and the bride,
But never a word to me."

Then, of lovers, another came wooing the maid,
But she answered him nay and nay,
The manfullest man and her servant true,
"Give me thy hand and thou shalt not rue,"
She murmured, "Alack, the day."

Her father arose in his pride and his wrath,
He was last of his race and name,
"Because that a daughter will peak and will pine
Must I never have child of my child to my line,
But die in my childless shame?"

They bore her a bride to the kirkyard gate,
It was a pitiful sight to see,
Her body they decked in their jewels and gold,
But the heart in her bosom sate silent and cold,
And she murmured "Ah, woe is me."

III.

They had not been wedded a year, a year,
  A year but barely two,
When the good wife close to the hearth-stone crept
And rocked her babe while the good man slept
  And the wind in the chimney blew.

Loud was the sea and fierce was the night,
  Gloomy and wild and dour;
From a flying cloud came a lightning flash,
A pane of the window fell in with a crash,
  And something rang on the floor.

O, was it a stone from the waste sea-beach?
  O, was it an earthly thing?
She stirred the peat and stooped to the ground,
And there in the red, red light she found
  The half of a broken ring.

She rose upright in a terror of fright
  As one that hath sinned a sin,
And out of the dark and the wind and rain,
Through the jagged gap of the broken pane,
  A man's white face looked in.

" Oh, why didst thou stay so long, Juan?
  Five years I waited for thee."
" I vowed by our troth, that living or dead
I should come back yet to thine arms and thy bed,
  And my vow I have kept, my chree."

" But I have been false to my troth, Juan;
  Falsely I swore me away."
" I have silks and satins and lace and gold,
I have treasure as deep as my ship will hold;
  And my barque lies out in the bay."

" But I have a husband that loves me dear ;
  I promised him never to part."
" Through the salt sea's foam and the earth's hot breath,
  Through the grapplings of hell and the gates of death
  I have come for thee, Joney, my heart."

" But I have a child of my body so sweet—
  Little Jannie that sleeps in the cot."
" By the glimpse of the moon, at the top of the tide,
  Ere the crow of the cock our vessel must ride,
  Or what will befall us, God wot."

" Now, ever alack, thou must kiss and go back ;
  My love, I am never for thee."
" As sure as yon ship to the billows that roll,
  By the plight of our troth, both body and soul
  You belong to me, graih my chree."

She followed him forth like to one in a sleep ;
  It was a woeful and wonderous sight.
The moon on his face from a rift in a cloud
Showed it white and wan as a face in a shroud,
  And his ship on the sea gleamed white.

IV.

" Now weigh and away, my merry men all."
  The crew laughed loud in their glee.
" With the rich man's pride and his sweet daughter,
  In the spite of wind and the wild water—
  To the banks of Italy !"

The anchor was weighed, the canvas was spread,
  All in the storm and the dark,
With never a reef in a stitch of sail,
But standing about to burst the gale
  Merrily sped the barque.

The first night out there was fear on the ship,
  For the lady lay in a swoon ;
The second night out she woke from her trance,
And the skipper did laugh and his men would dance,
  But she made a piteous moan.

" O, where is my home and my sweet baby—
  My Jannie I nursed on my knee ?
He will wake in his cot by the cold hearth-stone
And cry for his mother who left him alone ;
  My Jannie, I 'm wae for thee."

The skipper he shouted for music and song,
  And his crew they answered his call.
He clothed her in silk and satin and lace,
But still through the rout and riot her face
  Showed fit for a funeral.

And ever at night they sailed by the moon,
  Through the wild white foam so fleet,
And ever again at the coming of day,
When the sun rose out of the sea they lay
  In a mist like a winding sheet.

And still the skipper he kissed her and cried,
  " Be merry and let-a-be."
And still to soothe her he sat through the nights
With his hand in her hand, till they opened the lights
  By the banks of Italy.

Then his face shone green as with ghostly sheen,
  And the moon began to dip.
" O, think not you, I am the lover ye knew ;
I am a ghostly man with a ghostly crew,
  And this is a ghostly ship."

Then he rose upright to a fearsome height,
  And stamped his foot on the deck ;
He smote the mast at the topsail yards,
And the rigging fell like a house of cards,
  And the hulk was a splitting wreck.

O, then as she sank in the water's womb,
    In the churn of the choking sea,
She knew that his arms were about her breast,
    As close as his arms might be.
And he cried o'er the tramp of the champing tide
    On the banks of Italy,
" By the plight of our troth, by the power of our bond,
    If not in this world in the world beyond,
        Thou art mine, O graih my chree."

VI

CONTEMPORARY
ANGLO-CELTIC POETS
(Cornish)

The Splendid Spur.

Not on the neck of prince or hound,
  Nor on a woman's finger twin'd,
May gold from the deriding ground
  Keep sacred that we sacred bind :
          Only the heel
          Of splendid steel
Shall stand secure on sliding fate,
When golden navies weep their freight.

The scarlet hat, the laurell'd stave
  Are measures, not the springs of worth ;
In a wife's lap, as in a grave,
  Man's airy notions mix with earth.
          Seek other spur
          Bravely to stir
The dust in this loud world, and tread
Alp-high among the whisp'ring dead.

Trust in thyself,—then spur amain :
  So shall Charybdis wear a grace,
Grim Ætna laugh, the Libyan plain
  Take roses to her shrivell'd face.
          This orb—this round
          Of sight and sound—
Count it the lists that God hath built
For haughty hearts to ride a-tilt.

The White Moth.

If a leaf rustled, she would start :
And yet she died, a year ago.
How had so frail a thing the heart
To journey where she trembled so ?
And do they turn and turn in fright,
Those little feet, in so much night ?

The light above the poet's head
 Streamed on the page and on the cloth,
And twice and thrice there buffeted
 On the black pane a white-wing'd moth :
'Twas Annie's soul that beat outside,
 And " Open, open, open !" cried :

" I could not find the way to God ;
 There were too many flaming suns
For signposts, and the fearful road
 Led over wastes where millions
Of tangled comets hissed and burned—
I was bewilder'd and I turned.

" O, it was easy then ! I knew
 Your window and no star beside.
Look up and take me back to you !"
 He rose and thrust the window wide.
'Twas but because his brain was hot
 With rhyming ; for he heard her not.

But poets polishing a phrase
 Show anger over trivial things :
And as she blundered in the blaze
 Towards him, on ecstatic wings,
He raised a hand and smote her dead ;
 Then wrote, "That I had died instead."

Featherstone's Doom.*

I.

Twist thou and twine! in light and gloom
A spell is on thine hand ;
The wind shall be thy changeful loom,
Thy web, the shifting sand.

II.

Twine from this hour, in ceaseless toil,
On Blackrock's sullen shore ;
Till cordage of the hand shall coil
Where crested surges roar.

III.

'Tis for that hour, when, from the wave,
Near voices wildly cried ;
When thy stern hand no succour gave,
The cable at thy side.

IV.

Twist thou and twine! in light and gloom
The spell is on thine hand ;
The wind shall be thy changeful loom,
Thy web, the shifting sand.

---

* The Blackrock is a bold, dark, pillared mass of
schist, which rises midway on the shore of Widemouth
Bay, near Bude, and is held to be the lair of the troubled
spirit of Featherstone the wrecker, imprisoned therein
until he shall have accomplished his doom.

Trebarrow.

I.

Did the wild blast of battle sound,
Of old, from yonder lonely mound?
Race of Pendragon! did ye pour,
On this dear earth, your votive gore?

II.

Did stern swords cleave along this plain
The loose rank of the roving Dane?
Or Norman chargers' sounding tread
Smite the meek daisy's Saxon head?

III.

The wayward winds no answer breathe,
No legend cometh from beneath,
Of chief, with good sword at his side,
Or Druid in his tomb of pride.

IV.

One quiet bird that comes to make
Her lone nest in the scanty brake;
A nameless flower, a silent fern—
Lo! the dim stranger's storied urn.

V.

Hark! on the cold wings of the blast
The future answereth to the past;
The bird, the flower, may gather still,
Thy voice shall cease upon the hill!

Witch Margaret.

Who hath not met Witch Margaret?
  Red gold her rippling hair,
Eyes like sweet summer seas are set
  Beneath her brow so fair;
And cream and damask rose have met
  Her lips and cheek to share.

Come up! and you shall see her yet,
  Before she groweth still;
Before her cloak of flame and smoke
  The winter air shall fill;
For they must burn Witch Margaret
  Upon the Castle Hill.

.   .   .   .   .   .

They found on her the devil's mark,
  Wherein naught maketh pain,—
"Bind her and dip her! stiff and stark
  She floateth aye again;
Her body changeth after dark,
  When powers of darkness reign."

They drave the boot on Margaret
  And crushed her dainty feet;
The hissing searing-irons set
  To kiss her lips so sweet:
She hath not asked for mercy yet,
  Nor mercy shall she meet.

The silent sky was cold and grey,
  The earth was cold and white,
They brought her out that Christmas Day
  To burn her in our sight;
The snow that fell and fell alway
  Would cover her ere night.

X

All feebly as a child would go
  Her bleeding feet dragged by,
Blood-red upon the white, white snow
  I saw her footprints lie ;
And some one shrieked to see her so—
  God knows if it was I !

Upon her body, all in black,
  Fell down her red-gold hair ;
All bruised and bleeding from the rack
  Her writhen arms hung bare ;
Red blood dripped all along her track,
  Red blood seemed in the air.

The while they told her deeds of shame,
  She, resting in the snow,
Stretched out weak hands toward the flame,
  Watched the sparks upward go,
Till on the pale pinched face there came
  Some of the red fire's glow.

   .   .   .   .   .   .

Oh, is it blood that blinds mine eyes,
  Or is it driving snow?
And are these but the wild wind's cries
  That drive me to and fro,
That beat about mine ears and rise
  Wherever I may go?

It's red and black on Castle Hill !
  The people go to pray,
A little wind sighs on, until
  The ashes float away ;
And then God's earth is very still,
  For this is Christmas Day.

A Ballad.

The Autumn leaves went whispering by,
  Like ghosts that never slept.
Up through the dusk a curlew's cry
  From glen to hill-top crept.
The Dead Man heard the burn moan by
  And thought for him it wept.

Lapped in his grave, a night and day,
  The Dead Man marked the sound :
He knew the moon rose far away,
  Grey shadows gathered round,
Then down the glen, he heard the bay
  Raised by his great grey hound.

A stag crashed out, and thundered back
  —She never turned aside.
The swollen stream ran cold and black,
  —She leapt the waters wide,
Nor paused, nor left the shadowy track
  Till at the dark grave side.

"What brings you here, my great grey hound,
  What brings you here, alone?
True I am dead, but is there found
  Beneath my board no bone?
No rushy bed for your grey head
  Now I am dead and gone?"

"Your brother reads your title-deeds,
  Your wife counts out red gold,
And laughs in rich black widow's-weeds,
  Red-lipped and smooth and bold.
I want no bone, to gnaw alone,
  Now that your hand is cold."

The Dead Man laughed in scornful hate,
  While the great hound growled low,

"Last night I rose to Heaven's gate,"
  He said, "for I would know
The best or worst dealt out by Fate,
  And whither I must go."

He paused—"My grave is damp and cold;
  I feel the slow worms glide
Smoothly and softly through the mould,
  And nestle by my side.
What lives and moves, in wood and wold,
  Where love and laughter bide?"

"The wild fowl fly across, and call
  In from the grey salt sea;
I scent the red stag by the Fall,
  He fears no more from me.
The moon comes up, and over all
  She glimmers eerily."

The corpse replied, "At Heaven's gates
  They stand to let me through,
And there, years hence, a welcome waits
  False Wife and Brother too.
Do what you will, my hound, and still
  Heaven holds no place for you.

"With tooth and claw tear down to me,
  And Death shall be no tether.
The swift red deer once more shall flee,
  Panting through burn and heather:
And you and I once more shall be
  Hunting my hills together!"

        .   .   .   .

That night the deer across the wold
  From dark to dawning fled;
The lady dreamt that, shroud-enrolled,
  A corpse had shared her bed;
But by the grave wind-swept and cold,
  The great grey hound lay dead!

Hell's Piper.

O have ye heard of Angus Blair,
Who lived long since in black Auchmair?
And have ye heard old pipers tell
His story—how he piped in Hell?
When Angus piped the old grew young,
Crutches across the floor were flung;
Nay more, 'twas said his witching breath
Had robbed the grave, and cheated death.

Above all else, a march of war
Was what men praised and feared him for;
When that he played, like fire it ran
In blood and brain of every man;
Then stiffened hair began to rise,
Bent brows scowled over staring eyes;
Then, at his will, men spilt their blood
Like water of a winter flood,
Swearing, with Angus, ill or well,
They'd charge light-hearted into Hell.

Long years, through many a feast and fray,
Did Piper Angus pipe his way;
Till, swept upon the swirling tide
Of a night-charge, he sank and died.

That night the Piper rose to tread
The ways that lie before the dead.
He saw God's battlements afar
Blazing behind the utmost star,
And turning in the chill night air,
Thought he might find a shelter there.

But as he turned to leave the earth,
With all its music, maids, and mirth,
The battered pipes beneath his feet
Screamed out a wailing, last retreat;

Then Piper Angus paused, and thought
Of the wild work those pipes had wrought;
"But there," quoth he, "in peace and rest,
Up there, the holy ones, the blest,
Praise aye the Lord, and aye they sing,
While golden harps and cymbals ring.
To my wild march or mad strathspey
The heavenly host would say me nay,
And none would hear my chanter more
Unless the Lord went out to war.
But often have I heard men tell
How they would follow pipes to Hell:
That way I'll try: in Hell maybe
Some corner's kept for them and me."

So said, so done—for well content
Down the dark way to Hell he went.
The Chanter felt his finger-tips,
The Blow-pipe thrilled between his lips,
The Drones across his shoulder flung,
Moaned till the Earth's foundations rung,
The streamers flaunted on the blast
As, striding smoke and shadow past,
With bonnet cocked, and careless air,
Piping his march, went Piper Blair.

Down where the shackled earthquakes dwell
Are piled the reeking halls of Hell.
Their walls are steel, their gates are brass;
Round them four flaming rivers pass;
And sleepless sentinels are set
On every point and parapet,
To hedge the souls whose far-off cries
Up to the world may never rise.

That night, so still the whole place seemed,
You'd think all Hell had peace, and dreamed
For the dark Master, brooding aye
Over lost hope and ancient fray,

Had, from his vantage, pale and grim,
Perchance to please a passing whim,
Hissed down a word which quelled and cowed
And silenced all that shuddering crowd.
So now aloft upon his throne
He sat indifferent, alone,
While poor damned souls who dared not cry
In writhing droves went whirling by.
These, dumb, before he noted aught,
Some strange and wandering sound now caught.

And first a little note they heard
Far off—and like a lonely bird ;
And then it grew, and grew, and grew,
As near and nearer still it drew,
Until Hell's Lord in slow surprise
Turned on the gates his weary eyes.

Then they that bent beneath a load
Stood up, nor felt the fiery goad.
Then they that trod on forks of flame
Tramped to the wild notes as they came.
Then, look, old foes of long ago
Feel old revenge revive and glow.
Then, heedless of the flaming whip,
They roll in one another's grip
With shout and shriek and throttled jeer,
—And over all the pipes rang clear.

But from the march those pipes turned soon,
And sank, to sing another tune ;
A low lament, whose sobbing wail
Filled aching hearts and made them fail.
And they that fought a breath ago
Now wept at one another's woe.

A second change—a lilting air
Made Hell look bright, made Hell look fair,
And wretches gasping new from death
Followed the tune beneath their breath—

Then, piping yet, erect, alone,
The Piper stood before the throne.

Up rose the Master in his place,
Eyeing the Piper's careless face,
" No room, no room in Hell can be
For Piper Angus Blair," cried he ;
"Would to such sounds my host had trod
Ere I was hurled down here by God ;
Mine hadst thou been, before I fell,
I 'd rule in Heav'n now—not in Hell.
Then every night and every day
On Heav'n's high ramparts shouldst thou play,
But here—here 's neither war nor mirth,
Nor more in Heav'n ; so back to Earth."

Thus now, as over glen and brae
The wild wind wanders on its way,
Dead Piper Angus Blair goes too,
And pipes and pipes the whole world through.
Unseen, unknown he goes. To-day
He 'll pipe perchance for bairns at play
To set them dancing: maybe steal
To-night to watch a roaring reel.
There, when the panting pipers tire,
He joins, and sets all hearts afire ;
And ere the dawn his pipes have pealed
Fiercely across some stricken field.
But when each year is at its close
Right down the road to Hell he goes.
There the gaunt porters all a-grin
Fling back the gates to let him in,
Then damned and devil, one and all,
Make mirth and hold high carnival,
The while the Master sits apart
Plotting rebellion in his heart.
Till, when above the dawn is grey,
The Piper turns and tramps away.

VII

MODERN AND CONTEMPOR-
ARY BRETON

O Breiz-Izel, O Kaera bro!
Koat enn hi c' hreiz, mor enn he zro!

The Poor Clerk.

(Ar C'Hloarek Paour.)

My wooden shoes I've lost them, my naked feet I've
torn
A-following my sweeting through field and brake of
thorn;
The rain may beat, and fall the sleet, and ice chill to
the bone,
But they're no stay to hold away the lover from his own.

My sweeting is no older than I that love her so:
She's scarce seventeen, her face is fair, her cheeks like
roses glow.
In her eyes there is a fire, sweetest speech her lips doth
part;
Her love it is a prison where I've locked up my heart.

Oh, to what shall I liken her, that a wrong it shall not
be?
To the pretty little white rose, that is called Rose-
Marie?
The pearl of girls; the lily when among the flowers it
grows,
The lily newly opened, among flowers about to close.

When I came to thee a-wooing, my sweet, my gentle
May,
I was as is the nightingale upon the hawthorn spray :
When he would sleep the thorns they keep a-pricking in
his breast,
That he flies up perforce and sings upon the tree's tall
crest.

I am as is the nightingale, or as a soul must be
That in the purgatory fires lies longing to be free,

Waiting the blessèd time when I unto your house shall
come,
All with the marriage-messenger * bearing his branch of
broom.

Ah, me! my stars are froward : 'gainst nature is my
state ;
Since in this world I came I 've dreed a dark and dismal
fate :
I have nor living kin nor friends, mother nor father
dear,
There is no Christian on earth to wish me happy here.

There lives no one hath had to bear so much of grief
and shame
For your sweet sake as I have, since in this world I
came ;
And therefore on my bended knees, in God's dear name
I sue,
Have pity on your own poor clerk, that loveth only you !

---

* The bazvalan, the bearer of the rod of broom.

The Cross by the Way.

(Kroaz ann Hent.)

Sweet in the green-wood a birdie sings,
Golden-yellow its two bright wings,
Red its heartikin, blue its crest:
Oh, but it sings with the sweetest breast!

Early, early it 'lighted down
On the edge of my ingle-stone,
As I prayed my morning prayer,—
"Tell me thy errand, birdie fair."

Then sung it as many sweet things to me
As there are roses on the rose-tree:
"Take a sweetheart, lad, an' you may;
To gladden your heart both night and day."

Past the cross by the way as I went,
Monday, I saw her fair as a saint:
Sunday, I will go to mass,
There on the green I'll see her pass.

Water poured in a beaker clear,
Dimmer shows than the eyes of my dear;
Pearls themselves are not more bright
Than her little teeth, pure and white.

Then her hands and her cheek of snow,
Whiter than milk in a black pail, show.
Yes, if you could my sweetheart see,
She would charm the heart from thee.

Had I as many crowns at my beck,
As hath the Marquis of Poncalec;
Had I a gold-mine at my door,—
Wanting my sweetheart, I were poor.

If on my door-sill up should come
Golden flowers for furze and broom,
Till my court were with gold piled high,
Little I'd reck, but she were by.

Doves must have their close warm nest,
Corpses must have the tomb for rest;
Souls to Paradise must depart,—
And I, my love, must to thy heart.

Every Monday at dawn of day
I'll on my knees to the cross by the way;
At the new cross by the way I'll bend,
In thy honour, my gentle friend!

The Secrets of the Clerk.

Each night, each night, as on my bed I lie,
I do not sleep, but turn myself and cry.

I do not sleep, but turn myself and weep,
When I think of her I love so deep.

Each day I seek the Wood of Love so dear,
In hopes to see you at its streamlet clear.

When I see you come through the forest grove,
On its leaves I write the secret of my love.

—But a fragile trust are the forest leaves,
To hold the secrets close which their page receives.

When comes the storm of rain, and gusty air,
Your secrets close are scattered everywhere.

'Twere safer far, young clerk, on my heart to write.
Graven deep they 'd rest, and never take their flight.

Love Song.

In the white cabin at the foot of the mountain,
Is my sweet, my love :

Is my love, is my desire,
And all my happiness.

Before the night must I see her
Or my little heart will break.

My little heart will not break,
For my lovely dear I have seen.

Fifty nights I have been
At the threshold of her door; she did not know it.

The rain and the wind whipped me,
Until my garments dripped.

Nothing came to console me
Except the sound of breathing from her bed.

Except the sound of breathing from her bed,
Which came through the little hole of the key.

Three pairs of shoes I have worn out,
Her thought I do not know.

The fourth pair I have begun to wear,
Her thought I do not know.

Five pairs, alas, in good count,
Her thought I do not know.

—If it is my thought you wish to know,
It is not I who will make a mystery of it.

There are three roads on each side of my house,
Choose one among them.

Choose whichever you like among them,
Provided it will take you far from here.

—More is worth love, since it pleases me,
Than wealth with which I do not know what to do.

Wealth comes, and wealth it goes away,
Wealth serves for nothing.

Wealth passes like the yellow pears:
Love endures for ever.

More is worth a handful of love
Than an oven full of gold and silver.

Hymn to Sleep.

Keeper of the keys of Heaven,
Lingering near the starry Seven !
Guardian of the gates of Hell,
Hushed beneath thy drowsy spell !
 Fold thy wings and come to me,
 Sleep ! thou soul's euthanasy.

When the pilgrim of strange lore
Haunts thy pale phantasmal shore,
Dreams and absolution grant,
Priestess thou and hierophant !
 Fold thy wings and come to me,
 Sleep ! thou soul's euthanasy.

Builder of eternal towers !
Weaver of enchanted bowers !
Thou dost forge the fighter's arms,
Thee the lover woos for charms :
 Fold thy wings and come to me,
 Sleep ! thou soul's euthanasy.

Thou dost soothe the virgin's fears,
Thou dost staunch the widow's tears,
Smooth the wrinkled brows of Care,
Still the cries of wild Despair :
 Fold thy wings and come to me,
 Sleep ! thou soul's euthanasy.

Healer of the sores of shame !
Cleanser of the unholy flame !
Thou dost breathe beatitude
On the evil and the good :
 Fold thy wings and come to me,
 Sleep ! thou soul's euthanasy.

When the cup that Pleasure sips
Turns to wormwood on the lips;
When Remorse, with venomed mesh,
Frets and tears the writhing flesh:
　Fold thy wings and come to me,
　Sleep! thou soul's euthanasy.

Queller of the storms of Fate!
Quencher of the fires of Hate!
In thy peaceful bosom furled
Lies the turmoil of the world:
　Fold thy wings and come to me,
　Sleep! thou soul's euthanasy.

Calm as noon's abysmal blue,
Soundless as the falling dew,
Soft as snow with fleecy plumes,
Sweet as curling incense-fumes:
　Fold thy wings and come to me,
　Sleep! thou soul's euthanasy.

Keeper of the keys of Heaven!
(Cease your vigil, starry Seven)
Guardian of the gates of Hell!
(Loosen not the drowsèd spell)
　Fold thy wings and come to me,
　Sleep! thou soul's euthanasy.

The Burden of Lost Souls.

This was our sin. When Hope, with wings enchanted
    And shining aureole,
Hung on the blossomed steps of Youth and haunted
    The chancel of the soul ;

When we whose lips haply had blown the bugle
    That cheers the wavering line,
And solaced those to whom the world was frugal
    Of Love, the food divine ;

Whose hands had strength to strike men's chains asunder
    And heal the poor man's wrong,
Whose breath was blended with the chords that thunder
    Along the aisles of song ;

Whose eyes had seen and hailed the Light of Ages,
    In cloudiest heavens a star,
Whose ears had heard, on ringing wheels, the stages
    Of Freedom's trophied car :—

We turned, rebellious children, to the clamour
    And tumult of the world ;
We gave our souls in fee for Circe's glamour
    And white limbs lightly whirled ;

We drank deep draughts of Moloch's unclean liquor
    Even to the dregs of shame,
And blinded by the golden lights that flicker
    From Mammon's altar-flame

We burned strange incense, bowed before his idol
    Whose eucharist is fire,
And on the neck of passion loosed the bridle
    Of fierce and wild desire :—

Till now in our own hearts the ashy embers
    Of Love lie smouldering,
And scarce our Autumn chill and bare remembers
    The glory of the Spring ;

While faith, that in the mire was fain to wallow,
    Returns at last to find
The cold fanes desolate, the niches hollow,
    The windows dim and blind,

And, strown with ruins round, the shattered relic
    Of unregardful youth,
Where shapes of beauty once, with tongues angelic,
    Whispered the runes of Truth.

Confession.

Since I have lost the words, the flower
  Of youth and the fresh April breeze . . .
Give me thy lips; their perfumed dower
  Shall be the whisper of the trees!

Since I have lost the deep sea's sadness,
  Her sobs, her restless surge, her graves . . .
Breathe but a word; its grief or gladness
  Shall be the murmur of the waves!

Since in my soul a sombre blossom
  Broods, and the suns of yore take flight . . .
O hide me in thy pallid bosom,
  And it shall be the calm of night!

Discouragement.

Athwart the unclean ages whirled
  To solitary woods sublime,
Oh! had I first beheld this world
  Alone and free in Nature's prime!

When on its loveliness first seen
  Eve cast her pure blue eyes abroad:
When all the earth was fresh and green,
  And simple Man believed in God!

When sacred accents, vibrating
  Beneath the naked sun and sky,
Rose from each new-created thing
  To hail the Lord of Life on high;

I would have learned and lived in hope
  And loved! For in those vanished days,
Faith wandered on the mountain-slope . . .
  But now the world has changed her ways:

Our feet, less free, less fugitive,
  Tread beaten tracks from shore to shore . . .
Alas! what is the life we live?
  —A dream of days that are no more!

The Black Panther.

Along the rosy cloud light steals and twinkles;
The East is flecked with golden filigree :
Night from her loosened necklace slowly sprinkles
Pearl-clusters on the sea.

Clasped on the bosom of the sparkling azure
Soft skirts of flame trail like a flowing train,
And cast on emerald blades a bright emblazure,
Like drops of fiery rain.

The dew shines, like a sheaf of splendour shaken,
On cinnamon leaves and lychee's purple flesh ;
Among the drowsed bamboos the wind's wings waken
A myriad whisperings fresh.

From mounds and woods, from mossy tufts and flowers,
In the warm air, with sudden tremours thrilled,
Fragrance bursts forth in sweet and subtile showers,
With feverish rapture filled.

By virgin jungle-track and hidden hollow,
Where in the morning sun smoke tangled weeds,
And where live streams their winding channels follow
Through arches of green reeds,

Steals the black panther from her midnight prowling,
With dawn turned to the lair in which her cubs
Among smooth shining bones, with hunger growling,
Grovel beneath the shrubs.

Restless she slinks along, with arrowy flashes
That scan the shadows of the drooping wood.
The bright, fresh-sprinkled crimsoned dew that dashes
Her velvet skin is blood.

Behind she drags the relict of her quarry
  Torn from the stricken stag, a mangled spoil
That leaves a loathsome trail and sanguinary
  Along the moss-flowered soil.

Round her the tawny bees and light-winged dragons
  Flit fearless as she glides with supple flanks;
And clustering foliage from a thousand flagons
  Pours fragrance on the banks.

The python, through a scarlet cactus peering,
  Slowly above the bush lifts his flat head
And curious eyes, his scaly folds uprearing
  To watch her stealthy tread.

She glides in silence into the tall bracken,
  Then plunges lost beneath the lichened boughs:
Air burns in the vast light, earth's noises slacken,
  And wood and welkin drowse.

The Spring.

A live spring sparkles in the bosky gloom,
  Hidden from the noonday glare ;
The green reeds bend above its banks and there
  Blue-bells and violets bloom.

No kids that batten on the bitter herb,
  On slopes of the near hill,
Nor shepherd's song, nor flute-note sweet and shrill,
  Its crystal source disturb.

Hard by, the dark oaks weave a peaceful screen
  Whose shade the wild-bee loves,
And nestled in dense leaves the murmuring doves
  Their ruffled plumage preen.

The lazy stags in mossy thickets browse
  And sniff the lingering dew ;
Beneath cool leaves, that let the sunlight through,
  The languorous Sylvans drowse.

White Naïs, near the sacred spring that drips,
  Closing her lids awhile,
Dreams as she slumbers, and a radiant smile
  Floats on her purple lips.

No eye, kindling with love's desire, has scanned
  Beneath those lucent veils
The nymph whose snowy limbs and hair that trails
  Gleam on the silvery sand.

None gazed on the soft cheek, suffused with youth,
  The splendid bosom's swerve,
The ivory neck, the shoulder's delicate curve,
  White arms and innocent mouth.

But now the lecherous Faun, that haunts the grove,
  Spies from his leafy trench
Those supple flanks, kissed by the oozy drench
  As with a kiss of love;

Then laughs, as when the Satyr's wanton imps
  A wood-nymph's bower assail,
And, waking with the sound the virgin pale
  Flies like the lightning-glimpse.

Even as the Naiad, haunting the clear stream,
  Slumbers in woods obscure,
Fly from the impious look and laugh impure
  O Beauty, the soul's dream!

The Return of Taliesen.

On my lips the speech, in my ears the sound of the
    Armorican :
I hear the voice of Esus by the shores of the ocean,
And the songs which the great bard Ossian
        Resings by the ancient dolmen.

Many times since this, my twelfth rebirth on earth,
Have I seen the mistletoe grow green on the oak,
Seen the yellow crocus, the sunbright, and the vervein
        Bloom again in the woodlands :

But never shall I see again the white-robed Druid of old
Seek the sacred mistletoe as one seeketh a treasure ;
Never more shall I see him cut the living plant
        With his golden sickle.

Alas ! the valiant chiefs with the flowing locks !
All sleep in the cairns, beneath the fresh green grass ;
In vain my voice o'er the fields of the dead lamenting—
        "Vengeance ! Treason !

"Be swift, Revenge, on the feet of the sorrows of Arvor !"
Alas, dull echoes alone answer my wailing summons.
Treason, indeed, and Vengeance ! for lo, in the hallowed
    Némèdes
        The wayside flaunt of the Cross !

Tarann no longer sends forth his terror of thunder !
Camul no longer laughs behind the strength of his arm !
Tentatès, rising in wrath, has not yet crumbled the
    earth ;
        Esus is deaf to our call !

Whither, O whither fled are ye, ye powerful, redoubt-
    able gods ;
And ye, ye famous Druids, the glory and terror of Armor ?
Who has usurped, who has o'erwhelmed ye, unconquer-
    able knights,
        Warriors of the golden collar ?

Thou, who harkenest, I have been in the place of the
  Ancients !
I, alone among mortals, thence have issued alive :
Alas, the temple was deserted : I saw nought but some
  wind-haunted oaks
            Swaying in the silence.

All is fugitive ! pride, pleasure, the song, the dance,
Blithe joys of friendship, noble rivalries all :
The keen swift song of the swords, the whistling
  lances !
            Dreams of a dreamer all ! . . . But no,

A new dawn wakes and laughs on the breast of the
  darkness ;
Earth has her sunshine still, the grave her Spring ;
Many a time Dylan hath oared me afar in the death-
  barque,
            Many a death-sleep mine, and long !

For long I have slept with the heavy sleep of the dead,
Ofttimes my fugitive body has passed into divers forms,
I have spread strong wings on the air, I have swum in
  dark waters,
            I have crawled in the woods.

But, amid all these manifold changes, my soul
Remaineth ever the same : it is always, always "myself" !
And now I see well that this is the law of all that
  liveth,
            Though none beholdeth the reason, none the
            end.

Still stand our lonely menhirs, and still the wayfarer
  shudders
As in the desolate dusk he passes these Stones of
  Silence !
Thou speakest, I understand ! Thy Breton tongue
            Is that of the ancient Kymry.

Lights steal through the hours of shadow flame-lit for
  unknown saints,
As, in the days of old, our torches flared on the night :
Ah, before ever these sacred lamps shone for your meek
  apostles,
      They burned for Héol.

Blind without reason are we, thus changing the names
  of the gods :
Thus, mayhap, we think to destroy them, we who
  abandon their altars !
But, cold, calm, unsmiling before our laughter and
  curses,
      The gods wait, immortal.

Yea, while the sacred fires still burn along the hill-tops,
Yea, while a single lichened menhir still looms from the
  brushwood,
Yea, whether they name thee Armorica, Brittany, Breiz-
  Izèl,
      Thou art ever the same dear land !

Ah, soul of me ofttimes to thee, Land of mystery !
Ofttimes again shall I breathe in thy charmèd air !
Sure, every weary singer knoweth the secret name of
  thee,
      Land of Heart's Desire !

Enduring thou art ! For not the slow frost of the ages
Shall dim from thy past thy glory immortally graven !—
Granite thy soil, thy soul, loved nest of Celtic nations !—
      Sings the lost Voice, Taliesin.

By Menec'hi Shore.

Sad the sea-moan that echoes through my dream,
And sad the auroral sky suffused with gold,
Sad the blue wave that croons along the shore—

O Joy of Night in whose still calms I sleep!

Sadness of love, and O tired heart of man:
Sadness of hope, and all brave vows that be:
Sadness of joy itself, the joys we know!

Joy of Oblivion, is there bliss with thee?

Sad is the splendour, glory, the bright flame
And laughter of the soul, since underneath
Dreams and Desires veiled Mystery broods obscure . . .

O Joy of Death, with thee the Vials of Peace!

VIII

THE CELTIC FRINGE

z

Song.

Love, by that loosened hair
Well now I know
Where the lost Lilith went
So long ago.

Love, by those starry eyes
I understand
How the sea-maidens lure
Mortals from land.

Love, by that welling laugh
Joy claims his own
Sea-born and wind-wayward
Child of the sun.

The War-Song of Gamelbar.

Bowmen, shout for Gamelbar!
Winds, unthrottle the wolves of war!
Heave a breath
And dare a death
For the doom of Gamelbar!
Wealth for Gamel,
Wine for Gamel,
Crimson wine for Gamelbar!

Chorus:—Oh, sleep for a knave
With his sins in the sod!
And death for the brave,
With his glory up to God!
And joy for the girl,
And ease for the churl!
But the great game of war
For our lord Gamelbar,
Gamelbar!

Spearmen, shout for Gamelbar,
With his warriors thirty score!
Heave a sword
For our overlord,
Lord of warriors, Gamelbar!
Life for Gamel,
Love for Gamel,
Lady-loves for Gamelbar!

Horsemen, shout for Gamelbar!
Swim the ford and climb the scaur!
Heave a hand
For the maiden land,
The maiden land of Gamelbar!
Glory for Gamel,
Gold for Gamel,
Yellow gold for Gamelbar!

Armourers for Gamelbar,
Rivet and forge and fear no scar !
Heave a hammer
With anvil clamour,
To weld and brace for Gamelbar !
Ring for Gamel,
Rung for Gamel,
Ring-rung-ring for Gamelbar !

Yeomen, shout for Gamelbar,
And his battle-hand in war !
Heave his pennon ;
Cheer his men on,
In the ranks of Gamelbar !
Strength for Gamel,
Song for Gamel,
One war-song for Gamelbar !

Roncliffe, shout for Gamelbar !
Menthorpe, Bryan, Castelfar !
Heave, Thorparch
Of the Waving Larch,
And Spofford's thane, for Gamelbar !
Blaise for Gamel,
Brame for Gamel,
Rougharlington for Gamelbar !

Maidens, strew for Gamelbar
Roses down his way to war !
Heave a handful,
Fill the land full
Of your gifts to Gamelbar !
Dream of Gamel,
Dance for Gamel,
Dance in the halls for Gamelbar !

Servitors, shout for Gamelbar!
Roast the ox and stick the boar!
Heave a bone
To gaunt Harone,
The great war-hound of Gamelbar!
Mead for Gamel,
Mirth for Gamel,
Mirth at the board for Gamelbar!

Trumpets, speak for Gamelbar!
Blare as ye never blared before!
Heave a bray
In the horns to-day,
The red war-horns of Gamelbar!
To-night for Gamel,
The North for Gamel,
With fires on the hills for Gamelbar!

Shout for Gamel, Gamelbar,
Till your throats can shout no more!
Heave a cry
As he rideth by,
Sons of Orm, for Gamelbar!
Folk for Gamel,
Fame for Gamel,
Years and fame for Gamelbar!

Chorus :—Oh, sleep for a knave
With his sins in the sod!
And death for the brave,
With his glory up to God!
And joy for the girl,
And ease for the churl!
But the great game of war
For our lord Gamelbar,
Gamelbar!

Golden Rowan.

She lived where the mountains go down to the sea,
    And river and tide confer.
        Golden Rowan, in Menalowan,
Was the name they gave to her.

She had the soul no circumstance
    Can hurry or defer.
        Golden Rowan, of Menalowan,
How time stood still for her !

Her playmates for their lovers grew,
    But that shy wanderer,
        Golden Rowan, of Menalowan,
Knew love was not for her.

Hers was the love of wilding things ;
    To hear a squirrel chirr
        In the golden rowan of Menalowan
Was joy enough for her.

She sleeps on the hill with the lonely sun,
    Where in the days that were,
        The golden rowan of Menalowan
So often shadowed her.

The scarlet fruit will come to fill,
    The scarlet spring to stir
        The golden rowan of Menalowan,
And wake no dream for her.

Only the wind is over her grave,
    For mourner and comforter ;
        And "Golden Rowan, of Menalowan,"
Is all we know of her.

A Sea Child.

The lover of child Marjory
  Had one white hour of life brim full ;
Now the old nurse, the rocking sea,
  Hath him to lull.

The daughter of child Marjory
  Hath in her veins, to beat and run,
The glad indomitable sea,
  The strong white sun.

The Quest.

It was a heavenly time of life
  When first I went to Spain,
The lovely lands of silver mists,
  The land of golden grain.

My little ship through unknown seas
  Sailed many a changing day;
Sometimes the chilling winds came up
  And blew across her way.

Sometimes the rain came down and hid
  The shining shores of Spain,
The beauty of the silver mists
  And of the golden grain.

But through the rains and through the winds,
  Upon the untried sea,
My fairy ship sailed on and on,
  With all my dreams and me.

And now, no more a child, I long
  For that sweet time again,
When on the far horizon bar
  Rose up the shores of Spain.

O lovely land of silver mists,
  O land of golden grain,
I look for you with smiles, with tears,
  But look for you in vain!

Moth-Song.

What dost thou here,
Thou dusky courtier,
Within the pinky palace of the rose?
Here is no bed for thee,
No honeyed spicery,—
But for the golden bee,
And the gay wind, and me
Its sweetness grows.
Rover, thou dost forget;—
Seek thou the passion-flower
Bloom of one twilight hour.
Haste, thou art late!
Its hidden savours wait.
For thee is spread
Its soft, purple coverlet;
Moth, art thou sped?
—Dim as a ghost he flies
Through the night mysteries.

June.

Of silvery-shining rains
And noonday golds and shadows
June weaves wild-daisy chains
For happy meadows.

She stoops to set the stream
With scented alder-bushes,
And with the rainbow gleam
Of iris 'mid the rushes,
She scatters eglantine
And scarlet columbine.

Ah, June, my lovely lass,—
Sweetheart, dost thou not see
I stay to watch thee pass—
What hast thou brought to me?

Thy mystic ministries
Of glorious far skies,
Thy wild-rose sermons, Sweet,
Like dreams profound and fleet,
Thy woodland harmony
Thou givest me.

The vision that can see,
The loving will to learn,
How fair thy skies may be,
What in thy roses burn,
Thy secret harmonies,—
Ah, give me these!

Scent o' Pines.

Love, shall I liken thee unto the rose
    That is so sweet?
Nay, since for a single day she grows,
Then scattered lies upon the garden-rows
    Beneath our feet.

But to the perfume shed when forests nod,
    When noonday shines,
That lulls us as we tread the woodland sod,
Eternal as the peace of God
    The scent o' pines.

The Reed-Player.

By a dim shore where water darkening
    Took the last light of spring,
I went beyond the tumult, harkening
    For some diviner thing.

Where the bats flew from the black elms like leaves,
    Over the ebon pool
Brooded the bittern's cry, as one that grieves
    Lands ancient, bountiful.

I saw the fire-flies shine below the wood,
    Above the shallows dank,
As Uriel, from some great altitude,
    The planets rank on rank.

And now unseen along the shrouded mead
    One went under the hill;
He blew a cadence on his mellow reed,
    That trembled and was still.

It seemed as if a line of amber fire
    Had shot the gathered dusk,
As if had blown a wind from ancient Tyre
    Laden with myrrh and musk.

He gave his luring note amid the fern;
    Its enigmatic fall
Haunted the hollow dusk with golden turn
    And argent interval.

I could not know the message that he bore,
    The springs of life from me
Hidden; his incommunicable lore
    As much a mystery.

And as I followed far the magic player
    He passed the maple wood;
And, when I passed, the stars had risen there,
    And there was solitude.

The Celtic Cross.

Through storm and fire and gloom, I see it stand
    Firm, broad, and tall,
The Celtic Cross that marks our Fatherland,
    Amid them all !
Druids and Danes and Saxons vainly rage
    Around its base ;
It standeth shock on shock, and age on age,
    Star of our scatter'd race.

O Holy Cross ! dear symbol of the dread
    Death of our Lord,
Around thee long have slept our martyr dead
    Sward over sward.
An hundred bishops I myself can count
    Among the slain :
Chiefs, captains, rank and file, a shining mount
    Of God's ripe grain.

The monarch's mace, the Puritan's claymore,
    Smote thee not down ;
On headland steep, on mountain summit hoar,
    In mart and town,
In Glendalough, in Ara, in Tyrone,
    We find thee still,
Thy open arms still stretching to thine own,
    O'er town and lough and hill.

And would they tear thee out of Irish soil,
    The guilty fools !
How time must mock their antiquated toil
    And broken tools !
Cranmer and Cromwell from thy grasp retir'd,
    Baffled and thrown ;
William and Anne to sap thy site conspir'd,—
    The rest is known.

Holy Saint Patrick, father of our faith,
  Belov'd of God!
Shield thy dear Church from the impending scaith,
  Or, if the rod
Must scourge it yet again, inspire and raise
  To emprise high
Men like the heroic race of other days,
  Who joyed to die.

Fear! wherefore should the Celtic people fear
  Their Church's fate?
The day is not—the day was never near—
  Could desolate
The Destin'd Island, all whose clay
  Is holy ground:
Its Cross shall stand till that predestin'd day
  When Erin's self is drown'd.

MARY C. G. BYRON
(M. C. Gillington)

The Tryst of the Night.

Out of the uttermost ridge of dusk, where the dark and
the day are mingled,
The voice of the Night rose cold and calm—it called
through the shadow-swept air ;
Through all the valleys and lone hillsides, it pierced, it
thrilled, it tingled—
It summoned me forth to the wild sea-shore, to meet
with its mystery there.

Out of the deep ineffable blue, with palpitant swift
repeating
Of gleam and glitter and opaline glow, that broke in
ripples of light—
In burning glory it came and went,—I heard, I saw it
beating,
Pulse by pulse, from star to star,—the passionate heart
of the Night!

Out of the thud of the rustling sea—the panting,
yearning, throbbing
Waves that stole on the startled shore, with coo and
mutter of spray—
The wail of the Night came fitful-faint,—I heard her
stifled sobbing :
The cold salt drops fell slowly, slowly, gray into gulfs
of gray.

There through the darkness the great world reeled, and
the great tides roared, assembling—
Murmuring hidden things that are past, and secret
things that shall be ;
There at the limits of life we met, and touched with a
rapturous trembling—
One with each other, I and the Night, and the skies,
and the stars, and sea.

The Doom-Bar.

O d'you hear the seas complainin', and complainin',
    whilst it's rainin'?
Did you hear it mourn in the dimorts,* when the surf
    woke up and sighed?
        The choughs screamed on the sand,
        And the foam flew over land,
And the seas rolled dark on the Doom-Bar at rising of
    the tide.

I gave my lad a token, when he left me nigh heart-
    broken,
To mind him of old Padstow town, where loving souls
    abide;
        'Twas a ring with the words set
        All round, "Can Love Forget?"
And I watched his vessel toss on the Bar with the
    outward-turning tide.

D'you hear the seas complainin', and complainin', while
    it's rainin'?
And his vessel has never crossed the Bar from the purple
    seas outside;
        And down the shell-pink sands,
        Where we once went, holding hands,
Alone I watch the Doom-Bar and the rising of the tide.

One day—'twas four years after—the harbour-girls, with
    laughter
So soft and wild as sea-gulls when they're playing seek-
    and-hide,
        Coaxed me out—for the tides were lower
        Than had ever been known before;
And we ran across the Doom-Bar, all white and shining
    wide.

---

* Twilight.

I saw a something shinin', where the long, wet weeds
  were twinin'
Around a rosy scallop; and a gold ring lay inside;
      And around its rim were set
      The words "Can Love Forget?"—
And there upon the Doom-Bar I knelt and sobbed and
  cried.

I took my ring and smoothed it where the sand and
  shells had grooved it;
But O! St Petrock bells will never ring me home a
  bride!—
      For the night my lad was leavin'
      Me, all tearful-eyed and grievin',
He had tossed my keepsake out on the Bar to the rise
  and fall of the tide!

D' you hear the seas complainin', and complainin', while
  it's rainin'?
Did you hear them call in the dimorts, when the surf
  woke up and sighed?
      Maybe it is a token
      I shall go no more heart-broken—
And I shall cross the Doom-Bar at the turning of the
  tide.

The Seven Whistlers.

Whistling strangely, whistling sadly, whistling sweet
and clear,
The Seven Whistlers have passed thy house, Pentruan
of Porthmeor ;
It was not in the morning, nor the noonday's golden grace,
It was in the dead waste midnight, when the tide yelped
loud in the Race :
The tide swings round in the Race, and they 're plaining
whisht and low,
And they come from the gray sea-marshes, where the
gray sea-lavenders grow,
 And the cotton-grass sways to and fro ;
 And the gore-sprent sundews thrive
 With oozy hands alive.
Canst hear the curlews' whistle through thy dreamings
dark and drear,
How they 're crying, crying, crying, Pentruan of Porth-
meor ?

Shall thy hatchment, mouldering grimly in yon church
amid the sands,
Stay trouble from thy household ? Or the carven cherub-
hands
Which hold thy shield to the font ? Or the gauntlets on
the wall
Keep evil from its onward course as the great tides rise
and fall ?
The great tides rise and fall, and the cave sucks in the breath
Of the wave when it runs with tossing spray, and the
ground-sea rattles of Death ;
 " I rise in the shallows," 'a saith,
 " Where the mermaid's kettle sings,
 And the black shag flaps his wings ! "
Ay, the green sea-mountain leaping may lead horror in
its rear,
When thy drenched sail leans to its yawning trough,
Pentruan of Porthmeor !

Yet the stoup waits at thy doorway for its load of
   glittering ore,
And thy ships lie in the tideway, and thy flocks along
   the moor ;
And thine arishes gleam softly when the October moon-
   beams wane,
When in the bay all shining the fishers set the seine ;
The fishers cast the seine, and 'tis " Heva !" in the
   town,
And from the watch-rock on the hill the huers are
   shouting down ;
      And ye hoist the mainsail brown,
      As over the deep-sea roll
      The lurker follows the shoal ;
To follow and to follow, in the moonshine silver-clear,
When the halyards creek to thy dipping sail, Pentruan
   of Porthmeor !

And wailing, and complaining, and whistling whisht and
   clear,
The Seven Whistlers have passed thy house, Pentruan
   of Porthmeor !
It was not in the morning, nor the noonday's golden
   grace,—
It was in the fearsome midnight, when the tide-dogs
   yelped in the Race :
— The tide swings round in the Race, and they 're
   whistling whisht and low,
And they come from the lonely heather, where the fur-
   edged foxgloves blow,
      And the moor-grass sways to and fro,
      Where the yellow moor-birds sigh,
      And the sea-cooled wind sweeps by.
Canst hear the curlews' whistle through the darkness
   wild and drear,—
How they 're calling, calling, calling Pentruan of Porthmeor ?

NOTES

NOTES

ANCIENT IRISH AND SCOTTISH

THE MYSTERY OF AMERGIN.   PAGE 3

Of this strange pantheistical fragment, Dr Douglas Hyde writes:—" The first poem written in Ireland is said to have been the work of Amergin, who was brother of Evir, Ir, and Eremon, the first Milesian princes who colonised Ireland many hundred of years before Christ.   The three short pieces of verse ascribed to Amergin are certainly very ancient and very strange.   But, as the whole story of the Milesian invasion is wrapped in mystery and is quite possibly only a rationalised account of early Irish mythology (in which the Tuatha De Danann, Firbolgs, and possibly Milesians, are nothing but the gods of the early Irish euhemerised into men), no faith can be placed in the alleged date or genuineness of Amergin's verses.   They are, however, of interest, because as Irish tradition has always represented them as being the first verses made in Ireland, so it may very well be that they actually do present the oldest surviving lines in any vernacular tongue in Europe except Greek."

THE SONG OF FIONN.   PAGE 4

" The Song of Finn MacCool, composed after his eating of the Salmon of Knowledge."   This, if not the earliest, is almost the earliest authentic fragment of Erse poetry. The translation is after O'Donovan and Dr Douglas Hyde.

CREDHE'S LAMENT.   PAGE 5

From *The Colloquy of the Ancients* (called also " The Dialogue of the Sages," and by other analogues), translated by Standish Hayes O'Grady (*vide The Book of Lismore ; Silva Gadelica;* etc.).   See specific mention in Introduction.

CUCHULLIN IN HIS CHARIOT.   PAGE 6

(*Source :* Hector MacLean's *Ultonian Hero Ballads.* See Introduction.)

376 LYRA CELTICA

DEIRDRE'S LAMENT FOR THE SONS OF USNACH. PAGE 8

Of the many Irish-Gaelic and Scottish-Gaelic and English translations and paraphrases, I have selected the rendering of Sir Samuel Ferguson. The original Erse is of unknown antiquity. (See Introduction.)

THE LAMENT OF QUEEN MAEV. PAGE 10

This admirable translation is by Mr T. W. Rolleston (*vide* Note to p. 166), after the original in *The Book of Leinster*.

THE MARCH OF THE FAERIE HOST. PAGE 12

This striking poem is given as translated by Professor Kuno Meyer. It and other verses are to be found, in the original, in *The Book of Lismore* (15th century). The particular narrative therein deals with the visit of Laegaire mac Crimthainn to the land of Faerie. The episodic portion of this narrative has been translated and edited by Mr Standish Hayes O'Grady (see *Silva Gadelica*); but the general reader may be more interested in the brief and lucid commentary of Professor Kuno Meyer (see *The Voyage of Bran*—with Essay on the Celtic Elysium, by Mr Alfred Nutt—recently published by D. Nutt). Professor Meyer considers this and the other verses of "Laegaire mac Crimthainn" to be as old as the 10th century period. "The Faerie Host," as here given, is fragmentary, being part of an episode; but I have further curtailed it by three lines, for the sake of effect and unity of impression. The other three lines are—

" At all times melodious are they,
Quick-witted in song-making,
Skilled at playing *fiachell*."

VISION OF A FAIR WOMAN. PAGE 13

This characteristic Scoto-Celtic poem is supposed by some scholars to be very ancient. The Gaelic version permits of some doubt on the conjecture, but the text is not in this instance conclusive. The "Aisling" will be found in Smith's *Collection of Ancient Poems, from the Gaelic of Ossian, Ullin, Orran, and others* (1780)—the reputed originals of which were published in 1787. See, for easier reference, Nigel MacNeil's *Literature of the Highlanders*, p. 218.

THE FIAN BANNERS. PAGE 14

This paraphrase of an ancient poem is modern. The original is supposed to relate to the Scoto-Celtic and Viking wars of the 11th century. (See Nigel MacNeil's *Literature of the Highlanders*, p. 117.)

THE RUNE OF ST PATRICK ("THE FAEDH; OR, THE CRY OF THE DEER"). PAGE 17
This translation of the "Faedh," from *The Book of Hymns* (11th century), is by Charles Mangan.

COLUMCILLE CECENIT. PAGE 18
The version of Colum's Hymn here given is the translation of Dr Douglas Hyde, himself a poet, and one of the foremost living Irish folk-lorists. All students of Celtic literature should see his fascinating volume of metrical renderings of the old Erse, *The Three Sorrows of Story-Telling*. (*Vide* Notes to p. 126.)

COLUMCILLE FECIT. PAGE 20
This well-known poem is given as translated by Michael O'Curry, from an Irish MS. in the Burgundian Library of Brussels.

THE SONG OF MURDOCH THE MONK. PAGE 22
This "Monastic Shaving Song" is the version of Professor Blackie, as translated from *Bishop Ewing's Book*.

DOMHNULL MAC FHIONNLAIDH. "THE AGED BARD'S WISH." PAGE 23
Although this undoubtedly old Gaelic poem is attributed by its translators, Charles Edward Stuart and John Sobieski, to the early bard Domhnull _ ac Fhionnlaidh, there is no certainty (as they admit) either as to authorship or date. This version is taken from *Ballads and Songs* by Charles Edward Stuart and John Sobieski.

"OSSIAN SANG." PAGE 28
The original was jotted down in phonetic Gaelic by Dean Macgregor some 380 years ago.

FINGAL AND ROS-CRANA. PAGE 29
This is not part of the text of Macpherson's *Ossian* though the Englishing is by Macpherson, who attributes the original to Colgan, an ancient Scoto-Irish bard. It will be found in the Notes to *Temora*. (See Introduction.)

THE NIGHT-SONG OF THE BARDS. PAGE 31
Macpherson "translated" this, he avers, from an old Gaelic original. His version is to be found in the Notes to *Croma*.

OSSIAN. "COMALA." PAGE 35
I have selected this short poem as representative of

the semi-mythical Ossian of Macpherson. It is undoubtedly ancient substantially.

THE DEATH-SONG OF OSSIAN. PAGE 41

The close of "The Songs of Selma." (See foregoing Note.

ANCIENT CORNISH

THE POOL OF PILATE. PAGE 45

From the ancient Cornish drama, *The Resurrection of Christ* (*vide* section : "The Death of Pilate"). See the volume on the subject by Mr Edwin Norris, referred to in Note to "The Vision of Seth."

MERLIN THE DIVINER. PAGE 46

(*Vide* Introduction.) This, though it exists in the old Cornish dialect, is really an ancient Breton incantation. The Cornish variant is to be found in that invaluable depository of Armorican legendary lore, the *Barzaz Breiz*. The translation here given is by Thos. Stephens. (*Vide Thos. Stephens: a Memoir*. Wm. Rees, Llandovery, 1849.)

THE VISION OF SETH. PAGE 47

This dramatic fragment is from *The Ancient Cornish Drama*, edited and translated by Edwin Norris, Sec. R.A.S. (Oxford, 1859).

ARMORICAN

THE DANCE OF THE SWORD. PAGE 53

(*Vide* Introduction.) In Armorican, *Gwin ar C'Hallaoued: Ha Korol or C'Hlezf—i.e.* The Wine of the Gauls, and the Dance of the Sword. Supposed to be the fragment of a Song that accompanied the old Celtic sword-dance in honour of the Sun. [This and the following translation by the late Tom Taylor are, by courteous permission of Messrs Macmillan, quoted from *Ballads and Songs of Brittany* (selections from the *Barzaz Breiz* of the Vicomte Hersart de la Villemarqué).]

THE LORD NANN AND THE FAIRY. PAGE 55

(By the same, and from the same source.) The "Korrigan" of Breton superstition has his familiar congeners in Celtic Scotland and Ireland ; and is identical with the "elf" of Scandinavian mythology and of the Danish ballads. In this English version of "The Lord Nann" the metre and divisions into stanzas of the original Armorican have been adhered to. The triplet indicates antiquity in Cambrian and Armorican compositions.

ALAIN THE FOX.   PAGE 58

This and the following poem are from the same Franco-Breton source as their two predecessors, but are translated by Mr F. G. Fleay, M.A. (*The Masterpieces of Breton Ballads.* Printed for Private Circulation. Halifax, 1870).

BRAN (THE CROW).   PAGE 60

See foregoing Note.

EARLY CYMRIC

THE SOUL.   PAGE 67

This strange fragment is of unknown antiquity, and may well be, as affirmed, of as remote a date as the 6th or even 5th century. It is from that remarkable depository of early Cymric lore, *The Black Book of Caermarthen* (1154-1189).

LLYWARC'H HEN.   PAGE 68

The "Gorwynion" of Llywarc'h Hên, "Prince of the Cambrian Britons" (if it is really the work of that poet), is one of the most famous productions of early Cymric literature. Llywarc'h Hên's *floreat* is by some authorities placed in the middle of the 7th century, by others so early as the beginning of the 6th, and by others as really extending from early in the 6th till the middle of the 7th : the drift of evidence indicates the remoter date as the more probable. The translation here given was made about a hundred years ago by William Owen. It is not easy to find an English equivalent for "Gorwynion," a plural word which signifies objects that have a very bright whiteness or glare. Perhaps the word glitterings might serve, though, as has been suggested, the nearest term would be *Coruscants*. The last line of these verses generally contains some moral maxim, unconnected with the preceding lines, except in the metre. It is said that the custom arose through the desire of the bards to assist the memory in the conveyance of instruction by oral means. In the translation the rhymed or assonantal unity of the tercets is lost, with the result that the third-line maxim generally comes in with almost ludicrous inappositeness. According to the *Triads of the Isle of Britain*, Llywarc'h Hên passed his younger days at the Court of Arthur. In one triad he is alluded to as one of the three free guests at the Arthurian Court; in another, as one of the three counselling warriors. According to tradition, the bones of this princely bard lie beneath the Church of Llanvor, where, as averred, he was interred at the patriarchal age of 150 years. He was not one of the Sacred Bards, because of his military profession as a prince and knight; for these might not carry arms, and in their presence a naked sword even might not be held. The *Beirdd* were not poets and sages only, but were accounted and accepted as missioners of peace.

LLYWARC'H HEN.   PAGE 71

This is another series of "Gorwynion," attributed to Llywarc'h Hên by Mr Skene, who has translated it from *The Red Book of Hergest* (MS. compiled in 14th and 15th centuries). The English rendering of *The Red Book* was issued through Messrs Edmonston & Douglas of Edinburgh in 1868.

TALIESIN.   PAGE 73

"Song to the Wind" (*Vide* Introduction). "The Song about the Wind," of which only a section is given here, will be found in full in Skene's *Four Ancient Books of Wales*, Vol. I., page 535, and is the most famous poem by the most famous of Cymric bards. It was first translated, some forty-five years ago, by Lady Charlotte Guest, whose Englished renderings of the "Mabinogion" attracted the attention of scholars throughout the whole Western world. (Longmans, 1849 and later.) Emerson delighted in the "Song," and declared it to be one of the finest pieces of its kind extant in any literature. See also the *Myvyrian Archaiology*.

ANEURIN.   PAGE 75

Aneurin was one of the famous warrior bards of ancient Wales. His birth is noted as *Circa* 500 A.D., and in any case he flourished during the first half of the 6th century. Aneurin—like Taliesin, called "the monarch of the bards"—was a Briton of Manau Gododin, a principality or province of Cymric Scotland, now Mid-Lothian and Linlithgowshire. Manau Gododin stretched from the Carron of to-day (the Carun of Ossian), some miles to the north-west of Falkirk to the river Esk, that now divides Mid-Lothian and East Lothian. Manau Gododin was then much more Celtic (Pictish) than Gododin. "Breatan Cymru" (*i.e.* the country of the Welsh Britons) then comprised the larger part of southern Scotland—that is, from the north end of Loch Lomond, and from the upper reaches of the Gwruid (the Forth), to the Mull of Galloway on the south-west; eastward to a line drawn from the western Lammermuirs, by Melrose, Kelso, and Jedburgh, and so down by the Cheviots to Hexham, and thence south-westerly by Cumberland. The exception was the Pictish or Celtic province of Galloway—bounded on the west by Carrawg (that part of Ayrshire known as Carrick); on the north by Coel (Kyle); on the east by a line drawn from Sanquhar through Nithsdale and by Dumfries to Lochar-moss and the Solway; on the south-west, by Novant (Mull of Galloway); and on the south by the Solway Firth.

Aneurin was a contemporary of the princely poet, Llywarc'h Hên. He was called Aneurin y Coed Awr ap Caw o Gwm Cawlwyd—or, again, Aneurin Gwadrydd—both designations indicative of his greatness. It has been maintained that Aneurin is identical with the celebrated Gildas, "the author of the Latin epistle which Bede so blindly copied," both Aneurin and Gildas having been sons of Caw. He is supposed to be alluded to as the seventh bard, in a curious fragment preserved in the *Myvyrian Archaiology* (Vol. III.), which I excerpt here.

"The seven questions put by Catwg the Wise, to the Seven Wise Men of the College of Llanvuthan, and the answers of these men:

1. "What is the greatest wisdom of man?" "To be able to do evil and not to do it," answered *St Tedio*.
2. "What is the highest goodness of man?" "Justice," answered *Tahaiarn*.
3. "What is the worst principle of man?" "False-hood," answered *Taliesin*, chief of Bards.
4. "What is the noblest action of man?" "Correct-ness," answered *Cynan*, son of Clydno Eddin.
5. "What is the greatest folly of man?" "To desire a common evil, which he cannot do," answered *Ystyvan*, the Bard of Teilo.
6. "Who is the poorest man?" "He who is not con-tented with his own property," answered *Arawn*, son of Cynvarch.
7. "Who is the richest man?" "He who does not covet anything belonging to others," answered *Gildas* of Coed Awr.

" The Ode to the Months " is given in the translation of
William Probert (1820), according to whom the Ode contains moral maxims and observations which were known
and repeated long before Aneurin lived, and were put into
verse by him as an aid to the memory : " valuable, because
they show the modes of thinking and expression which the
primitive inhabitants of Britain used nearly 2000 years ago."

DAFYDD AP GWILYM.   PAGE 78

(Fl. 14th century.) In his love of Nature, and in the
richness of his poetic imagination (as well, so say those
who can read Welsh fluently, as in his poetry), Dafydd
ap Gwilym is the Keats of Wales. The romance of his
life and wild-wood experiences has yet to be written : and
we still await an adequate translator—though, to judge
from some recent renderings by Mr Ernest Rhys, in an
interesting short study of Dafydd, recently published
in *The Chap Book* (Stone & Kimball, Chicago) we
may not have to wait much longer. He was a love-
child : of noble parentage, though born under a hedge
at Llandaff. His mother wedded after his birth ; but he
remained the " wilding " throughout his life. He became
the favourite of Ivor Hael of Emlyn, with whose daughter
Morvydd he fell in love. He wooed and won her " under
the greenwood tree," but only to lose her shortly afterward,
when she was forcibly married to a man called Bwa Bach.
Dafydd stole her from her legitimate husband, but was
captured and imprisoned. His ultimate release was due
to the payment of the imposed fine, the sum having been
got together by the men of Glamorgan. His most ardent
love-poetry is addressed to this fair Morvydd.

RHYS GOCH OF ERYRI.   PAGE 82

There are two famous poets of the name of Rhys Goch ;
probably both belong to the 14th century (and Wilkins
certainly disputes the claim of Rhys Goch ap Rhiccart
to be of the 12th century). This Ode is an illustration of
the sound answering the sense. Rhys was in love with
the fair Gwen of Dol, and sent a peacock to her. His
rival, also a bard, composed a poem to the Fox, beseeching
it to kill his rival's present, and, singularly enough, the
bird was destroyed by a fox, and the rival bard was happy.
Stung by this misadventure, Rhys composed the above,
which, in the original, so teems with gutturals that Sion

Tudor called it the "Shibboleth of Sobriety, because no man, when drunk, could possibly pronounce it."

RHYS GOCH AP RHICCART. PAGE 83

See foregoing Note.

IRISH (MODERN AND CONTEMPORARY)

A. E. PAGES 87-91

From *Homeward Songs by the Way* (Whaley, Dublin). This little book, published in paper covers, and apparently with every effort to avoid rather than court publicity, almost immediately attracted the notice of the few who watch contemporary poetry with scrupulously close attention. The author, who is well known in Dublin literary society, prefers to disguise his identity in public under the initials A. E., though it is no longer a secret that Mr G. W. Russell is the name of this poet-dreamer, who, like Blake, of whom he is a student and interpreter, has also a faculty of pictorial expression of a rare and distinctive kind.

WM. ALLINGHAM. (1824-1889.) PAGES 92-94

Every lover of Irish poetry is familiar with "The Fairies" of the late William Allingham. He is an Irish rather than distinctively a Celtic poet in the strict sense of the word; but every now and again he strikes the genuine Celtic note, as in his well-known "Fairies," and the little poem called the "Æolian Harp," by which he is also represented here. Much the best critical summary of his life-work is to be found in the brief memoir by Mr W. B. Yeats in Miles' *Poets and Poetry of the Century*, Vol. V., p. 209. Among the innumerable love songs of the Irish peasantry there are few more beautiful than Allingham's "Mary Donnelly." As Mr Yeats says, he was "the poet of little things and little moments, and neither his emotions nor his thoughts took any wide sweep over the world of Man and Nature." His "Laurence Bloomfield" is already practically forgotten; but many of the lighter and often exquisitely deft lyrics of his early life will remain in the memory of the Irish people, and one or two at least in English literature.

THOMAS BOYD. PAGE 95

So far as I know, Mr Thomas Boyd has not published any volume of verse. Some of his poems have appeared in

United Ireland, among them the beautiful lines, "To the Lianhaun Shee."

EMILY BRONTË. (1818-1848.)   PAGE 97

It may be as well to explain to those readers who take it for granted that Emily Brontë is to be accounted an English poet, that she was of Irish nationality and birth. The name Brontë, so familiar now through the genius of herself and her sister, was originally Prunty. Everything from her pen has a note of singular distinction; but perhaps she could hardly be more characteristically represented than by the poem called "Remembrance." The, in quantity, meagre poetic legacy of the author of *Wuthering Heights* is comprised (under her pseudonym, Ellis Bell) in the volume *Poems by Currer, Ellis, and Acton Bell.*

STOPFORD A. BROOKE.   PAGE 98-100

"The Earth and Man" and "Song" (from the poem called "Six Days") are from Mr Stopford Brooke's volume, *Poems* (Macmillan & Co.). These seem to me fairly representative of the distinctive atmosphere which Mr Brooke conveys in all his poetry. See particularly his *Riquet of The Tuft* (1880) and *Poems* (1888).

JOHN K. CASEY.   PAGE 101-3

Most of Mr Casey's poems appeared above the signature "Leo." Born in 1846, the son of a peasant, his early efforts to make literature his profession were handicapped by inevitable disadvantages. In 1876 he was arrested as a Fenian conspirator, and imprisoned. This, combined with the influence of his unselfish patriotism and the popularity of many of his lyrics, gave him a recognised place in the Irish Brotherhood of Song.

GEORGE DARLEY. (1795-1846.)   PAGE 104

This remarkable poet, who has so strangely lapsed from public remembrance, was in his own day greatly admired by his fellow-poets and the most discerning critics of the period. Mrs Browning, and Robert Browning still more, were deeply impressed by what is now his best known production—*Sylvia: a Lyrical Drama* (1836); and Alfred Tennyson was so struck by the quality of the young poet's work that he volunteered to defray the cost of publishing his verse. Lord Tennyson frequently, in conversation, alluded to George Darley as one of the "hopelessly misapprehended men"; and we have Robert Browning's own authority, says Darley's latest biographer, Mr John

NOTES 385

H. Ingram, for stating that *Sylvia* did much to determine
the form of his own early dramas. *Sylvia*, again, charmed
Coleridge; and in 1836, Miss Mitford, whom Mr Ingram
calls a leading spirit among the *literati* of her day, writes:—
" I have just had a present of a most exquisite poem, which
old Mr Carey (the translator of Dante and Pindar) thinks
more highly of than any poem of the present day—' Sylvia,
or The May Queen,' by George Darley. It is exquisite—
something between the 'Faithful Shepherdess' and the
' Midsummer Night's Dream.'"

Darley was the eldest child of Arthur Darley, of the
Scalp, County Wicklow. The poet, however, was not
born there, but in Dublin, in the year 1795. While
he was a child, his parents emigrated to the United
States; and the boy spent the first ten years of his life
at the family home in Wicklow. In due time, and subse-
quent to the return of his parents from America, he went
through the usual scholastic routine, though he did not
graduate at Trinity College, Dublin, till his twenty-fifth
year—a delay in great part due to what, then and later,
he considered a disastrous impediment of speech. From
the loss of a scholarship to the social deprivations
he underwent in London, this infirmity, he declared,
was his evil fortune. His first book, *The Errors of
Ecstasie*, was published (1822) in London, where he had
settled. Needless to say, as this volume consists mainly
of a dialogue between a Mystic and the Moon, the
reading public remained in absolute ignorance of the
new poet. His second book (1826) consisted of a series
of prose tales and verses, collectively entitled — *The
Labours of Idleness ; or, Seven Nights' Entertainments*—
set forth as by "Guy Penseval." Three years later
appeared his chief work, *Sylvia*. Notwithstanding its
divers shortcomings, some of them frankly acknowledged
by the author himself, *Sylvia* is a creation of genuine
imagination, and possesses a haunting and quite distinctive
charm. Both the merits and demerits of his too often
uncontrolled style are adequately indicated in the criticism
of Mr Ingram : "[frequently] his wild Celtic fancy breaks
its curb and carries him into clouds of metaphor as marvellous as they are musical, although often the flight ends
by a hasty and undignified descent to commonplace earth."
There is no commonplace, however, in his exquisite faëry
verse, which, in the words of the same critic, "is among

2 B

the loveliest in the language; at times is even sweeter than Drayton's, and is as fantastic as Shakespeare's own."

For ten years the poet kept silence; but in 1839 he issued his fragmentary and extraordinary *Nepenthe*—a poem which, with all its brilliant quality and daring richness of imagery, might well be taken as an example of the Celtic genius *in extremis*—so unreservedly does he give way to an uncontrolled imagination. Perhaps the best thing said about *Nepenthe* is in a letter from the author himself, wherein he writes : —"Does it not speak a heat of brain mentally Bacchic?"

Nothing that Darley published afterwards enhanced his reputation. Lovers of his best work, however, should read the posthumous volume of his " Poems " edited by R. and M. J. Livingstone—a rare volume, as it was printed for private circulation. It contains some of the songs from an unpublished lyrical drama called *The Sea Bride* ; and it is from this that the " Dirge," quoted at page 104 in this book, comes. In this posthumous collection also is included the following striking and characteristic lyric :—

THE FALLEN STAR.

A star is gone ! a star is gone !
　There is a blank in Heaven,
One of the cherub choir has done
　His airy course this even.

He sat upon the orb of fire
　That hung for ages there,
And lent his music to the choir
　That haunts the nightly air.

But when his thousand years are passed,
　With a cherubic sigh
He vanished with his car at last,
　For even cherubs die !

Hear how his angel brothers mourn—
　The minstrels of the spheres—
Each chiming sadly in his turn
　And dropping splendid tears.

The planetary sisters all
　Join in the fatal song,
And weep this hapless brother's fall
　Who sang with them so long.

But deepest of the choral band
　The Lunar Spirit sings,
And with a bass-according hand
　Sweeps all her sullen strings.

From the deep chambers of the dome
Where sleepless Uriel lies,
His rude harmonic thunders come
Mingled with mighty sighs.

The thousand car-borne cherubim,
The wandering eleven,
All join to chant the dirge of him
Who fell just now from Heaven.

After a life of great intellectual activity, but of singular isolation and of misanthropic unhappiness, George Darley died in London on the 23rd of November 1846, in his fifty-first year. For further information as to the personality and writings of this strange, undeservedly neglected, but unbalanced man of genius, the reader may be referred to the delightful edition of *Sylvia*, with Introduction, by Mr John H. Ingram, published by Mr J. M. Dent (1892).

AUBREY DE VERE. PAGE 105-6

Mr Aubrey De Vere is one of the most scholarly poets of Ireland. All his work is informed with a high and serious spirit ; and though the bulk of it is not distinctively Celtic, either in sentiment or utterance, not even distinctively Irish, he has written some poems which are as dear to Nationalists and Celticists as is almost any other verse by contemporary poets. Mr Aubrey De Vere is the younger brother of Sir Stephen De Vere, Bart. (the translator of Horace, and himself a poet of distinction), and son of Aubrey De Vere, the poet friend of Wordsworth. He was born in 1814, and has lived most of his life, with long intervals in London and in several parts of Europe, at his birthplace, Curragh Chase, Adare, Co. Limerick. Among his most noteworthy writings are :—*The Waldenses* (1842) ; *The Search after Proserpine* (1843) ; *Poems* (1853) ; *The Sisters* (1861) ; *The Infant Bridal: and other Poems* (1864) ; *Irish Odes* (1869) ; *The Legends of St Patrick* (1872) ; *Alexander the Great*, a poetical drama (1874) ; and another drama, *St Thomas of Canterbury* (1876) ; *Antar and Zara: and other Poems* (1877) ; *Legends of the Saxon Saints* (1879) ; and *The Foray of Queen Meave*, based upon an ancient Irish epic (1882). Since then Mr Aubrey De Vere has published a Selection of his poems and one or two books of a religious nature. His best prose work is to be found in his *Essays chiefly on Poetry* (1887), and *Essays chiefly Literary and Ethical* (1889).

388   LYRA CELTICA

FRANCIS FAHY.   PAGE 107
Author of *Irish Songs and Poems*, published under the
pseudonym "Dreolin." Mr Fahy is a member of the group
of notable lyrists whose captain is Sir Samuel Ferguson.

SIR SAMUEL FERGUSON. (1810-1886.)   PAGE 109
This celebrated poet and archæologist was born in Belfast.
He has aptly been called a man of encyclopædic learning;
but this learning did not prevent his becoming perhaps the
foremost Irish poet of the Middle Victorian period. His
most ambitious poetic work is *Congal: an Epic Poem*
(1872)—a work full of lofty imagination and epical music,
but unfortunate in its metrical setting. His short poem,
"The Forging of the Anchor," is one of the most celebrated and popular poems of our era. Even yet, the
influence of his *Lays of the Western Gael* (1865) is considerable, and for good. "Cean Dubh Deelish" (darling dark
head), of which several able, and one or two good translations have been made, finds its happiest interpreter in
Ferguson. How many poets and lovers have repeated
these lines—

> "Then put your head, darling, darling, darling,
> Your darling black head my heart above;
> Oh, mouth of honey, with thyme for fragrance,
> Who, with heart in breast, could deny you love?"

                                              PAGE 110
"Molly Asthore" is also a paraphrase. The original is
ascribed to a celebrated Irish Gaelic bard, Cormac O'Con.

                                              PAGE 112
"The Fair Hills of Holy Ireland," is familiar to Irish
men and women in every part of the world.

ALFRED PERCIVAL GRAVES.   PAGE 113
One of the best known names of Ireland of to-day. Mr
Graves, born in Dublin in 1846, is thoroughly national, and
nis delightful work is perhaps as adequately typical of the
Irish spirit as that of any one man could be. His lyric
faculty—or at any rate his movement, his verve—is unsurpassed by any living Irishman. These few examples of his
poetical writings should win him many more readers. His
first book, *Songs of Killarney*, was published over twenty
years ago. Since then he has issued *Irish Songs and
Ballads, Songs of Old Ireland*, and (1880) his best known

collection, *Father O'Flynn : and other Irish Lyrics. Irish Songs and Airs* is the title of his promised contribution to Sir Gavan Duffy's Irish Library.

GERALD GRIFFIN. (1803-1840.)   PAGE 121

The author of the lovely song, " Eileen Aroon " (Nellie, my Darling), was born in Limerick. His chief work is his novel, *The Collegians*, which has been pronounced to be "the most perfect Irish novel published." I have heard that Tennyson once " went mooning about for days," repeating with endless gusto, and with frequent expressions of a wish that he was the author of, the closing lines :—

> Youth must with time decay,
>   Eileen Aroon !
> Beauty must fade away,
>   Eileen Aroon !
> Castles are sacked in war,
> Chieftains are scattered far,
> Truth is a fixèd star,
>   Eileen Aroon !

NORA HOPPER.   PAGE 123 ETC.

This young Irish poet made an immediate impression by her *Ballads in Prose* (John Lane). Both in prose and verse she displays the true Celtic note, and often the unmistakable Celtic intensity. The lovely lyrics "April in Ireland," and "The Wind among the Reeds," are from *Ballads in Prose.* "The Dark Man" has not hitherto appeared in print, and I am indebted to Miss Hopper for her permission to quote it here. It is, I understand, to be included in her shortly forthcoming volume, to be published by Mr John Lane.

DOUGLAS HYDE, LL.D.   PAGE 126

Dr Hyde, one of the foremost living expositors of Gaelic folklore in Ireland, was born about thirty-five years ago in the Co. Roscommon, where he has since resided. He graduated at Trinity College, Dublin, after an exceptionally brilliant University career. He is now President of the Gaelic League, and one of the acknowledged leaders of the Gaelic wing of the Celtic Renascence; but from the first he was in the front rank of those who are working for the preservation of the ancient Irish language and the rescue of its beautiful fugitive literature. Although best known by his Irish Tales, taken down at first hand from the peasantry, and other Folk-

390 LYRA CELTICA

collections, and his invaluable and unique *The Love Songs
of Connacht* (Connaught), he is himself a poet of mark.
(See, also, Note XI., *supra*.) Those who are in a position
to judge declare his Gaelic poetry, which appears in the
Irish Press above the signature "An Chraoibhin Aoibhinn,"
to be of altogether exceptional excellence. The work Dr
Douglas Hyde does deserves the most cordial recognition.
No man has worked more whole-heartedly, more enthusias-
tically, and with more far-reaching success for the cause of
the Irish-Gaelic language, folk-lore, and literature, and, it
may be added, the best interests of the Irish of the soil.

The songs by which he is represented in this volume are
from the *Love Songs of Connacht* (Fisher Unwin, 1893), a
book which is not only indispensable to the Celtic scholar,
but should be in the hands of every lover of Celtic literature,
old-time or new. All are translations, though perhaps
paraphrastic rather than metaphrastic. Both in their music
and in their intensity—in, also, their peculiar lyric lilt—
they are distinctively West Irish. The collection from
which these poems are drawn was issued as *The Fourth
Chapter of the Songs of Connacht*. The preceding three
appeared in the now defunct *Nation*. They were all originally written in Irish ; but very wisely, or at any rate for
us very fortunately, Dr Hyde interpolated translations. In
these he has endeavoured to reproduce the vowel-rhymes
as well as the exact metres of the original poems. We
must hope to see the reprint, in like fashion, of the predecessors of this volume.

LIONEL JOHNSON. PAGE 133

Though come of a Dublin family, and otherwise Irish by
descent, Mr Johnson was born at Broadstairs in Kent
(1867). He first became known to the reading public, as
a poet, by his contributions to *The Book of the Rhymers'
Club*, notable for their distinction of touch. Since then
Mr Johnson has published much in prose and verse, though
in book form he has not, I think, produced any other
prose work than his admirable study of Thomas Hardy,
or any other volume of poetry than his *Poems*. His work
is not characterised by distinctively Celtic quality, though
occasionally, as in "The Red Wind" and "To Morfydd,"
the Celtic note makes itself audible. No doubt—to judge
from internal evidence in his later writings—Mr Johnson's
poetic work, at least, will develop more and more along
the line of his racial bent.

DENIS FLORENCE MACCARTHY. (1817–1882.) PAGE 135

Mr Maccarthy, who was a barrister in Dublin, and one of the main supports of the *Nation*, is best known by his fine translations of Calderon's Dramas. The "Lament," by which he is here represented, has always seemed to me his most haunting lyrical achievement. It is necessary to add, however, that this poem is somewhat condensed from the original—which is weakened by diffuseness. The score or so of lines beginning "As fire-flies fade," have been favourites with many poets of Maccarthy's own time and later.

JAMES CLARENCE MANGAN. (1803-1849.) PAGE 137

While it is not the case, as sometimes averred, that Mangan was, or is, to Ireland what Burns is to Scotland, it is indisputable that the claim may be made for him rather than for any other Irish poet of the Early Victorian period. In fire and energy his faculty is unsurpassed by any of his poetic countrymen, though we may dispute Sir Charles Gavan Duffy's assertion that Mangan "has not, and perhaps never had, any rival in mastery of the metrical and rhythmical resources of the English tongue." Mangan was the child of a small tradesman of Dublin, where, in 1803, he was born. From childhood, fate dealt hardly with him. Abandoned in his early boyhood, he was indebted to a relative for his education; but when, in his fifteenth year, he became a copyist in a lawyer's office, at a small pittance, his kindred discovered him and compelled him to share his meagre gains with them. For ten years thereafter he toiled in this bitter bondage. In his own words :—"I was obliged to work seven years of the ten from five in the morning, winter and summer, to eleven at night; and during the three remaining years, nothing but a special Providence could have saved me from suicide." No wonder that, from an early period in his life, he found relief from his misery in drink; but it was misery and unbroken ill-fortune and adversity, much more than the curse of his fatal habit, that really killed him. There is a period in his life which is a blank, "a blank into which he entered a bright-haired youth and emerged a withered and stricken man." His first chance for a happier life came with his appointment to a minor post in the University Library of Dublin, and it was during this time that most of his best work was done. His highest level is reached

in his brilliant free paraphrases of German originals:
Anthologia Germania (1845). His later years were
darkened by the worst phases of his malady, and he died
(as in most part he had lived, in misery and poverty) in
Meath Hospital, in his forty-seventh year. He has written
one lyric that Irishmen will always account immortal:
"Dark Rosaleen" — a wild and passionate rhapsody on
Ireland herself. "Dark Rosaleen," "Silk of the Kine,"
"The Little Black Rose," "Kathleen Ny Houlahan" —
these were at one time the familiar analogues of Ireland.
Of his Oriental paraphrases the most stirring is "The
Karamanian Exile." Strangely enough, Mangan's Irish
renderings are less happy than those poems which he based
upon German and Oriental originals; but sometimes, as in
the beautiful "Fair Hills of Éiré, O!" after the Irish of
Donough mac Con-Mara, he has bequeathed a memorable
lyric. Of poems that are strictly original, nothing seems
to me more characteristic of Mangan than "The One
Mystery" (see p. 142).

ROSA MULHOLLAND.   PAGE 144

This accomplished prose - writer and poet was born
in Belfast. Since her *Vagrant Verses* (1886) she has
published many stories and poems, and is a regular contribu-
tor to the leading Irish periodicals. Her "Fionnula" is
one of the happiest renderings of the legend of the Swan
Daughters of Lir ; but is too long for quotation in the text.
"The Wild Geese," by which she is represented here, is
eminently characteristic. Her latest poem, and one of her
best, appears under the title "Under a Purple Cloud"
in the autumn number of *The Evergreen*. It is a vision of
Earth personified, and opens thus :

> Under a purple cloud along the west
> The great brown mother lies and takes her rest,
> A dark cheek on her hand, and in her eyes
> The shadow of primeval mysteries.
>
> Her tawny velvets swathe her, manifold,
> Her mighty head is coifed in filmy gold,
> Her youngest babe, the newly-blossomed rose
> Upon her swarthy bosom feeds and grows.
>
> With her wide darkling gaze the mother sees
> Her children in their homes, the reddening trees,
> Roofing wet lawns, fruit-laden lattices,
> Blue mountain domes, and the grey river-seas.

NOTES

THE HON. RODEN NOËL. (1834-1894.) PAGE 146

Mr Roden Noël was son of the first Earl of Gainsborough, grandson of Lord Roden of Tullymore in Ireland, and nephew to the present Marquis of Londonderry. By birth, descent, training, and sympathy, he considered himself an Irishman : though he was half English by blood, and lived the greater part of his life in England, while his intellectual homage was largely evoked by Hellenic mythology and lore, and by Teutonic mysticism and speculation. It was this confused blending of influences which, perhaps, militated so strongly against the concentration of his brilliant abilities into long-sustained and organic creative effort. With all his shortcomings, he still remains a poet of genuine impulse and occasionally of high distinction ; and some of his lyrics and ballads, of a more essentially human interest than his more ambitious work, are likely to be held in honourable remembrance. The "Lament for a Little Child" (see p. 146) has passed into literature ; as, indeed, may perhaps be said of the book whence it comes : *A Little Child's Monument* (1881). In one of his Cornish poems he begins thus :—

> " For me, true son of Erin, thou art rife,
>   Grand coast of Cornwall, cliff, and cave, and surge,
>   With glamour of the Kelt."

I do not think there is much "glamour of the Kelt" in Roden Noël's work, but it may be discerned in one or two poems in each of his volumes, and in many of his lyrics and irregular lyrical compositions there is much of Celtic intensity and dream. Few poets have written of the sea with more loving knowledge and profound sympathy ; hence it is that he is represented here by one characteristic sea-poem, called " The Swimmer "—as autobiographical as anything of the kind can be. The swimmer's joy was Roden Noël's chief physical delight. All who knew the man himself remember him as one of the personalities of his time, and as a man of individual distinction and charm. Besides the book already mentioned, his chief poetic volumes are *Beatrice and Other Poems* (1868) ; *Songs of the Heights and Deeps* (1885) ; and *A Modern Faust* (1888). See also the Selection from his poems published in the Canterbury Poets Series (edited, with a Critical Introduction, by Mr Robert Buchanan), and the posthumous volumes *My Sea* and *Selected Lyrics* (Elkin Mathews).

CHARLES P. O'CONOR.   PAGE 158

Besides this typical Irish song, Mr O'Conor has written other winsome lyrics of the same kind. One of the best is that called " Erinn " beginning—

" O, a lovely place is Erinn, in the summer of the year,
Roseen dhu ma Erinn."

This and " Maura Du of Ballyshannon " are from his *Songs of a Life* (Kentish Mercury Office, 1875).

JOHN FRANCIS O'DONNELL.   PAGE 160

This pretty Spinning Song is characteristic of the always deft and generally delicate and winsome lyrical writing of Mr Francis O'Donnell.

JOHN BOYLE O'REILLY.   PAGE 161

This prolific writer, often designated an Irish-American poet, through the accident of his enforced exile to, and long residence in, the United States, is inadequately represented by the brief lyric, " A White Rose "; but it is significant of his best achievement, for he is always at his happiest in brief, spontaneous lyrics, often in a Heinesque vein. John Boyle O'Reilly was born at Dowth Castle in Ireland. In his early manhood he enlisted in a hussar regiment ; and it was while as a hussar that he was arrested on the charge of spreading republican principles in the ranks, and was sentenced to be shot. This sentence was commuted to twenty years of penal servitude ; when the unfortunate man, victim of that disastrous as well as iniquitous tyranny which has characterised the English official attitude towards the Celtic populations, was taken to the convict settlements of Western Australia. Thence, in time, he escaped, and after hairbreadth escapes reached Philadelphia. From there he went to Boston, where he settled ; and in a few years, by virtue of his remarkable gifts as a poet, a prose-writer, and a brilliant journalist, became an acknowledged power in trans-Atlantic literature. A novel of his, *Moondyne*, is widely and deservedly celebrated. Of his poetical works, the best are *Songs of the Southern Seas*, *Songs, Legends, and Ballads*, and *In Bohemia*.

ARTHUR O'SHAUGHNESSY. (1844-1881.)   PAGE 162

O'Shaughnessy is to be ranked as an English rather than as an Irish poet ; for the national sentiment played a minor, indeed hardly a perceptible part in his poetic life. The Celtic part of him found its best expression in his translations

of the *Lays of Marie* (particularly the difficult and extraordinary "Bisclaveret"), powerful paraphrases rather than
translations. The poem by which he is represented here
shows the influence of Edgar Allan Poe, but is founded
upon a Celtic legend. In his early youth he was appointed
to a subordinate position in the Library of the British
Museum, and was afterwards promoted to the Natural
History Department. His first literary success was his
Epic of Women (1870), a volume of exceptional promise,
which, however, was never adequately fulfilled. His
Lays of France (1872) was followed by *Music and Moonlight* (1874) and a posthumous volume, *Songs of a
Worker* (1881). Always delicate, his death without any
previous breakdown surprised none of his friends. I
recollect that on the Saturday preceding his death, which I
think was on a Wednesday, he came into the rooms of his
brother-in-law, and fellow-poet and friend, Philip Bourke
Marston, and asked me to come to his residence on the
following Wednesday, to hear him read from the proofs of
his new book. That evening he went to a theatre, came
home on the top of an omnibus, caught a chill, and died
before any of his friends knew that he was seriously indis-
posed. The best critical and biographical accounts of this
charming if insubstantial poet, are to be found in Dr
Garnett's memoir in Miles' *Poets and Poetry of the
Century*, Vol. VIII., and in the biographical edition of his
poems recently put forth by Mrs Louise Chandler Moulton.
Of the poem here given, Dr Garnett speaks as a "miracle
of melody," and as one of the pieces in which "the poet's
inward nature has perhaps most clearly expressed itself."

FANNY PARNELL. (1855-1883.)   PAGE 165

A remarkable poem by a remarkable woman. Frances
Isabelle Parnell was the sister of Charles Stewart Parnell,
and grand-daughter of Charles Stewart (from whom the
great Irish patriot derived his baptismal names), the historic
commander of the U.S. Frigate *Constitution*. Miss
Parnell's poems, which always appeared above the signature
of Fanny Parnell, have not yet been published collectively.
She was secretary of the Ladies' Land League, and was
as intensely wrought by the fervour of patriotism as was her
famous brother.

T. W. ROLLESTON.   PAGE 166

The sometime editor of the *Dublin University Review*, and

one of the most valued present members of the Irish Literary Society, was born at Shinrone, King's County, in 1857. Mr Rolleston has had a cosmopolitan training since he left Trinity College, and has in particular been influenced by his long residence in Germany; but he has remained a Celtic poet and ardent Celticist through every intellectual development. While resident in Germany and in London, he wrote his *Life of Lessing* and his introductions to Epictetus and Plato. He is now responsibly connected with the Irish Industries Association, but is more and not less engrossed by his Celtic studies. If there were a few more poet-scholars who could translate or paraphrase so beautifully as Mr Rolleston has paraphrased the Irish of Enoch o' Gillan (see p. 166) and other poems, there would be a wider public in England for the lovely work of early Irish poetry. "The Lament of Queen Maev," given here in the Ancient Irish section, is also a translation by Mr Rolleston.

DORA SIGERSON.   PAGE 167

This young and promising writer comes of poetic stock. Her sister Hester is also a writer of verse, and her father, Dr Sigerson, is one of the foremost workers in the Gaelic Revival. Miss Dora Sigerson's only published book as yet bears the modest title *Verses*. It is, perhaps, more significant in its promise than in its achievement; and I find nothing in it so mature as the poem by which she is represented here, taken from a recent issue of the *Chap Book* (Stone & Kimball, Chicago). The following lines, from *Verses*, may be given as an example of her poetic first-fruits :—

IN SOUTHERN SEAS.

In southern seas we sailed, my love and I,
In southern seas.
Death joined no chorus as the waves swept by,
No storm hid in the breeze.
Low keeled our boat until her white wings dipped half wet with spray,
And seeking gulls tossed on the passing wave laughed on our way,
The rhyme of sound, the harmony of souls—of silence too;
Your silence held my thoughts, my love, as mine of you ;
The wingèd whispering wind that blew our sails was summer sweet—
I found my long-sought paradise crouched at thy feet.

In northern seas I weep alone, alone,
In winter seas.
Death's hounds are on the waves, with many moans
Death's voice comes with the breeze,
My helpless boat, rocked in the wind, obeys no steadfast hand,
Her swinging helm and ashing sheet have lost my weak command ;

The shrieking sea-birds seek the sheltering shore,
The writhing waves leap upward, and their hoar
Strong hands tear at the timbers of my shuddering craft.
I cry in vain, the Fates have seen and laughed,
Time and the world have stormed my summer sea—
I ate my fruit, the serpent held the tree.

DR GEORGE SIGERSON.   PAGE 168

The distinguished translator and editor of *The Poets and
Poetry of Munster* was born near Strabane, Co. Tyrone, in
1839. Much of his original work has appeared above his
Irish pen-name " Erionnach " ; and from first to last Dr
Sigerson's name is indissolubly associated with the wide-
reaching Celtic Renascence in Ireland.

DR JOHN TODHUNTER,   PAGE 170

One of the foremost contemporary poets of Ireland, was
born in Dublin in 1839, and, like so many of his literary
compatriots, was educated at Trinity. He then pursued his
medical studies in Paris and Vienna ; returned to Dublin and
practised awhile as a physician ; succeeded Prof. Dowden as
Professor of English Literature in Alexandria College ; and,
since 1875, has devoted himself exclusively to literature.
Some of his lyrical pieces are known to all lovers of poetry
—*e.g.* " The Banshee " ; and for the rest he has won a
distinctive place for himself by work at once varied in theme
and beautiful in treatment. Though he has won deserved
reputation as a playwright for the contemporary stage, as
well as in the poetic drama, he seems to me to be at his best
when most Celtic in feeling and expression. He is represented here, not by pieces so well known as "The Banshee"
or any part of *The Three Sorrows of Story - Telling*, but
by two typical Irish poems, and one lovely fragment
(see p. 173) from *Forest Songs*. Personally, I consider the
" Love Song " given at page 170 to be one of the finest
compositions of its kind in modern Celtic literature. I have
regretfully refrained from quoting two other poems by Dr
Todhunter, one familiar to every Irishman, " The Shan Van
Vocht of '87," beginning—

There's a spirit in the air,
    Says the *Shan Van Vocht*,
And her voice is everywhere,
    Says the *Shan Van Vocht* ;
Though her eyes be full of care,
Even as Hope's, born of Despair,
Her sweet face looks young and fair,
    Says the *Shan Van Vocht*.—

and the other, which I think the strongest of his short lyrical

poems, " Aghadoe "—of which I may give the two concluding quatrains—

I walked to Mallow town from Aghadoe, Aghadoe ;
Brought his head from the gaol's gate to Aghadoe,
Then I covered him with fern, and I piled on him the cairn,
Like an Irish king he sleeps in Aghadoe.

Oh ! to creep into that cairn in Aghadoe, Aghadoe !
There to rest upon his breast in Aghadoe,
Sure your dog for you could die with no truer heart than I,
Your own love, cold on your cairn, in Aghadoe.

KATHERINE TYNAN.   PAGE 174

The author of *Louise de la Vallière* (1885), *Shamrocks* (1887), *Ballads and Lyrics* (1891), and later volumes
in prose as well as verse, is one of the best known representatives of the Irish poetic fellowship. Mrs Hinkson
(though best known by her maiden name) is distinctively
Irish rather than Celtic, and pre-eminently a Catholicist in
the spirit of her work. She has a St Francis-like love of
birds and all defenceless creatures and humble things, and
has a most happy lyric faculty in dealing with aspects and
objects which excite her rhythmic emotion. In lyric quality
and in her all-pervading sense of colour, she is, however,
characteristically Celtic. Miss Tynan was born in Dublin
in 1861, but since her marriage a few years ago to Mr
Hinkson (himself one of the Dublin University *Young
Ireland* men) she has resided in or near London. Some of
her work has a lyric ecstasy, of a kind which distinguishes
it from the poetry of any other woman-writer of to-day.

CHARLES WEEKES.   PAGE 179

Mr Weekes is one of the small band of Irish poet-
dreamers who may be particularly associated with Mr W.
B. Yeats and Mr G. W. Russell (" A.E. "). His book,
Reflections and Refractions, contains fine achievement as
well as noteworthy promise.

WILLIAM BUTLER YEATS.   PAGE 181

Born (of an Irish father, and or a Cornish mother come
of a family settled in Ireland) at Sandymount, Dublin, in
1866 ; but early life chiefly spent in Sligo, and on the
Connaught seaboard. Of late years, Mr Yeats has passed
much of his time in London, but is never absent from
Ireland for any long period—

" .   .   .   .   . for always night and day
    I hear lake-water lapping with low sounds on the shore ;
While I stand on the roadway, or on the pavements grey,
    I hear it in the deep heart's core."

W. B. Yeats is the prince of contemporary Irish poets. While no one is more essentially Celtic, and none is more distinctively national, his poetry belongs to English literature. Mr Yeats himself would be the last man to nail his flag to the mast of parochialism in literature. He is one of the two or three absolutely poetic personalities in literature at the present moment; and in outlook, and, above all, in atmosphere, stands foremost in the younger generation. It is noteworthy that the two most convincingly poetic of all our younger poets, since the giants who (with the exception of George Meredith, A. C. Swinburne, and William Morris) have gone from our midst, are predominantly Celtic; W. B. Yeats and John Davidson—and noteworthy, also, that both are too wise, too clear-sighted, too poetic, in fact, to aim at being Irish or Scoto-Celtic at the expense of being English in the high and best sense of the word. This, fortunately, is consistent with being paramountly national in all else. In the world of literature there is no geography save that of the mind.

Mr Yeats' poetic work is best to be read, and perhaps best to be enjoyed, in the revised collective edition of his poems, in one volume, published recently by Mr Fisher Unwin. His first volume of verse, *The Wanderings of Oisin*, was published in 1889. This was followed (in 1892) by *The Countess Kathleen: and Various Legends and Lyrics; The Land of Heart's Desire*, and two short prose tales (in the Pseudonym Library), *John Sherman* and *Dhoya*. Two new books are promised in 1896 (through Mr Elkin Mathews), *The Shadowy Waters* (a poetic play), and *The Wind Among the Reeds* (poems). He has also published several volumes of selected Irish tales and legendary lore; edited, in conjunction with Mr E. J. Ellis, the *Works of William Blake* (3 vols., 1893); and *A Book of Irish Verse* (Methuen, 1895), an interesting rather than an adequately representative anthology of nationalistic Irish poetry. All that is most distinctive in Mr Yeats' own original work is to be found in his *Poems* (Collective Edition, in 1 vol., Fisher Unwin, 1895), and the prose volume entitled *The Celtic Twilight* (Lawrence & Bullen, 1893), one of the most fascinating prose-books by a poet published in our time.

LATER SCOTO-CELTIC

THE PROLOGUE TO GAUL. PAGE 189

Comes from the *Sean Dana*: *vide* Dr John Smith's *Collection of Ancient Poems* (1780), (*vide* Note to page 13 *supra*, and also Introduction).

IN HEBRID SEAS. PAGE 191

This stirring Hebridean poem is given as from the ancient Gaelic. Probably by this is meant merely old Gaelic, mediæval or even later. The translation is by Mr Thomas Pattison, and is included in his *Gaelic Bards*. He has the following note upon it: "This effusion, although in its original form it is only a kind of wild chant—almost indeed half prose—yet it is the germ of the ballad. It occurs in many of the tales contained in that collection, the repository of old Gaelic lore, the *Popular Tales of the West Highlands*, sometimes more and sometimes less perfect. The original will be found in the second volume of the Tales. . . . The vigorous and elastic spirit that pervades these verses must have strung the heart of many a hardy mariner who loved to feel the fresh and briny breeze drive his snoring birlinn bounding like a living creature over the tumbling billows of the inland loch or the huge swell of the majestic main."

LULLABY. PAGE 193

Supposed to be the composition of the wife of Gregor MacGregor after the judicial murder of her husband.

DROWNED. PAGE 194

This folk-poem, the antiquity of which may be anywhere from a hundred to two hundred years or more, is given in the translation of the Rev. Dr Stewart of Nether Lochaber.

ALEXANDER MACDONALD. PAGE 195

This celebrated Gaelic poet was born in the first half of the 17th century. In the Highlands and Western Isles he is invariably styled *Mac Mhaighstir Alastair—i.e.* the son of Mr Alexander. Alastair the Elder resided at Dalilea in Moydart of Argyll, and was both Episcopal clergyman and official tacksman. He was a man of immense strength and vigour, and his muscular Christianity may be inferred from the saying current in Moydart that "his hand was heavier on the men of Suainart than on the men of Moydart." Alexander Macdonald had a good education for his time—

first under his father, and later, for a year or so, at Glasgow University. Poverty, however, compelled him to leave Glasgow and retire to Ardnamurchan, where, as his bio- grapher, Mr Pattison, says, he lived, teaching and farming, and composing poetry, until the advent of the year 1745. In this momentous year he left not only his farm and his teaching, but even his eldership in the Established Church, and forsook all to join Prince Charlie, and to take upon him the onus of a change to the detested Roman Catholic faith. He was a Jacobite of the Jacobites, and his fiery and warlike songs were repeated from mouth to mouth through- out Celtic Scotland. It is supposed that he had a commis- sion in the Highland army of the Prince, though whether he served as an officer is uncertain ; at any rate, after the battle of Culloden he had to share the privations of his leaders, and he lived in hiding in the woods and caves of the district of Arisaig. On one occasion, when lurking among these caves with his brother Angus, the cold was so intense that the side of Macdonald's head which rested on the ground became quite grey in a single night. When the troubles were over he went to Edinburgh, where he taught the children of a staunch Jacobite, but soon returned to his beloved West, where he remained till his death. Mac- donald's first published book was a *Gaelic and English Vocabulary* (1741), nor was it till ten years later that his poems were published in Edinburgh—said to be one of the earliest volumes of original poems ever published in Gaelic. Pattison declares that he is the most warlike, and much the fiercest of the Highland poets ; and altogether ranks him as, if not the foremost, certainly second only to the famous Duncan Bàn MacIntyre. His poem called " The Birlinn of the Clan-Ranald " is by this critic, and most others, ranked as the finest composition in Modern Gaelic ; certainly many Highlanders prefer it even to the "Coire Cheathaich," or the still more famous " Ben Dorain " of Duncan Bàn. Assuredly no one could read this poem " Of the hurling of the birlinn through the cold glens of the sea, loudly snoring," without being stirred by its vigour and power. The portion here given is merely a fragment, for the original is much too long for quotation—indeed, it is said to be the longest poem in Gaelic, except such as are Ossianic. For a full account of Macdonald and his poems, including the translation of the greater part of " The Manning of the Birlinn," see Pattison's *Gaelic Bards*.

ANGUS MACKENZIE.   PAGE 201

"The Lament of the Deer" is the work of a favourite
Highland poet whose name is particularly familiar in the
Northern Highlands. Angus Mackenzie was head forester
of Lord Lovat, and most of his poems have the impress of
his well-loved profession. "The Cumha nam Fiadh" was
composed during the recovery from a severe illness, when
the poet's chief regret was his inability to be with Lovat
and his Frasers at the hunting of the stag. The translation
here given was made by Charles Edward and John Sobieski
Stuart, and is to be found in their *Lays of the Deer
Forest* (Blackwood, 1848).

DUNCAN BÀN MACINTYRE.   PAGE 203

A name loved throughout the Highlands and Islands.
Even the most illiterate crofters are familiar with Duncan
Bàn and much of his poetry, and there are few who could
not repeat at least some lines of "Ben Dorain." The
Hunter Bard of Glenorchy, as he is often called—though
his best title is the affectionate Gaelic "Duncan of the
Songs"—was born on the 20th of March 1724, at Druim-
liaghart in Glenorchy, Argyll. His first song was composed
on a sword with which he was armed at the battle of
Falkirk—where he served on the Royalist side as substitute for a gentleman of the neighbourhood. "This sword,"
says his biographer, Thomas Pattison, "the poet lost or
threw away in the retreat. On his return home therefore,
the gentleman to whom it belonged, and whose substitute
he had been, refused to pay the sum for which he had
engaged Duncan Bàn to serve in his stead. Duncan con-
sequently composed his song on 'The Battle of the
Speckled Kirk'— as Falkirk is called in Gaelic—in which
he good-humouredly satirised the gentleman who had sent
him to the war, and gave a woful description of 'the black
sword that worked the turmoil,' and whose loss, he says,
made its owner 'as fierce and furious as a grey brock in his
den.' The song immediately became popular, and incensed
his employer so much that he suddenly fell upon the poor
poet one day with his walking-stick, and, striking him on
the back, bade him 'go and make a song about that.' He
was, however, afterward compelled by the Earl of Bread-
albane to pay the bard the sum of 300 merks Scots (£16, 17s.
6d.), which was his legal due." Although in his later years
he was for a time one of the Duke of Argyll's foresters,

most of his later life was spent in Edinburgh, where he was one of the City Guard. In that city he died in 1812, in his eighty-ninth year, and lies in Greyfriars Churchyard. In all there have been seven editions of his *Gaelic Songs.* " Ben Dorain" has been translated several times, most successfully by Thomas Pattison and the late Professor Blackie. The version here given is that of the former ; while the following poem ("The Hill Water," page 208) is that of Professor Blackie.

Translations of both "Ben Dorain" (in full) and of "Coire Cheathaich" (The Misty Corrie) are included in Pattison's *Gaelic Bards.* Professor Blackie's version of "Ben Dorain" is in his well-known book, *Altavona.*

MARY MACLEOD. PAGE 210
The most famous of Hebridean poets was born in Harris of the Outer Hebrides in 1569. She may be regarded either as the last of the poets of the Middle Scoto-Celtic period, or, more properly, as the first of the moderns. She is generally spoken of in the Western Isles as Màiri nighean Alastair Ruaidh (Mary, daughter of Alexander the Red). "Although she could never either read or write, her poetry is pure and chaste in its diction, melodious, though complicated, in its metre, clear and graceful, and frequently pathetic" (Pattison). She died at Dunvegan, in the Isle of Skye, in 1674, at the great age of 105. For some reason, Mary Macleod was banished from Dunvegan by Macleod of Macleod, but his heart was melted by the song here given, and the exile was recalled, and that, too, with honour, and enabled to live in Macleod's country thenceforth in prosperity and happiness.

MODERN AND CONTEMPORARY SCOTO-CELTIC

MONALTRI. PAGE 217
These lines tell their own tale. The translation given is that of Thomas Pattison.

HIGHLAND LULLABY. PAGE 218
This lullaby first appeared in the *Duanaire*, edited by D. C. Macpherson (1864). It is supposed to be sung by a disconsolate mother whose babe has been stolen by the fairies. In each verse she mentions some impossible task she has performed, but still she has not found her baby. *Coineachan* is a term of endearment applied to a child. (Quoted by "Fionn" in the *Celtic Monthly* for September 1893.)

BOAT SONG. PAGE 219

This boat song, so familiar to West Highlanders, is in the rendering of Professor Blackie.

JOHN STUART BLACKIE. (1809-1895.) PAGE 222

The late Professor Blackie was born in Glasgow and brought up for the law. This he forsook for literature, and ultimately, in 1852, was appointed to the Greek Chair in Edinburgh University. All particulars of the brilliant Professor's life and writings will be found in the recently-published biography by Miss Anna Stoddart. Professor Blackie's name will always be held in affectionate regard for his unselfish efforts to preserve and cultivate the Gaelic language and literature, and because of his having been mainly instrumental in founding the Chair of Celtic Literature in the University of Edinburgh. His poetical writings are mostly to be found in *Lays and Legends of Ancient Greece* (1857), *Lyrical Poems* (1860), and *Lays of the Highlands and Islands* (1872).

ROBERT BUCHANAN. PAGE 224

The foremost Scoto - Celtic poet of our time, was born in Glasgow, 1841. It would be needless to give particulars concerning the life and work of so eminent a contemporary. Lovers of the Celtic Muse will doubtless be familiar (or if not, ought to be) with Mr Buchanan's *Book of Orm*. Much of his early poetry is strongly imbued with the Celtic atmosphere. Those who have read his several volumes of verse need no further guidance, but readers unacquainted with the poetical work of one of the foremost poets of our day should obtain the collective edition of his poems published by Messrs Chatto & Windus. "The Flower of the World" (page 224), "The Dream of the World without Death" (pages 228-234) are from *The Book of Orm*; "The Strange Country" comes from *Miscellaneous Poems and Ballads* (1878-1883). No more memorable poem than "The Dream" has been written by an Anglo-Celtic poet.

LORD BYRON. (1788-1824.) PAGES 238-239

Byron is represented in *Lyra Celtica* by virtue of his Celtic blood and undoubtedly Celtic nature, rather than because there is much trace of Celtic influence in his poetry. The two lyrics given here may be taken as fairly representative of that part of his poetical work which may with some reason be called Celtic, though, of course, there is nothing

NOTES 405

in them which radically differentiates them from the lyrics of any English poet. More than one eminent critic, foreign as well as British, has claimed for Byron that he was the representative Celtic voice of the early part of the century; but Byron was really much more the voice of his own day and time than anything more restricted.

CRODH CHAILLEAN. PAGE 240

This familiar Highland Milking Song is given in the translation of Dr Alexander Stewart of Nether Lochaber.

MACCRIMMON'S LAMENT. PAGE 241.

Perhaps the most famous pipe-tune in the Highlands is the "Cumha mhic Criomein," composed by Donald Bàn MacCrimmon, on the occasion of the Clan MacLeod, headed by their chief, embarking to join the Royalists in 1746. The Lament is said to have been composed by Donald Bàn under the influence of a presentiment that he as well as many others of the clan would never return; a presentiment fulfilled, for he was killed in a skirmish near Moyhall. The tune and the chorus are old, but it is commonly believed the poem was composed by Dr Norman Macleod; at any rate, they first appeared in a Gaelic article on the MacCrimmons, which he contributed in 1840 to "Cuairtear nan Gleann" ("Fionn," the *Celtic Monthly*). The translation here given is that of Professor Blackie.

IAN CAMERON ("IAN MOR"). PAGE 242

Translated from the Gaelic by Miss Fiona Macleod.

JOHN DAVIDSON. PAGE 243

Mr Davidson was born at Barrhead, near Paisley, on April 11th, 1857. After his preliminary education at the Highlanders' Academy, Greenock, he went to Edinburgh University. For a time he taught in Greenock, and also gained a certain amount of literary experience in occasional contributions to the *Glasgow Herald* and other papers. In 1886 he published *Bruce: a Drama*, followed by *Smith: a Tragedy* (1888), *Scaramouch in Naxos: and other Places* (1889), *In a Music Hall, and other Poems* (1891), *Fleet Street Eclogues* (1893), *Ballads and Songs* (1894), *Second Series of Fleet Street Eclogues* (1895), besides several volumes of prose papers and fiction. Although *Bruce* was Mr Davidson's first published work, he had begun to write at a much earlier period: his *An Historical Pastoral* was composed in 1877; *A Romantic Farce* in 1878;

while *Bruce* was written four years before its publication. Mr Davidson's later poetical writings have been mainly in the form of songs and lyrical ballads, and these have placed him in the foremost rank of the younger poets of to-day. He has the widest range, the largest manner, and the intensest note of any of the later Victorians. The two poems by which he is represented here are eminently characteristic, and none the less Celtic in their essential quality from the fact that the one deals with a loafer of the London streets and the other with a scenic rendering of an impression gained in Romney Marsh. Mr Davidson's latest writings are " The Ballad of an Artist's Wife," not as yet issued in book form, and the just published second series of the *Fleet Street Eclogues* (John Lane). Both " A Loafer " and " In Romney Marsh " are from *Ballads and Songs*.

JEAN GLOVER. (1758-1800.)   PAGE 246
    The author of " O'er the Muir amang the Heather " was the daughter of a Highland weaver settled in Kilmarnock. She married a strolling actor, and her fugitive songs became familiar throughout the West of Scotland. "O'er the Muir amang the Heather " has become a classic.

GEORGE MACDONALD.   PAGE 247
    This popular Scottish novelist and poet was born at Huntly, in Aberdeenshire, December 10, 1824. As a novelist he has almost as large an audience as have any of his contemporary romancists. His poems are less widely known, though in them he has expressed himself with great variety and subtlety. The Celtic element is not conspicuous in Dr Macdonald's work either in prose or verse ; but sometimes, as in the little song " Oimè," quoted here, it finds adequate expression. This song is from his early volume *Within and Without*.

RONALD CAMPBELL MACFIE.   PAGE 249
    The author of *Granite Dust* (Kegan Paul) is one of the most promising of the younger Celtic Scots.

WILLIAM MACDONALD.   PAGE 250
    One of the band of young writers associated with *The Evergreen* (Patrick Geddes and Colleagues, Edinburgh). Mr Macdonald has not yet issued his poems in book form.

AMICE MACDONELL.   PAGE 251
    Miss Macdonell has not, so far as I know, published a volume. "Culloden Moor" appeared in the *Celtic Monthly* in June 1893.

NOTES

ALICE C. MACDONELL.   PAGE 252

Miss Alice Macdonell of Keppoch has contributed many
poems to Scottish and other periodicals. "The Weaving of
the Tartan" appeared in the *Celtic Monthly* for December
1894.

WILLIAM MACGILLIVRAY. (1796-1852.)   PAGE 254

The author of "The Thrush's Song" was not a poet,
but occasionally indulged in the pleasure of verse-making.
He was a well-known Highland ornithologist, and it may
be added that his attempt at an onomatopoeic rendering of
the song of the thrush has been pronounced by Buckland
and other ornithologists to be remarkably close.

FIONA MACLEOD.   PAGE 255

Miss Macleod is one of the younger writers most inti-
mately associated with the Celtic Renascence in Scotland.
"The Prayer of Women" (see page 255) is from *Pharais :
a Romance of the Isles* (Frank Murray, Derby, 1894) ; "The
Rune of Age" and "A Gaelic Milking Song" are from *The
Mountain Lovers* (John Lane) ; the "Lullaby" and the two
songs of Ethlenn Stuart are from her last volume, *The Sin-
Eater : and other Tales* (Patrick Geddes and Colleagues,
Edinburgh). "The Closing Doors" has not been published hitherto. The brief lyric, "The Sorrow of Delight,"
was contributed to an as yet unpublished fantastic sketch,
The Merchant of Dreams, written in collaboration with
a friend. Such of the poems scattered through her several
volumes, and others, as she wishes to preserve in connected
form, will be published by Miss Macleod early in 1896
(Patrick Geddes and Colleagues), under the title of *Lyric
Runes and Fonnsheen.*

NORMAN MACLEOD.   PAGE 266

There is no Highlander held in more affectionate remembrance and admiration than the late Dr Norman Macleod :
and with justice; for no one worked more arduously, under-
standingly, and sympathetically for the cause of the Gaelic
language, Gaelic literature, and the Gaelic people than the
famous poet-minister, who, to this day, is commonly spoken
of as "The Great Norman." It was, however, Dr Norman
the elder who wrote "Fiunary,"—and not, as commonly
stated, the late Dr Norman. His "Farewell to Fiunary"
is probably the most universally-known modern poem in

the West Highlands. (For critical remarks as to the authenticity of this poem, see Dr Nigel M'Neil's *Literature of the Highlanders*, pp. 283-286.)

SARAH ROBERTSON MATHESON.   PAGE 267

Mrs Robertson Matheson, some of whose poems in periodicals have attracted the attention of lovers of poetry, is chief secretary and treasurer of the Clan Donnachaidh Society. The fine lyric, "A Kiss of the King's Hand," appeared in the *Celtic Monthly* for May 1894 ; but I regret that version has inadvertently been followed, for it twice misspells *tae* for "to," and in the third line of the third quatrain has a misreading ("jewels" instead of "ruffles").

It may interest many readers to know that "A Kiss of the King's Hand" decided the descendant of Flora Macdonald to leave Mrs Robertson Matheson the last heirloom of Scottish romance, the "ring of French gold" given by Prince Charlie to Flora, and holding the lock of hair cut from "the king's head" by her and her mother.

DUGALD MOORE.   PAGE 268

"The First Ship" is so remarkable a poem that it is difficult to understand how it has met with so little recognition, and escaped most, if not all, of the Scottish and British anthologists. Dugald Moore was the son of Highland parents, and was born in Glasgow in 1805. His first book was entitled *The Bard of the North*, and consisted of a series of poetical tales illustrative of Highland scenery and character (1833). *The Hour of Retribution* and *The Devoted One* appeared respectively in 1835 and 1839. Moore died unmarried in the 36th year of his age (Jan. 2, 1841), and was buried in the Necropolis of Glasgow. It is a pity that the poem could not have appeared without its fourth stanza, which is inferior to the others.

LADY CAROLINE NAIRNE. (1766-1845.)   PAGE 269

Needless to say anything here concerning the "Flower of Strathearn." Baroness Nairne was mainly Celtic in blood and wholly Celtic in genius. "The Land o' the Leal" is now one of the most famous and most loved lyrics in the English language. (Readers may be referred to *Life and Songs of Baroness Nairne*, 1868.)

ALEXANDER NICOLSON.   PAGE 270

Besides this fine poem, "On Skye," Sheriff Nicolson has translated the "Birlinn" of Alexander Macdonald, and has

NOTES

written many moving verses full of Gaelic sentiment of a robust kind.

SIR NOËL PATON.   PAGE 272

Joseph Noël Paton was born at Dunfermline on the 13th of December 1821; and while his father was also of partial Celtic origin, Sir Noël is, through his mother, the descendant of the last of the Scoto-Celtic kings. Of his career as a painter it is not necessary to speak here. His two volumes of poetry are *Poems by a Painter* (1861) and *Spindrift* (1867). The best account of the life and work of this distinguished Scot is the monograph recently published by Mr David Croal Thomson, as the "Art-Annual" of *The Art Journal*. The two poems by which Sir Noël is represented in this book are not to be found in either of his volumes, and their appearance here is due to the courtesy of the author.

WILLIAM RENTON.   PAGE 274

Mr Renton was born in Perthshire, of Scoto-Celtic parents. "Mountain Twilight" is taken from his first volume of poems called *Oils and Water Colours* (Hamilton, Edinburgh, 1876). Mr Renton's only other volume of verse is his *Songs* (Fisher Unwin, 1893).

LADY JOHN SCOTT.   PAGE 275

The author of "Durisdeer" was of mixed Highland and Lowland descent. Her poem has a permanent place in our literature because of its haunting passion and pain.

EARL OF SOUTHESK.   PAGE 276

Lord Southesk (James Carnegie) was born in 1827. He first made his name in literature by his strange and vigorous *Jonas Fisher* (1875). This was followed by *Greenwood's Farewell* (1876), and *The Meda Maiden* (1877); though most of the poems contained in these two volumes, with several others, are comprised in *The Burial of Isis* (1884).

JOHN CAMPBELL SHAIRP.   PAGE 277

This able Scottish writer was of Celtic origin through his mother. Readers unacquainted with the poems of the late Principal Shairp, and ex-Professor of Poetry at Oxford, will do best to turn to the posthumous volume, edited, with a memoir, by Francis Turner Palgrave, entitled *Glen Dessary* (Macmillan, 1888).

UNA URQUHART.   PAGE 279
I know nothing else of Gaelic or English verse by this
young writer. "An Old Tale of Three," as it appears here,
is a rendering of the original by Miss Fiona Macleod.

LOST LOVE.   PAGE 280
The author of this poem is unknown. The original is in
the Gaelic of the Western Isles, and is one of the several
fugitive songs rescued by Thomas Pattison. The version
given here, however, is not identical with his, the first and
last quatrains having been added by another hand.

CONTEMPORARY ANGLO-CELTIC POETS (WALES)

GEORGE MEREDITH.   PAGE 283
Mr George Meredith, who recently has been addressed
in a dedication as "The Prince of Celtdom," is rather
the sovereign of contemporary English literature. Although of Welsh descent and sympathies, and with a
nature pre-eminently Celtic in its distinguishing characteristics, Mr Meredith was born in Hampshire on February 12th, 1828. Part of his early education was received
in Germany, and after his return to England it was
intended that he should pursue the legal profession : an
intention set aside on account of an irresistible bias toward
literature. His first published writings were in verse : and
now this early little book, *Poems*, published in his twenty-
third year (1851) is one of the rarest treasures for the biblio-
phile. It is dedicated to Thomas Love Peacock, whose
intellectual influence upon the young writer is obvious.
In 1850 the poet married the daughter of Peacock, but
it was not till a year or two later that he definitely set
himself to the profession of literature as also a means of
livelihood. It is characteristic of him that his first prose
book should be one of his most individual writings ; for
The Shaving of Shagpat might have been written at
almost any period of its author's career. A fascinating and
perplexing production it must indeed have seemed at that
time, published as it was in a year which, with the exception
of two radically distinct American works of pre-eminent
note, Longfellow's *Hiawatha* and Walt Whitman's
Leaves of Grass, was a singularly barren one. The fantasy
has always remained a favourite with staunch Meredithians.
It was followed two years later by the somewhat akin *Farina*;

and two years passed again before that first important work appeared which so profoundly affected the minds and imagination of Mr Meredith's contemporaries—the now famous *Ordeal of Richard Feverel*, (1859). Since that date Mr Meredith has given us what many consider the greatest literary legacy of our time ; and unquestionably he has had no compeer in brilliant delineation of life at white heat. It is unnecessary to specify the works of an author with which all lovers of literature must be familiar ; but a word must be added as to the delight which the reading world has known this year in the publication of *The Amazing Marriage*, one of the most brilliant and vivid of all Mr Meredith's romances, and, in its display of his characteristic quality at his best, ranking with *Harry Richmond*, *The Egoist*, and *Diana of the Crossways*. As a poet George Meredith is less widely known, or, rather, is less widely accepted. There are, nevertheless, many who regard his poetic achievement as perhaps the most essential part of what he has given us. In depth of thought, in clarity of vision, and in remarkable expressional subtlety,—often, if not invariably, set forth in a lyric utterance whose only fault is that of an occasional apparent incoherence due to rapidity of thought and eagerness of rhythmic emotion—he stands here, as in all else, alone. From that extraordinarily powerful study of contemporary life, expressed emotionally and rhythmically in singularly convincing verse, *Modern Love*, to his latest volume, *The Empty Purse*, there is a range of rhythmic and lyric beauty which may well be a challenge to posterity to redeem the relative neglect of the mass of Mr Meredith's contemporaries. I am not of those who consider Mr Meredith's least popular poems as mere cryptic utterances in verse ; for everywhere I find the lyric spirit,—hampered, at times, it is true, by a wind-rush of images, and by a sudden drove of unshepherded words. But who could read " Love in the Valley," " The Lark Ascending," " The Woods of Westermain," " The South-Wester," " The Hymn to Colour," to mention five only, without recognising that here indeed we have one of the great poets of our time. The poems by which, owing to the gracious courtesy of Mr Meredith—who has consented to forego for once his great objection to the appearance of any of his poems in miscellaneous collections—he is here represented, are from his later volumes. The "Dirge in Woods," " Outer and Inner," and the superb " Hymn to Colour," are

from *A Reading of Earth* (1888), the volume which contains
" Hard Weather," " The South-Wester," " The Thrush in
February," " The Appeasement of Demeter," " Woodland
Peace," the noble ode " Meditation under Stars," and that
flawless and memorable sonnet, " Winter Heavens." The
" Night of Frost in May " is from the volume entitled *The
Empty Purse* (1892). Mr Meredith's other volume of poetry,
the favourite with most of his readers, is *Poems and Lyrics of
the Joy of Earth* (1883). This book includes "The Woods
of Westermain," " The Day of the Daughter of Hades,"
" The Lark Ascending," " Phœbus with Admetus," " Mel-
ampus," " Love in a Valley," and the group of sonnets
beginning with " Lucifer in Starlight," and ending with
" Time and Sentiment." All Mr Meredith's poetical
writings are now published by Messrs Macmillan.

SEBASTIAN EVANS.   PAGE 292

Born in 1830, the grandson of the Rev. Lewis Evans,
a well-known Welsh astronomer, and the son of the Rev.
Arthur Benoni Evans, a linguist, scholar, and author. He
was not the only one of this parentage who came to some
distinction, for his brother, John Evans, F.R.S., became
President of the Society of Antiquaries, and his sister, Anne,
had some repute as a poetess and musician. Sebastian
Evans won a fair measure of fugitive fame by his *Brother
Fabian's Manuscript and Other Poems* (Macmillan, 1865).
In the early '70's Dr Evans published his second volume,
In the Studio: a Decade of Poems (Macmillan). The
true note of his strangely subtle and illusive muse is not that
of either irony or audacity as commonly supposed, but rather
a living belief in the passage of the contemporary mind and
aspiration from the sureties of the ancient faith to the
assurance of a still finer faith to come. Among his short
poems perhaps the most indicative is that entitled " The
Banners "—

Lordly banners, waving to the stars,
  Flap upon the night-wind, heavy with the dew,
Trustful youth is wending to the wars,
  Strong in ancient faith to battle with the new.

Lordly banners, trodden in the clay,
  Lie upon the mountain dank with other dew,
Hapless Youth hath lost the bloody day,
  Ancient faith is feeble, stronger is the new.

Lordly banners, other than of yore,
  Flap upon the night-wind, heavy with the dew :
Youth to battle girdeth him once more,
  New and Old are feeble,—mighty is the True !

EBENEZER JONES. (1820-1860.)   PAGE 293

Of Welsh parentage and descent, Ebenezer Jones was born in Islington, London. Much has been written upon the famous Chartist poet, both in his relation to the socialistic movements in which he participated, and in literary criticism of his two at one time much discussed volumes, *Studies of Sensation and Event* (1843), and *Studies of Resemblance and Consent* (1849); but perhaps the best critical summary of his life-work is that of Mr Wm. J. Linton in Miles' *Poets and Poetry of the Century*, Vol. V. The two poems by which Ebenezer Jones is represented here are respectively from his second and first volumes.

EMILY DAVIS (MRS PFEIFFER). (1841-1890.)   PAGE 296

Mrs Pfeiffer, many of whose poems achieved a wide popularity, was the daughter of a Welsh gentleman settled in Oxfordshire, and an officer in the army. She was born in Wales. Of her several volumes of verse, the first was *Gerard's Monument*, etc. (1873), and the best are *Sonnets and Other Songs*, *Under the Aspens* (1884), and *Sonnets* (1887).

ERNEST RHYS.   PAGE 297

"The House of Hendra" is not given here intact: for the whole poem, see *A London Rose*, etc. (Elkin Mathews). Mr Rhys is the most noteworthy of the younger generation of Welsh poets and romancists, and may well be accepted as the leader of the Neo-Celtic movement in Wales. He has in a more marked degree than almost any of his compatriots of his own period the gift of style; and already his enthusiasm, knowledge, and fine and notable work in prose and verse have brought him to the front as the recognised representative of young Wales. Of Welsh parentage, Mr Rhys was born in London in 1860, spent much of his boyhood in South Wales, and his youth and early manhood in the north-country, where he intended to follow the profession of a mining engineer. However, he came to London in the early 'eighties and settled down to literary work. His first publication in book form was *The Great Cockney Tragedy* (1891). His poems first became known to the outside reading world through his contributions to *The Book of the Rhymers' Club* (1893). In the following year he published his first and as yet sole volume of verse: *A London Rose: and Other Rhymes*, whence comes the fine

"House of Hendra" by which he is represented here. Besides other writings, in prose, Mr Ernest Rhys was editor of the "Camelot Series" of popular reprints and translations in 65 volumes (1885-1890), and now is critical editor of *The Lyric Poets* (Dent), one of the most delightful poets-series extant.

CONTEMPORARY ANGLO-CELTIC POETS (MANX)

THOMAS EDWARD BROWN.   PAGE 307

Was born at Douglas, in the Isle of Man, in 1830. After a career of exceptional distinction at Oxford, he was appointed Vice-Principal of King William's College in the Isle of Man (1855). Since 1863 he has been assistant-master of Clifton College. The book by which Mr Brown is best known is his admirable *Fo'c'sle Yarns* (Macmillan, 1881 and 1889), though the first of his tales in verse included therein, "Betsy Lee," appeared in *Macmillan's Magazine* in 1873 where it at once attracted wide attention. He has also published *The Doctor* (1887) and *The Manx Witch* (1889). The author of *Fo'c'sle Yarns* is by far the most noteworthy poetic representative of the Isle of Man. In range, depth of insight, dramatic vigour, keen sympathy, and narrative faculty, all transformed by the alchemy of his poetic vision, he is not only the foremost Manx poet, but one of the most notable of living writers in verse. It is probably because most of his poems deal almost wholly with Manx scenes and characters, and are for the most part written in the Manx dialect, that he is so little talked of by literary critics and so little known to the reading world at large. Than "Betsy Lee" (*Fo'c'sle Yarns*) there is no more moving, human, and beautiful poem, of the narrative kind, written in our time. The fragmentary lines by which the author is represented here were selected from one of his most characteristic Manx poems, and give a good idea of the common parlance of the islanders of to-day. It is from *The Doctor: and Other Poems* (Swan Sonnenschein, 1887).

HALL CAINE.   PAGE 309

This fine Manx ballad of "Graih my Chree" appeared this year in the first number of *London Home*, to the editor and proprietor of which, as well as to Mr Hall Caine, I am indebted for the permission to include "Love of my Heart" here.

Mr Caine, so celebrated as a novelist, has published no
volume of poems; but at rare intervals something of
his in verse has appeared. I think that his earliest
appearance as a poet was in *Sonnets of this Century*
(1886, and later editions), where he is represented by two
fine sonnets, "Where Lies the Land to which my Soul
would go?" and "After Sunset." Mr Caine's own first
acknowledged book was an anthology of sonnets (*Sonnets
of Three Centuries*, Stock, 1882), published in the author's
twenty-seventh year. Of his many books, the best known
are his *Recollections of Dante Gabriel Rossetti*; and his
romances, *The Shadow of a Crime*, *The Deemster*, *The
Bondman*, *The Scapegoat*, and *The Manxman*. Mr Hall
Caine is himself a Manxman, crossed with a strong
strain of Cumberland blood. Both in his strength and
weakness he is eminently Celtic, after his own kind; for
he could belong to no other Celtic people than either the
Manx or the Welsh. He has, and not without good reason,
been called the Walter Scott of Man. Certainly, *The
Deemster* and *The Manxman* alone have revealed Manx-
land and Manx life and character to the great mass of
English readers.

CONTEMPORARY ANGLO-CELTIC POETS
(CORNISH)

ARTHUR THOMAS QUILLER COUCH.   PAGE 317

So well known as "Q," was born at Bodwin, in Cornwall, of an old Cornish family, in 1863. He left Trinity
College, Oxford, for London; but, after a brief experience
of literary life in the metropolis, returned to the "Duchy,"
and has since resided there, mainly at Fowey. He is not
only the most noteworthy living Cornishman of letters, and
the romancer *par excellence* of contemporary Cornwall and
Cornish life, but is acknowledged as one of the best
story-tellers of the day. His first book was *The Splendid
Spur* (1889), a stirring romance, which was followed
by *The Delectable Duchy*, *Noughts and Crosses*, and
I Saw Three Ships. He has published little poetry;
and even in his slender volume, *Green Bays* (1893), there
are not more than one or two poems, the other verses being
for the most part what are called "occasional." If, however, he had written nothing in verse except the lyric called
"The Splendid Spur," he would be accounted a poet for

remembrance. "The White Moth" is the most distinctively Celtic poem he has written. In the main, he is more Cornish than Celtic—in this a contrast to Dr Riccardo Stephens, who is far more distinctively Celtic than Cornish.

ROBERT STEPHEN HAWKER. (1804-1875.)   PAGE 319

The celebrated vicar of Morwenstow (born at Plymouth) came of an old Cornish family, and spent the greater part of his life in the Duchy. In 1834 he became Vicar of Morwenstow, a remote parish on the Cornish sea-board. His best-known book is *Cornish Ballads* (1869); but the reader who may not be acquainted with his writings should consult the *Poetical Works, and Other Literary Remains, with a Memoir* (1879). Hawker has much of the sombre note which is supposed to be characteristic of Celtic Cornwall.

RICCARDO STEPHENS.   PAGE 321

Dr Stephens is a Cornishman settled in Edinburgh, where he practises as a physician. He has not, as yet, published any of his poems in book form ; but, none the less, has won (if necessarily, as yet, a limited) reputation by his exceedingly vigorous and individual poems. He has written several "Castle Ballads" (of which the very striking " Hell's Piper" given here is one)—poems suggested by legendary episodes connected with Edinburgh Castle, or perhaps only vaguely influenced by that romantically picturesque and grand vicinage—for Dr Stephens is one of the many workers, thinkers, and dreamers who congregate in the settlement founded by Professor Patrick Geddes on the site of Allan Ramsay's residence—"New Edinburgh," as University Hall is sometimes called, an apt name in more ways than one. Dr Stephens is a poet of marked originality, and his work has all the Celtic fire and fervour, with much of that sombre gloom which is held to be characteristically Cornish. " Hell's Piper " has lines in it of Dantesque vigour, as those which depict, among "the shackled earthquakes," the "reeking halls of Hell," and the torture - wrought denizens of that Inferno. "The Phantom Piper" will never be forgotten by any one who has once read and been thrilled by this highly-imaginative poem.

MODERN AND CONTEMPORARY BRETON

THE POOR CLERK (IN BRETON, "AR C'HLOAREK PAOUR")
PAGE 331

is rather a mediæval than a modern folk-poem. The translation is that of the late Tom Taylor (*Ballads and Lyrics*,
Macmillan), who has the following note upon it:—"The
Klöarek is a seminarist of Tréguier, a peasant who has a
turn for books, or shows some vocation for the priesthood.
Their miserable life, hard study, and abnegation of family
life are provocative of regretful emotion, passionate and
mystic asceticism. The Klöarek is the poet and hero of
most of the Breton *Sônes*; Tréguier, therefore, is the nursery
of the elegaic and religious popular poetry of Brittany."

THE CROSS BY THE WAY (KROAZ ANN HENT). PAGE 332
Vide preceding Note. This translation is from the same
source as last.

THE SECRETS OF THE CLERK, AND LOVE SONG.
PAGES 335-337

See Note to "The PoorClerk." The first of these poems was
probably composed in the transition period—late mediæval
or early modern. Both are given in the rendering of Mr
Alfred M. Williams (*vide* " Folk-Songs of Lower Brittany "
in *Studies in Folk-Song and Popular Poetry* (1895)). " The
Love Song " is modern—probably *circa* 1800, or even 1750.

HERVÉ NOËL LE BRETON. PAGE 338
For all particulars concerning this poet I must refer
interested readers to Mr W. J. Robertson's brief memoir
in that most delightful of all books of translation, *A
Century of French Verse* (A. D. Innes & Co., 1895). This
is without exception the ablest work of its kind we have.
It is the production of one who is unmistakably himself a poet, who has the rare double power to translate
literally, and at the same time with subtle art and charm, so
that the least possible loss in translation is involved. In
addition to these often exquisitely felicitous, and always
notably able and suggestive renderings, Mr Robertson has
prefixed to each representative selection a brief critical and
biographical study of the poet represented—short *études*
of remarkable insight and critical merit. Of Hervé Noël le
Breton he gives some interesting particulars. The poet is

of the ancient Armorican race, and was born in Nantes in
1851. He has not yet published any volume; and it is
from an unpublished collection, *Rêves et Symboles*, that Mr
Robertson has drawn. Strangely enough, neither in Tiercelin's Breton Anthology nor anywhere else can I find any
allusion to Hervé Noël le Breton : and his name is unknown
to M. Louis Tiercelin, M. Anatole le Braz, and M. Charles
Le Goffic, respectively the most eminent living Breton
anthologist, Breton folk-lorist, and Breton poet-romancist
and critic. For several reasons I take it that Le Breton is
an assumed name ; and it is even possible that the Armorican
blood is only in the brain, and not in the body of the author
of *Rêves et Symboles*. "The Burden of Lost Souls" is in
three parts, of which that given here is the first. Here is
the second :

THE BURDEN OF LOST SOULS.

II.

This is our doom. To walk for ever and ever
　The wilderness unblest,
To weary soul and sense in vain endeavour
　And find no coign of rest ;

To feel the pulse of speech and passion thronging
　On lips for ever dumb,
To gaze on parched skies relentless, longing
　For clouds that will not come ;

Thirsty, to drink of loathsome waters crawling
　With nameless things obscene,
To feel the dews from heaven like fire-drops falling,
　And neither shade nor screen ;

To fill from springs illusive riddled vessels,
　Like the Danaïdes,
To grapple with the wind that whirls and wrestles,
　Knowing no lapse of ease ;

To weave fantastic webs that shrink and crumble
　Before they leave the loom,
To build with travail aëry towers that tumble
　And temples like the tomb;

To watch the stately pomp and proud procession
　Of splendid shapes and things,
And pine in silent solitary session
　Because we have no wings ;

To woo from confused sleep forlorn the dismal
　Oblivion of despair ;
To seek in sudden glimpse of dreams abysmal
　Sights beautiful and rare,

NOTES

419

And waking, wild with terror, see the vision
Cancelled in swift eclipse,
Mocked by the pallid phantoms of derision,
    With spectral eyes and lips;

To turn in endless circles round these purlieus
    With troops of spirits pale.
Whose everlasting song is like the curlew's,
    One ceaseless, changeless wail.

Mr Robertson gives four poems by this poet : "*La Plainte des Damnés*," "*Vers les Étoiles*," "*Le Tombeau du Poète*," and "*Hymne au Sommeil.*" His translation of the last-named also appears in this anthology.

VILLIERS DE L'ISLE-ADAM. (1838-1889.)   PAGE 342
    This famous French novelist and poet was born at St Brieuc, in Brittany, of parents who were each of old Breton stock.   The full details of the life and work of Philippe-Auguste-Mathias de Villiers de l'Isle-Adam, son of the Marquis Joseph de Villiers de l'Isle-Adam and his wife Marie Françoise le Nepveu de Carfort, can be read in the recently - published *Life*, by the late Vicomte Robert du Pontavice de Heussey—an English translation of which, by Lady Mary Lloyd, was issued last year by Mr Heinemann.   This distinguished writer lived in mis-fortune, and died amid darker shadows than those he had too long been bitterly acquainted with.   His first volume of poems was published when he was little more than twenty years old—as Mr Robertson says, "one of the most remarkable ever written by so young a poet."   The young Breton poet came under the strong personal influence of Baudelaire, and in the process he lost much of his native Celtic fire and spirituality.   Besides the poems given here, " Confession " ("*D'aveu*") and " Discouragement " ("*Découragement*"), Mr Robertson translates, in his *Century of French Verse*, "*Eblouissement*" and "*Les Présents.*"

LECONTE DE LISLE. (1818-1894.)   PAGE 344
    "The great Creole poet, Charles Marie René Leconte, known as Leconte de Lisle, was the child of a Breton father and a Gascon mother, and was born at St Paul, in the isle of Bourbon (*Réunion*) in 1818.   He had the Celtic clearness of vision and love of beauty, and the vigour and courage of the Pyrenean race.   In his youth he travelled through the East Indies, and the vivid im-pressions of tropical colour and warmth which are visible

in his poetry derive their value from the personal observ-
ation of Nature in those regions" (W. J. Robertson, *A
Century of French Verse*). Leconte de Lisle, one of
the greatest of modern French poets, is assured of im-
mortality by his beautiful trilogy: — *Poèmes Antiques*
(1852), *Poèmes Barbares* (1862), and *Poèmes Tragiques*
(1884). The reader who, unfamiliar with this poet, wishes
to know more of Leconte de Lisle and his work, cannot
do better than turn first to Mr Robertson's biographical
and critical memoir in *A Century of French Verse*.
There, too, he will find five poems from *Poèmes
Antiques*, including the long "*Dies Iræ*"; two from
Poèmes Barbares, and two from *Poèmes Tragiques*. Of
the two given here, the first ("The Black Panther") is
from *Poèmes Barbares*, and "The Spring" ("*La Source*")
from *Poèmes Antiques*. Leconte de Lisle strove after
an ideal perfection of form. The spirit of that almost
flawless work of his, is of intellectual emotion rather than
of passion; but in colour, and splendour of imagery, no
romanticist can surpass him. He is of the great minds
who create, calm and serene. He is often classed with
the two great master-spirits of modern German and French
literature; but, while he has neither the lyric rush nor epic
sweep of Victor Hugo, nor the philosophical modernity
and innate human sentiment of Gœthe, he is much more
akin to the latter than to the former. For the rest, to
quote Mr Robertson, "he gives the noblest expression
to human revolt and desire, to ideal dreams, and to the
pure and sometimes pathetic love of external nature."

LEO-KERMORVAN.   PAGE 348

Leo-Kermorvan has been represented here as one of the
most distinctively Celtic of the contemporary Breton poets.
In translating his "Taliesen," as well as Louis Tiercelin's
"By Menec'hi Shore," I have endeavoured to convey the
atmosphere, as well as to be literal; and, partly to this end,
and partly because of a personal preference for unrhymed
metrical translation, have not ventured to make a rhymed
paraphrase. M. Kermorvan is a poet worthy to be named
with his two most notable living compatriots, Tristran
Corbière and Charles Le Goffic.

LOUIS TIERCELIN.   PAGE 351

(See foregoing note.) M. Tiercelin is a Breton poet and
critic, perhaps best known as co-editor of the *Parnasse de la*

NOTES

421

Bretagne. No more characteristic Breton poem, apart from folk-poetry, could close *Lyra Celtica.* It is the keynote of the poetry that is common to all the Celtic races.

THE CELTIC FRINGE

BLISS CARMAN.   PAGE 355

Mr Bliss Carman, the trans-Atlantic poet who, it seems to me, has the most distinctive note of any American poet (and the word "American" is used in its widest sense), is of Scoto-Celtic descent through his father's side, and of East-Anglian through the maternal side; but was born of a family long settled in Canada—viz., at Fredericton, New Brunswick, in 1861. His poetry is intensely individual, and with a lyric note at once poignant and reserved. Work of very high quality is expected of him, on both sides of the Atlantic; for his beautiful lyrics and poems have appeared in the periodicals of both countries. His slight volume, *Low Tide on Grand-Pré* (1893), is published in this country by Mr Nutt. About half of the *Songs from Vagabondia* (written in collaboration with Mr Richard Hovey) are of his authorship. This book, published in 1894 by Messrs Stone & Kimball of Chicago, is to be had here through Mr Elkin Mathews. It is from the *Songs* that the stirring war-chant of "Gamelbar" comes.

ELLEN MACKAY HUTCHINSON.   PAGE 361

This distinguished American lady is descended from old Highland stock. I know of no other book by her than *Songs and Lyrics* (Boston, Osgood & Co., 1881), but that is one which all lovers of poetry should possess. Miss Hutchinson's name is best known in connection with that colossal and invaluable work, the *Cyclopædia of American Literature* (eleven vols.), in which she was the collaborator of Mr Edmund Clarence Stedman.

HUGH M'CULLOCH.   PAGE 364

This descendant of an old Highland family is the author of *The Quest of Heracles* (Stone & Kimball, Chicago, 1894).

DUNCAN CAMPBELL SCOTT.   PAGE 365

Mr Scott is a member of one of the many Scoto-Celtic families settled in Canada. He was born at Ottawa in 1862, and is the author of *The Magic House* (1893).

THOMAS D'ARCY M'GEE. (1821-1868.)   PAGE 366

This distinguished Irishman is to be accounted only an adopted American. He emigrated to the States in 1842, edited *The Boston Pilot*, and in 1857 went to Montreal and entered the Canadian Parliament. It was when returning from a night-session that he was assassinated in Ottawa by Fenian malcontents.

MARY C. G. GILLINGTON (MRS BYRON) AND ALICE E. GILL-
INGTON.   PAGES 368-373

These two sisters, whose names have become so deservedly well-known by their contributions to British and American periodicals, are of Celtic blood, though born and resident in England. They are included here as representative of the Anglo Celtic strain so potent in England itself. The elder, Mrs Byron, was born in Cheshire in 1861. Their joint volume, *Poems*, was published in 1892. Mr Elkin Mathews has just published a volume entitled, *A Little Book of Lyrics*, by Mrs Byron.